ANSWERS FOR THE
Honest Skeptic

ANSWERING SKEPTIC OBJECTIONS TO BIBLICAL CHRISTIANITY

PART 3: THE CONFLICTING WORLD RELIGIONS

TED EVEN

Copyright © 2024 by Ted Even

ISBN 978-1-963917-36-9 (paperback)
ISBN 978-1-963917-37-6 (hardback)
ISBN 978-1-963917-38-3 (ebook)
Library of Congress Control Number: 2024908331

All rights reserved. No part of this publication may be reproduced, distributed, or transmitted in any form or by any means, including photocopying, recording, or other electronic or mechanical methods without the prior written permission of the publisher.

Printed in the United States of America

To my Lord and Savior, Jesus Christ—to him
who has created all,
be all glory forever and ever!

As it concerns those whom he created, this book is dedicated to
Nancy:

My sweetheart, my best friend, and my wife.

Without her love, patience, and encouragement,
this large endeavor would have been much more difficult.

Preface

 Please note that many of the objections within this work are so involved that they could well be a whole book all on their own. So, while this author has certainly purposed to make each objection thorough enough to do justice to the subject, at the same time, I have also endeavored to make the answer to each one as short as possible. Perhaps all objections which have been covered do not necessarily either apply to you or spark your interest. That's perfectly okay. We'll just say they were written for some other reader than yourself, shall we? Ultimately, I have tried to answer most all of the common objections which the honest skeptic may wrestle with. But please feel free to read and contemplate the answers to just those objections which may spark your personal interest.

 However, if you wish to just start at the beginning and read all of them, that would be my first recommendation, simply because there is *new information* within each objection which is vital in one's search for the overall truth. Admittedly, there is also some overlap of information with some of the objections, just because repetition can be a good teacher concerning those things which are of more importance. However, no matter whether the whole book is read or just in parts, it is my sincere desire that you would not only meet the real Jesus; but also understand that he is all about perfect love towards you and all men. And as your creator, he only wants the best for you…which not only includes a right and loving relationship with him but also his awesome eternal life which is truly beyond our comprehension.

 For those of you who may already know Christ and have always just wondered about many of the topics covered in this work, it is sincerely my hope that your faith in Christ will be truly strengthened and you will be able to honestly defend it to a greater capacity in these last days we are living in before the return of Christ. All scriptures are italicized, and the Bible versions being quoted from are the King James Version, Amplified Version, Revised Standard Version, New International Version, New King James Version, and the New Living Translation.

INTRODUCTION

During the Middle Ages, knights were the most courageous warriors in this world. Knights were gallant, strong, and kept their honor by defending the honor of their king. Dressed in their suits of armor, they were unafraid to face the mightiest of opponents in defense of their kingdom. Since any lasting kingdom must be established in truth if it is to endure, it was indeed even a spiritual battle between truth and deception which also raged in the hearts of those knights which did do mortal combat for their king.

You may well be thinking, *Yes, that was then, but now the world has changed and the days of such chivalry are long gone and over.* But are they? Is the battle between good and evil really over? Is the battle between truth and deception over? I think not. Are even real kings and kingdoms upon this earth just faded memories of the past? I think not. For in truth, my friend, it has long been predicted within the Holy Scriptures of that ancient book we call the Bible that there is a real physical but eternal kingdom of God which will soon be established upon the whole earth! And even now, Christ, the King of kings, continues to send out his knights into that same battle between truth and deception that men may know him and dwell in his eternal kingdom to come.

Many have held belief that it is heaven itself which will be the main eternal dwelling for all men of sound faith and character. But what are such misguided notions founded upon? For the holy scriptures themselves have always taught that the earth we dwell on will endure forever and that the *meek shall inherit* it (Psalms 78:69; Revelation 11:15; Matthew 5:5). Surprised? In fact, the Bible teaches us that this soon coming kingdom on earth will not only be eternally inhabited by all those who have believed in Christ but will be the awesome and beautiful likes of which this world has never seen! Indeed, as it is written:

> *Eye has not seen, nor ear heard, neither has it entered into the heart of man the things which God has prepared for them that love him.* (1 Corinthians 2: 9)

If you do not yet believe in the Bible, perhaps you just haven't encountered the basic honest evidence which soundly validates it. For example, did you know this remarkable book has already foretold in their exact order the last three world-dominating kingdoms on earth within only a few of its great prophecies? Hundreds and hundreds of years before their fulfillment, these major world empire predictions were given to the Jewish prophet, Daniel, during the Babylonian kingdom (about 606 BC). They explicitly foretold that the next world-dominating kingdoms following Babylon would be none other than the Medo-Persian kingdom, then the Greek kingdom, and then the Roman kingdom: in that exact order (Daniel 2:38–45, 7:3–9, 8:1–21). And just as history cannot lie, those prophecies through Daniel which spanned roughly 2,000 years after his time proved 100 percent accurate without flaw!

But let us not stop there, for these were not the only world-dominating kingdoms which were foretold to come within those awesome prophecies. Following the Roman empire which we already know to be history by at least 500 years, the Prophet Daniel also foretold that an eventual short kingdom will be ruled by that man known as the Antichrist with the ten nations which will give him their aid (Daniel 8:23–25; Revelation 17:10–13). While this most wicked kingdom is by far the shortest of all (only three and a half years long), unlike all kingdoms before it, it is foretold to literally dominate all peoples, tongues, and nations on earth with its one-world government and nearly cause the extinction of the human race (Revelation 13: 7; Isaiah 24:6; Matthew 24:22)!

But before the world will be destroyed by the Antichrist, many prophecies within the Bible also foretell that Christ himself, the King of kings, will once again step back into human history and throw down the Antichrist from his wicked throne to finally establish his everlasting realm on earth which has no end (Daniel 2:34–35, 2: 44–45; Revelation 19:11–21).

Nearly 3,000 years of human history has transpired since those amazing prophecies were given to the Prophet Daniel, and three of the five predicted world-dominating kingdoms have proven 100 percent accurate in their exact succession. And now the world races towards a one-world government which the Bible tells us is a prerequisite to the rule of the Antichrist. Coincidence? I think not.

My friend, no other so-called holy book in the world has even dared to lay out 3,000 years of human history in advance to prove its divine authorship through such large prophecies. And what of these next two world-dominating kingdoms to come? Was it just the Prophet Daniel who specifically foretold of them? Nay, my friend, for it was at least twenty some other prophets and apostles of the Holy Bible who also foretold of these very same two coming kingdoms!

And considering these major prophecies are accompanied by many smaller detailed prophecies attached to them, which have also proved accurate so far, it is quite amazing to say the least. The mathematical probabilities of these small and large predictions all coming true together in their exact foretold sequence by mere random reckless chance could hardly account for all their accurate fulfillments so far! After all, thousands of human freewill decisions were also involved in these major prophecies all coming true, and only someone who is all-knowing could have known which world-dominating empires would commence in the exact order they did.

However, if, in fact, our eternal God and creator, who is all-knowing, desired to clearly reveal himself to his own creation by foretelling the detailed future far in advance, then such astounding prophecies (along with hundreds of others within the Holy Bible) begin to make some real sense.

Depending upon one's source and how that source chooses to divide up Bible prophecy, the exact number of predictive prophecies contained within the Bible can vary. Nevertheless, did you know that the Bible itself contains *roughly* 2,500 predictions of the future, and all but about 500 of them have already been fulfilled with undeniable historical accuracy? Would it not then be rather heedless and hasty to just throw such power of prediction aside? For why would the Bible's potential to accurately predict our future be any less than its potential to have already predicted the past with accuracy?

Indeed, my friend, if one was to bring such powerful evidence of these many fulfilled prophecies into any earthly civil court for examination, would not the burden of proof that this great book is false be upon the unbeliever? And so, with at least the fair trial it deserves in any civil court, shall we not bring this uncommon book under our honest examination together?

Of course, if you have already predetermined that any honest evidence presented would matter not and sway you not, then shall we not fairly conclude that your present stance is just one of mere emotion? However, if honest evidence does indeed hold sway in your good heart, then, my friend, you would quickly prove your good worth in any lasting kingdom. Nevertheless, at this present time, it might just be you who is the honest skeptic, saying within yourself, "I cannot yet believe in your Christ, his coming kingdom, nor the Holy Bible which tells of them, for as of yet, I've not encountered the sound evidence required for them." Well, my friend, it has long been said that a skeptic retains his honor as long as he remains an *honest skeptic*, for the honest heart will always find the truth no matter how long the journey to get there.

> A skeptic retains his honor as long as he remains an honest skeptic, for the honest heart will always find the truth no matter how long the journey to get there.

Let us then fairly face the facts. Honest evidence for the truth will only guarantee one's belief in the truth if they themselves are honest with that evidence. But all the honest evidence in the world presented to those dishonest would accomplish about as much as putting good coin in a bag with holes. However, since honesty is a personal choice of the human free will, then all men can be basically honest enough to arrive at the truth if they should so choose. And if you be that honest skeptic, undoubtedly, your sincere objections to the Bible could well vary. Therefore, it is precisely for those valid objections which this extensive work was penned to address. What, therefore, is your weapon of choice, my friend? Shall we not ride out together with a sincere heart to do battle against the very lies and deceptions which do hinder the truth of reality? Let us then once and for all place the claims of this ancient book on fair trial and address with honesty those objections of the unbelieving skeptic which have been so prevalent among men. What say you?

Foretold by the one who is Ancient of Days almost twenty centuries ago, the basic account within the Holy Scriptures which predict God's coming kingdom on earth has echoed down through the long deplorable corridors of humanity, still awaiting its awesome fulfillment in an exact time undisclosed to man. However, as time continues to elude those who would restrain it, the irreversible signs of our present day, which continue to just confirm Bible prophecy, have plainly mounted up to confuse scoffers and skeptics alike, reminding even an unsuspecting generation such as ours of those awesome words which rumble down out of eternity:

"Surely I come quickly"
—Revelation 22:20

Table of Contents

Part 3 - The Conflicting World Religions

Objective 41 13
There Are So Many Religions in the World Which All Claim to be Right; How Can You Know Which One Is the Truth?

Objective 42 40
I'm A Humanist

Objective 43 53
I Believe in Hinduism

Objective 44 83
I Believe in Buddhism

Objective 45 104
I Believe in the New Age Movement

Objective 46 133
I'm a Muslim

Objective 47 156
I'm Jewish and Believe in the Old Testament Only

Objective 48 174
I've Been Accused of Being in a Cult, But I'm Not So Convinced Yet

Objective 49 199
I'm a Catholic

Objective 50 229
I'm a Mormon

Objective 51 254
I'm a Jehovah's Witness

Objective 52 .... **272**
I'm a Seventh-Day Adventist

Objective 53 .... **292**
I Believe in Satanism

Objective 54 .... **311**
I Believe in Scientology

Objective 55 .... **323**
I Believe in Freemasonry

Objective 56 .... **330**
I Believe in Nothing

Objective 39 .... **338**
As Long as You Are Sincere, What Does It Really Matter What You Believe?

Part 3: The Conflicting World Religions

Objection 41

There Are So Many Religions in the World Which All Claim to be Right; How Can You Know Which One Is the Truth?

Part I: Narrowing Down All the Religions of the World

The true faith

Yes, our world today is more crowded than ever with diverse religions and or belief systems which all lay claim to reality. However, as we already mentioned in previous objections in Part 2 of our series, upon honest and careful examination, one will quickly discover that all the independent different religions in the world certainly cannot be right. For even though they may have *some* similarities, just because their *basic doctrines alone all greatly conflict with each other*, we can be sure that not even two different religions in the world could even be right and representative of reality. Why? Simply because the real truth which is representative of reality can never contradict itself!

Quite logically, any supposed truth which *contradicts itself* must really be regarded as either nonreality or deception. And of course, their conflicting basic doctrines are exactly why all the different religions in the world have all split from each other in the first place and cannot reasonably *coexist* under one title.

For a simple example, if the Catholic religion teaches that one can only have eternal life by following their certain ordinances, and the

Objection 41
Which Religion Is True Among Many?

Muslim religion teaches that one can only have eternal life by following their certain ordinances, which are quite different than the Catholic ordinances, then we must reasonably and logically conclude that either one of them is wrong or both of them are wrong, for it is just not sanely possible to believe both are an accurate representation of reality if they basically contradict each other!

Are you with me so far? So, if not even two religions in the world can be right because of their conflicting basic doctrines, there remains then only *two reasonable basic options left* as it regards all the religions in the world which have different basic doctrines that conflict with each other: either *one of them is the truth* or *none of them are the truth!*

And, again, this is simply because the truth itself can never ever contradict itself and still remain the truth. My friend, this may surprise you, but it is just simple sane logic if we are honest with ourselves! If the life-giving truth ever could basically contradict itself and still remain the truth, then everything else in life is all rather meaningless indeed, simply because everything could contradict itself and would cause mass confusion because it did! Not to mention no one could ever discover any certain life-giving truths or anything that could help anyone!

Additionally, this whole simple reality of their having to be only a single true faith also fully cooperates with the fact that if you go back just a couple hundred years, there was really only a handful of different religions in the world compared to the thousands we see today! So we must then ask ourselves the very reasonable question, what did the whole world do for truth and salvation *before* all the later religions developed in our world if, in fact, all these later religions are the truth? If there is a God, he sure must be dropping the ball if any of these later religions are in fact the truth!

So, sadly, what must we conclude? Any way one would sanely choose to look at it, there's a whole lot of religious/spiritual deception going on in our world today, all of which makes perfect sense with what the Holy Bible has always taught: that all false doctrines and religions are ultimately hatched by the demonic realm to deceive mankind away from our one true creator and the eternal salvation he has for us (1 Timothy 4:1–2). And since the great number of deeply flawed religions in the world can be reasonably explained by the demonic realm being behind them, we should not be surprised to see many of the world religions and/or belief systems miserably fail the reasonable tests we can apply to them!

A loving reminder: However, just so my loving intentions cannot be misunderstood, it must be clearly stated up front that it is certainly not the adherents of any false religion (or belief system) which the true Church is against, but only those false teachings within that religion or belief system which deceive men away from the one and only true God and his eternal salvation (Ephesians 6:12). As the Bible clearly teaches that God himself does not *"wish that any should perish,"* neither should any who truly follow him want anyone to perish either (2 Peter 3:9). And this is why in many verses like Jude v. 3 and Ephesians 5:11, God's Word teaches all Christians to *"earnestly contend for the faith which was delivered to the saints (through Christ)"* and to *"expose"* the *"works of darkness,"* simply because the eternal life of men is truly at stake!

You see, God loves everyone, and everyone *has the right to know* if a religion or belief system is truly steering people away from him and his eternal salvation. In fact, if the true Church *did not expose false belief systems,* which do not pass the reasonable tests which we can apply to them, then it most certainly would be a reflection of its love! Would not a loving mother warn her children of spoiled food in the fridge? Of course she would because love just does that, even if she knew the spoiled food was a favorite and her kids would be disappointed! And, unfortunately, as we've already explained through simple reasoning, there is a whole lot of spoiled spiritual food in the world which is quite deadly if truly believed!

Therefore, my dear reader, please know that our discussion of all these various different religions or belief systems is very much a *love* issue. However, with all that said, even though one confirms that a given religion is false by way of combing through the honest evidence, that is certainly not to say that there could not be some (or even many in some cases) true believers in Christ within that false religion. This is especially true with those false religions which are *closest* to the biblical truth. In such cases, the Bible teaches us that *"the Lord knows them that are his"* (2 Timothy 2:19).

However, if, in fact, there are true believers in Christ within any false religion, it is certainly despite their official doctrines, not because of them! And to be sure, God would have such a true believer in Christ

Objection 41
Which Religion Is True Among Many?

leave that false religion before they lose their own stability in Christ (please see Romans 16:17; 1 Corinthians 5:11, 13; 2 Corinthians 6:14, Galatians 5:19–21; 1 Timothy 6:3-11; 2 Timothy 3:2–5; Titus 3:9–11)! To start with, let's just look at some more simple examples which easily expose the fact that the basic doctrines of all the different independent religions in the world most certainly conflict with each other.

> Just because of their conflicting basic doctrines, no two different religions in the world could possibly be right just according to simple sane logic!

Comparing atheistic belief systems with theistic belief systems

For the simplest example of all, it is sanely impossible to be an atheist who doesn't believe in a personal God and at the same time believes in any other religion which maintains there most certainly is a personal God behind it all. Let's be, again, honest: both of these types of belief systems simply cannot be the one true belief system representative of reality to the *honest* soul!

Comparing monotheistic religions

Additionally, even when comparing the different religions which all *do believe in a personal God,* it is even equally impossible to believe in all of them for the same basic reason. The following are just several among many examples of basic doctrinal differences between even monotheistic religions which are *honestly* irreconcilable:

1. According to the Muslim faith, Jesus Christ was just a prophet. But according to the Bible, Jesus Christ is God almighty who created everything that exists (Colossians 1:16–17). Thus, it is honestly impossible to believe in both of these religions just on this one point alone!
2. According to the Jehovah's Witnesses, Jesus Christ was actually Michael, the archangel, and the very first being God ever created. But, again, according to the Holy Bible, Jesus Christ is God, and Michael, the archangel, is only an angelic being who Jesus created (John 10:30–33).
3. According to the Moonies or Unification religion, Jesus Christ

is not God nor is he the creator. He was just a perfect man. But, again, according to the Bible, Jesus Christ is both our God and creator (John 1:1–17).
4. According to the Jewish faith, Jesus Christ was nothing more than a false prophet. But, again, according to the Bible, Jesus Christ was not only God and creator of all but also the Jewish Messiah (Isaiah 53; Daniel 9:24–26).
5. The Roman Catholic religion may say Jesus Christ is God and creator, but ironically, when it comes to Catholic tradition (laid out in their Catechism) and the word of the pope conflicting with what Jesus taught in the Holy Bible, the words of Christ are traditionally trumped by the pope and/or Catholic tradition. So who then, really, is God in the Catholic religion? The pope or Jesus? Again, one cannot believe in the Holy Bible and at the same time believe in all the Catholic traditional doctrines which clearly conflict with it.

Comparing polytheistic religions

And, of course, even when one compares polytheistic religions, there is very little unity and common ground to be found between them either. Greek mythology is very different than the Viking religion in that they both have different gods who all have different purposes, etc. And both of those are quite different than the polytheistic native American Indian religion. And, of course, all polytheistic religions are even quite different than the Hindu religion which literally believes in millions of gods. And all of these religions also obtain *their idea of salvation* quite differently as well.

So our point is that all the different religions of the world split from each other for good reason: because they are just too different to even coexist under one title! Even though some of them may certainly have *some* similarities, you'll always find that their *basic doctrines* conflict with each other as it concerns *who God is* or *who man is* and *how their idea of salvation is obtained*. And this plainly being the case then, what can we reasonably conclude?

Again, it is not only impossible to *honestly* harmonize all the different religions of the world (like some false religions actually pretend to do), but it is even impossible to *believe in any two of them*, simply because,

Objection 41
Which Religion Is True Among Many?

once again, their basic doctrines all conflict with each other. If you can believe in all of them even though all their basic doctrines conflict with each other, then you can obey two bosses at work telling you to do two *opposing* things. Then you can also believe a red traffic light is green and a green one red while driving through town. Then you can also believe 5+2 = 6 just as much as 5 + 1 = 6. Then you can also believe all the conflicting testimonies in a murder mystery.

As you can see, the list goes on for some time for similar examples of insanity! So quite reasonably, if it is actually impossible to believe in *any two conflicting religions* in the world, then very logically, this narrows all the basic different religions in the world down to our only two options which remain. Either only *one of them* is the truth or *none of them* are the truth. And if, in fact, only one is correct, then we can, of course, also be sure that all the rest, while they may undoubtedly have *some* truth in them, cannot basically represent the truth of reality and are ultimately deceptions which lead men away from the one true faith!

> All the different religions of the world split from each other for good reason: because they are too different to coexist. Logically, then, either only one of them is the truth, or none of them are the truth.

And before we could blindly rule out *all* religions or arrogantly just assume that *none of them are the truth*, any belief system (just like any person in court) deserves a fair trial, does it not? Besides, since all mankind and the universe got here somehow, it would certainly seem that just *assuming* none of them are the truth isn't a very viable option. For let's be, once again, honest: there must be *some* explanation for the very same reality we all live in, especially since it has never been observed in science that anything ever came from nothing! Therefore, it is much more reasonable to believe that there is a one true faith to discover, rather than believing *all religions are wrong*.

But even if it does reasonably exist, just how could man ever identify *the one true faith* which is representative of reality anyway? What reasonable criteria would the true religion have to meet in order for it to *honestly* represent reality? And if it is the one true faith, shouldn't it uniquely stand out from all others in some good and important ways? Is there a way to reasonably test the one true faith before we would put our trust in it? If there is such a thing as a one true faith, what then is a reasonable explanation for all the many conflicting religions in the world? In this third part of our series, we'll be exploring the answers to all these very important and reasonable questions.

Part II: The Uniqueness of Biblical Christianity

We must remember that every one of the different religions and/or belief systems of the world all claim to be the one true faith, which we've already concluded is absolutely impossible. And we've also reasonably concluded that it only makes good sense that there is a one true faith to discover which is representative of the same reality we all experience every day. And because *all but one* belief system in our world must be false by necessity, it is also perfectly reasonable to expect the *real* one true faith to *uniquely stand out in its credibility* from all others, which are, in fact, just counterfeits and deceptions. And as we've touched upon in previous objections, only biblical Christianity uniquely stands out from all other so-called true faiths of the world in the following awesome ways which truly sets it *major leagues apart* from them:

1. *Only Christ among all other so-called gods (of any other religion in the world) came down to earth and had historical eyewitnesses to actually testify to his divinity.* Jesus Christ truly stands *alone* in recorded human history as not only the only one who *seriously claimed* to be the one and only God and creator of all things but also the only one who even began to display all the divine attributes of God Almighty in front of thousands of real historical eye witnesses (both friendly and hostile) in order to back up his claims! While professional historians consider the New Testament to be one of the most reliable historical documents which we possess, it cannot be confirmed by any reliable historical witnesses that any other so-called god of any other religion has been seen, touched, and talked to on earth while displaying all the divine attributes of God. Jesus Christ truly stands alone and is unique in this very basic respect!

Objection 41
Which Religion Is True Among Many?

Only Christ among all other so-called gods came down to earth and had many historical eye witnesses to actually witness his divinity.

As we already discussed in Objection #12, no so-called god of any polytheistic religion has ever visited mankind in this regard and displayed their obvious divine power with real historical eyewitnesses. This is also historically true for the gods of Hinduism or Mormonism as well, even though there are millions to choose from within both of those belief systems!

But, also, this could be said of all other religions which just claim a single monotheistic God as well. For example, Allah, the god of Islam, has never visited mankind on earth and displayed his divinity as Christ did. Nor can it be said that the Jesus of all the so-called Christian *cults* visited humanity when Christ did, simply because Christ himself never once promoted their particular religion by title, or any of their unique doctrines!

For example, when Jesus came to earth, he did not set up nor even talk about the Mormon Church. If the extra books (*Pearl of Great Price*, *Doctrines and Covenants*, and *The Book of Mormon*) of the Mormons are so critical to man's spiritual welfare, then why didn't Jesus (or even his apostles) ever refer to them even one single time? Nor did they set up, nor even talk about the Jehovah's Witnesses church. If, in fact, these *very small religions* are the truth, then why didn't Jesus even mention them once by name or *any* of their unique doctrines? It is most certainly an honest question for the honest soul!

When Jesus came to earth, he did not even set up or talk about the Catholic Church by name either. If the Catholic Church is truly the only one true church, you have to *honestly* explain why Jesus never mentioned it once by name or any of their unique doctrines, if, in fact, he wanted the whole world to be saved! If popes, cardinals, praying to Mary, purgatory, the Jesuit order, the seven sacraments, the use of holy water, and all the many other unique teachings of the Catholic religion are so critical to the one true church, then why didn't Jesus (or even any of his apostles) ever even mention any of these special doctrines even one single time?! And the same could be asked about the teachings of all other so-called Christian *cults* which clearly deviate from the basic teachings New Testament.

The simple truth is that none of the many contradicting religions in the world have ever demonstrated the real power of God to mankind as Christ and the apostles did many times over to clearly back up the fact that theirs is the one true faith which obviously comes from the one true God. The bottom line is that only true biblical Christianity reveals the one true God to all mankind through Christ who physically came down to earth and walked among men clearly displaying all the divine attributes we would expect of our perfect eternal creator.

2. *Only biblical Christianity teaches that the eternal life of God Almighty is an unearned gift to be humbly received by 100 percent faith in Christ and not some reward to be won through human effort (Ephesians 2:8–9).* All other religions or belief systems in the world teach that man has to *at least partially* earn their idea of heaven in some way or another *through human effort.* Some religions might teach that faith in Christ is *part* of your ticket to heaven (like the Catholic religion, Mormon religion, or Seventh Day Adventists), but at the same time, they will also teach that you must also keep their certain unique laws in order to obtain their version of heaven as well (like keeping the Ten Commandments).

Yes, we should all try our best (with God's help) to live God's law, but if, in fact, that was a hard fast requirement for eternal life, no one who has ever lived (not even Christ's apostles) would be able to obtain it! Since we've already pointed out thoroughly in Objection #19 that no one can even come close to keeping all of God's perfect moral standards, why would our perfect creator (who already knows we cannot keep his perfect moral stands) even begin to make that even a *partial requirement* to obtain his eternal life? And this is exactly what proves all the man-made religions in the world false because they make the obvious mistake of asking the impossible!

But at the same time, it just makes perfect sense that our perfect creator (representing the one true faith) would not ask us to keep his perfect moral standards to obtain his eternal life, simply because he would already be quite aware that we simply could not really keep them in order to earn his eternal life. And as even our Objection #19 more thoroughly discussed, even the best of men cannot even come

Objection 41
Which Religion Is True Among Many?

close to keeping all the perfect moral standards of our creator.

So for all the conflicting false religions of the world, to attach man's salvation to such a thing is to set the stage for immediate failure! As the saying goes: *"Faith disconnected from reality is faith misplaced."* For example, if you believe there is a chair behind you to sit on, and when attempting to sit down, there really isn't one there, your faith will be painfully misplaced, simply because it wasn't actually connected to reality! And, unfortunately, this is the very same kind of *painful misplaced faith* all the contradicting false religions of the world promote in order to obtain their idea of eternal life.

> Only biblical Christianity teaches that the eternal life of God Almighty is an unearned gift to be humbly received by 100 percent faith in Christ and not some reward to be won through human effort.

Even humanistic belief systems like Darwinian evolution, which may reject an afterlife altogether, still teach that human effort is to be relied upon for human survival. But biblical Christianity sets mankind free from all that striving and works for his own survival in this life and eternal life beyond. And, really, when you think about it, it only makes decent sense that a perfect God would certainly know we simply cannot do what only he can to obtain his eternal life. But just upon basic examination of just what is required for their salvation, no other religion in the world gets that, other than biblical Christianity! If salvation comes through man's performance of keeping God's perfect moral standards, then not only is there no hope for any man to obtain the salvation of God, but Christ also died on the cross in vain because he did not actually *finish* the work of man's salvation, if we must also help him with our good works!

But as it is, Jesus did completely finish the work of our salvation on the cross as he plainly said just before he died: *"It is finished"* (John 19:30)!

> Faith disconnected from reality is simply faith misplaced.

> 3. *Only biblical Christianity has a reliable historical record of each and every generation which goes all the way back to the very first man and woman created by God.* The genealogy

lists of both the Old and New Testaments combined give us each and every generation from Christ all the way back to Adam and Eve, which confirms that creation itself is only about 6,000 years old (see Genesis chapters 5, 10, 11, and Matthew 1:1–17). My friend, no other major religion or belief system in the world *even attempts* to field a complete and accurate record of human genealogy all the way back to the beginning of the human race! But if they are the one true faith, which represents the true God of all creation, one must reasonably ask, why don't they give us something which is so basic and reasonable to man's existence?

If our one and only true creator did start the one and only true faith, it only makes sense that preserving such records would be only reasonable if he wanted humanity to believe in him! And the fact that biblical Christianity does have such a record is certainly a reasonable prerequisite to the one true faith because, really, only the one true faith could have such records when you reasonably think about it! To date, no historian has found error in the Bible's genealogical records when cross-examining them with other historical records whenever they can.

Judaism does have its list of each and every generation from Abraham back to Adam and Eve in Genesis chapters 5, 10, 11, but because Judaism rejects the New Testament and holds only to the Old Testament, only biblical Christianity has the complete list of each and every generation from Christ all the way back to Adam and Eve. Judaism may be able to patch together some of the generations from Christ (who they don't believe in) back to Abraham, but the Old Testament still lacks the inspired consecutive list of each and every generation from Christ back to Abraham which only the New Testament contains.

4. *Interestingly enough, biblical Christianity is really the only religion in the world which accurately predicted over 2,000 years ago that the world would be filled with many conflicting different religions, just before the return of Christ!* Did you know that such a 2,000-year-old prediction is simply not found in any other founding written documents of any other religion in the world? And, again, all the small

Objection 41
Which Religion Is True Among Many?

Christian cults which may just *use* the Holy Bible in part along with their other special added books and literature cannot fairly claim that their religion predicted all the conflicting religions in the world through the Holy Bible because neither Christ nor his apostles breathed a word about their particular religion either by name or unique doctrine. Besides, *any* religion which uses the Holy Bible in addition to their other books and literature will most *always* believe in their other books and literature in any case when they disagree with the Holy Bible.

Thus, while they may *use* the Holy Bible for what they can get out of it in order to promote their own religion, they cannot reasonably claim that the Holy Bible is theirs as a founding doctrinal document of their religion, especially in light of the fact that the Holy Bible existed long before their particular religion even got started in the world!

In the 1600s, when America was first being established, it is common knowledge among historians that the world at large did not have all the different conflicting religions which we see today. The main religions in both Europe and the Americas were basically Catholic and Protestant, and if there were others, they were only subdivisions of those two. And, of course, there was eastern religions of both Hinduism and Buddhism, but today, it is quite different as we see, literally, *thousands of different religions* in the world which clearly conflict with each other in their basic doctrines.

My point is that, clearly, no honest historian would doubt that there has most certainly been an explosion of false conflicting religions in the world during the last century! The following are just some verses within the Holy Bible which collectively predict that during the last days before the return of Christ, there will most certainly be a *massive explosion* of conflicting false religions, which we now observe in our world today:

"[W]hat will be the sign of your coming, and of the end of the age?

Then many false prophets will rise up and deceive many." (Matthew 24:3,11; see also parallel accounts in both Mark 13:4–6 and Luke 21:7–8)

"Now the Spirit (of God) expressly says that in latter times (before the return of Christ) some will depart from the faith, giving heed to deceiving spirits and doctrines of demons." (1 Timothy 4:1)

"But know this, that in the last days (before the return of Christ) perilous times will come: For men will be lovers of themselves, lovers of money, boasters, proud, blasphemers, disobedient to parents, unthankful, unholy, unloving, unforgiving, slanderers, without self-control, brutal, despisers of good, traitors, headstrong, haughty, lovers of pleasure rather than lovers of God, having a form of godliness, but denying its power. From such people turn away! For of this sort are those who creep into households and make captives of gullible women loaded down with sins, led away by various lusts, always learning and never able to come to the knowledge of the truth." (2 Timothy 3:1–7)

"But evil men and imposters (of the true faith) will (in the last days according to context: see 2 Timothy 3:2-7) grow worse and worse, deceiving and being deceived." (2 Timothy 3:13)

"For the time will come (in the last days before the return of Christ according to context: see 2 Timothy 3:1-7) when they will not endure sound doctrine, but according to their own desires, because they have itching ears, they will heap up for themselves teachers; and they will turn their ears away from the truth." (2 Timothy 4:3–4)

"Knowing this first: that scoffers will come in the last days (before the return of Christ), walking according to their own lusts, and saying, Where is the promise of his coming?" (2 Peter 3:3–4)

"Little Children, it is the last hour; and as you have heard that the Antichrist is coming, even now many Antichrists have come, by which we know it is the last hour. They went out from us, but they were not of us; for if they had been of us, they would have continued with us." (1 John 2:18–19)

"[I] found it necessary to write to you exhorting you to contend earnestly for the faith which was once for all delivered to the saints. For certain men have crept in unnoticed, who long ago were marked out for this condemnation, ungodly men, who turn the grace of our Lord into lewdness and deny the only Lord God and our Lord Jesus Christ... But you, beloved,

Objection 41
Which Religion Is True Among Many?

remember the words which were spoken before the apostles of our Lord Jesus Christ: how they told you that there would be mockers in the last time (before the return of Christ) who would walk according to their own ungodly lusts." (Jude vs. 3–19)

And not only is biblical Christianity unique in that it, over 2,000 years ago, predicted the many conflicting false religions which we see in the world today, but it also predicted along with them an increase in immorality, wars, famines, diseases, earthquakes, and a one-world government forming in preparation for *the Antichrist*, all after Israel has regathered as a nation (Matthew 24:6–8; Revelation 13:3–7; Matthew 24:32–34)!

My friend, no other religion in the world has predicted all these major things to happen *all at one time* (just before the return of Christ) so long ago. And amazingly enough, all this is exactly what we've seen happen in our world just during the last seventy years or so! Mere coincidence? The notion seems rather absurd, don't you think? It makes much more sense to believe that the fulfillments of such major predictions (which includes the explosion of false religions) all coming true together at the same time is just more evidence that biblical Christianity is, in fact, the one true faith. After all, what other religion or belief system has accurately predicted all this just as the Bible has, much less predicted it two thousand years ago?

Part III: Testing All Religions In Search of the One True Faith

It seems everything in our fallen world has to be tested before it can be trusted. Whether it is the car you drive before it leaves the factory or the spouse you marry, it seems as time goes on, there are just more and more rules and laws safe-guarding and testing all things of society so they can be trusted to give life and not harm to the human race. So if all other things of the rational world, which are vital to man's survival and well-being in society must be tested before they can be trusted, how much more should our spiritual beliefs be tested before we can really trust them, especially if they boldly prescribe the way of our eternal life? For what if one is truly deceived about something so important?

Our spiritual beliefs are extremely important, not only because they speak for our afterlife, but even in this life, it has been largely observed that it is our spiritual beliefs which most often are the unseen driving influence behind the rest of our rational life which, in turn, directly affects our well-being. Thus, the testing of any spiritual belief system is not anything anyone should be offended by or take personal as it is meant only to be an objective and practical investigation with the loving motive to protect the human race from real harm, not only in this life but in the next!

> If all other things of the rational world, which are vital to man's well-being, must be tested before they are trusted, how much more should our spiritual beliefs be tested before we trust them, especially if they boldly prescribe the way of our eternal salvation?

But just how can we possibly test an invisible set of spiritual beliefs to see if it is the one and only truth anyway? Many may not know it, but very easily. One just has to know the simple tests the one true faith should very reasonably pass if, in fact, it is the reliable truth which gives men life. And, of course, one must be completely *honest* with themselves in the process when testing any religion; otherwise, the process is quite meaningless indeed. It would be about as meaningless as setting out to sea in a boat which has a decent hole in its bottom! Thus, if we are ever going to find the truth, it only makes good sense that *honesty* itself is only a reasonable prerequisite.

The following incomplete but quite adequate list of testing methods are actually not only reasonable but have always been quite effective and completely satisfactory to the conscience of man. And because *all but one* religion (or spiritual belief system) must reasonably and logically be false due to all their conflicting basic doctrines, we, of course, must fully expect to see *all religions but one miserably fail* the following tests which we'll be discussing! We will discuss at least ten different basic reasonable tests which can expose any religion as false and at the same time help us to also confirm the one true faith which belongs to our one true perfect and eternal creator.

In the following Objections #42 through #55, we'll be specifically discussing many of the main false religions in the world and how they obviously fail the following very reasonable tests:

Objection 41
Which Religion Is True Among Many?

Test #1: Testing a religion against the true moral condition of man

Let's start with one of the most obvious tests first: discerning the true moral condition of man. Does mankind have many moral failures throughout his (or her) entire life or not? Is there even such a thing as morality? Well, as we already thoroughly confirmed in Objection #19, there most certainly is such a thing as morality when you are the one being violated by someone immoral! And as we also confirmed in Objection #19, we certainly all do morally fail many times throughout our life time if we are honest enough to compare ourselves with the perfect moral standards of God and not just with the gutter drunks and bank robbers of society!

As it concerns our civil court laws, the moral failure of man may simply be defined as a crime. And a civil crime is usually defined as some act which is deemed *harmful to mankind* and breaks a civil law in an obvious way; thus, even civil crimes are a moral failure in the eyes of the world. As it concerns the Bible-believing Church, moral wrongs are not only those civil law-breaking things harmful to our fellow man but are also all those things we do or don't do which fails the perfect moral standards of our perfect creator. Within the Bible, the moral failure of man may be referred to as sin, iniquity, or even transgression, but ultimately, those are all just different terms for when we break God's perfect moral standards.

Yes, in Objection #19, we firmly establish the fact that all men fail the moral laws of God many times even in a given day. Because the range of moral wrong within the Church (that which breaks God's perfect law) is much more extensive than the range of moral wrongs (or crimes) according to civil law (that which obviously hurts mankind), it is fair to say that civil law crimes are then just a large *subset* within what the Bible calls sin (the breaking of God's perfect law). However, no matter how you define moral wrongs (crimes or sin), both the Church and state of any society all down through recorded human history has always maintained the reality of man's moral failure! And whether Church or state, they both agree within the *very conscience* of all men that any moral wrong is something harmful to mankind. And whether one believes in the Bible or not, all people consistently fail to live according to even their own standards and conscience as well and consistently fail to treat others the way they would want to be treated themselves.

Therefore, let's again be basically honest. If a certain spiritual belief system, which claims to represent reality for the whole world, insists that there is no such thing as sin or moral wrongs, when the plain historical evidence within every society that has ever existed shows otherwise, then that right there is the very first test they fail. Very reasonably, should we not reject that belief system in as much as it has rejected all the honest evidence for the plain moral failure of mankind throughout our entire history? And because all but one religion (or spiritual belief system) must reasonably and logically be false due to all their conflicting basic doctrines, it should not surprise us to find that *more than one false religion* out there actually teaches that there is simply no such thing as moral wrongs or sin. And this alone should rule them out as the one true faith in the hearts and minds of those honest with themselves on this issue.

> If a certain spiritual belief system insists that there is no such thing as sin or moral wrongs, when the plain historical evidence within every society that has ever existed shows otherwise, then that right there is the very first test they fail.

Test #2: Testing a religion against self-contradictions

Any religion can be tested against its own claims to see if it contradicts itself. If a certain faith, religion, or belief system obviously contradicts itself, then it too can be easily ruled out as the one true faith. Every man in his or her conscience knows that any belief system which represents the truth cannot obviously contradict itself any more than the truth can contradict itself or a perfect eternal God could ever contradict himself. This means that any given religion professing to be the truth simply cannot have any *unsolvable contradictions*. And, again, because all but one religion must logically be false due to all their conflicting basic doctrines, it should not surprise us to find that many conflicting religions in the world do in fact have many *unsolvable* contradictions which would rule them out as the one true faith. However, as we've already pointed out in Objection #24, these *unsolvable contradictions* are much different than *apparent contradictions*, which are reasonably solved when honestly examined further.

Objection 41
Which Religion Is True Among Many?

Similarly, if a particular religion is, in fact, the one true faith, it should equally not surprise us if we cannot find any unsolvable contradictions within it, which is just what we should expect with the truth coming from an eternal creator who must reasonably be morally perfect. But why would the one true faith even have to have *apparent contradictions* which must be studied out to be solved? For a decent explanation of this subject, please refer back to objection #24 in part 2 of our series.

> Every man in his or her conscience knows that any belief system which represents the truth cannot obviously contradict itself any more than the truth can contradict itself.

The bottom line is if a religion or even a main doctrine of that religion has *unsolvable contradictions with no reasonable or honest explanation or solution*, then that religion can be safely ruled out, even if you find only *one* such contradiction. Why? Because most every religion (or belief system) which represents either a perfect God or the complete truth which attempts to define reality for all mankind should not contradict itself *even once* if it is truly trustworthy. If it does, then obviously, it cannot be trusted to give man goodness, much less eternal life!

The truth is that even just *one* unsolvable contradiction should break our trust, just like only *one* hole in the bottom of a big beautiful boat should be unacceptable to us if we are going out to sea in it! In fact, even imperfect civil organizations cannot have ongoing dishonest or deceitful contradictions within them without breaking trust with human society. So how much more is trust broken if a religion claims to represent the truth and the only way to eternal life for the whole human race and it clearly contradicts itself without a reasonable solution? However, as we'll discuss, one need not worry about any religion having just one single unsolvable contradiction, for as we'll show, if any religion or belief system truly has one unsolvable contradiction, it undoubtedly has many more as well upon further investigation.

Test #3: Testing a religion against the well-known facts of history

Any religion which touches upon the subject of history can be tested against the well-known facts of history to see if its claims are really trustworthy and its source is the one true God who is both perfect and eternal. For example, if the New Testament clearly teaches that Pilate, the Governor of Judea, had Christ crucified and secular history did not even bear witness to the fact that Pilate was the governor at that time, then the gospels of the New Testament would be seriously discredited. But, of course, secular history affirms the many historical aspects of the New Testament, and because of that, the New Testament is just affirmed as the one true faith all the more. However, as we'll soon demonstrate, other so-called true religions certainly do not fare so well when tested against the well-known facts of recorded history.

Test #4: Testing a religion against the well-known facts of science

Any religion which touches upon science can be tested against the well-known facts of science to see if its claims are really trustworthy and its source is reliable. For example, the only explanation offered in the Hindu religion for what holds up our planet earth is that the earth actually rests on the back of four massive elephants, which in turn are standing on the back of a great cosmic sea turtle which is swimming across the sea of the cosmos. The Chinese and Native American Iroquois Indians both have somewhat similar explanations for the planetary heavens. These religions may refer to such beliefs of theirs as mere myths, but nevertheless, because their myths are the only explanations they are able to give, it is certainly no feather in their cap if they contradict true science, which was later discovered!

Obviously, these ancient beliefs were started long before modern science and such explanations offered by the leaders of those religions were just chickens they assumed would never come home to roost. But I think modern science can now safely rule such ridiculous beliefs out!

Let's face it, what good is even a myth if that myth clearly steers men away from reality backed by true science? While we may look at such beliefs today with humor, what really does it say about those faiths which claim to have the spiritual truth *and their version of eternal life* for all mankind? Are we not rather forced to conclude that those religions cannot honestly be a reliable source of *spiritual truth* if, in fact, they are clearly wrong about such *physical realities* within the field of natural science?

Objection 41
Which Religion Is True Among Many?

On the other hand, when the Bible does touch upon the subject of science, its claims have only been validated over and over again. And unlike most other religions, the Bible makes itself quite vulnerable simply because it has made so many scientific claims hundreds and even thousands of years before man discovered them to be so! Similar to the cosmic sea turtle, there was a time when the European scientific world seriously believed the world to be flat! However, if they had just read Isaiah 40:22 (written roughly 700 years before Christ), they most certainly would have known that it had to be a round *sphere*.

In fact, Job 26:10 and Prov. 8:27 also use the same Hebrew word "khug" for circle, which in context means "sphere". In Genesis chapter 1, it teaches that the earth began as water only. And our sciences have always observed that water suspended in space always takes the form of a sphere due to the surface tensions of water molecules. Thus, we also see that the earth's shape must be spherical just going by God's description of how the earth was made. When dry land appeared, Gen. 1:9 describes all the land as existing "in one place" while all waters are gathered in the same manner. Geometrically, this can only happen on a sphere, and therefore Gen. 1 also implies a spherical earth. Even today, some still absurdly insist that the earth is flat. But not only have many scientists of the past centuries confirmed the spherical shape of the earth taught within God's word through simple experiments and mathematical proofs, but also our more recent high altitude aircraft and satellites orbiting our planet have just confirmed their findings many times over. And even our simple observations from the ground agree with scripture and our modern science, for when standing on the shore looking out on the horizon, one can easily see that the spherical curvature of the earth cuts off the bottom of ships in the distance. Also, if both the moon and earth were not spherical, then they would not maintain the same basic shape as we observe them constantly rotating from all different directions via satellites. Obviously a flat earth would have to drastically change basic shape as we observe it rotating from a satellite which is also orbiting the earth!

> Are we not rather forced to conclude that those religions cannot honestly be a reliable source of spiritual truth if, in fact, they are clearly wrong about physical realities within the field of natural science?

Test #5: Testing a religion against well-known geography

If a religion which claims to be the truth and even mentions certain places of geography in its writings which simply don't exist or are even out of place, this too should be a red flag. Men truly inspired of the one true God simply cannot make such mistakes! For example, in 1832, Joseph Smith, a self-proclaimed prophet of God, prophesied that the Mormons would build the city of New Jerusalem in western Missouri before Joseph Smith's generation would die off. Of course, this geographical city has never been found anywhere at all within the United States during or after Joseph Smith's generation. However, on the other hand, no geographical claim of the Bible has been proven false to this day.

Test #6: Testing a religion against archaeological discoveries

Archaeologists should be able to basically confirm the basic historical claims of the one true faith. If well-known archaeological discoveries clearly conflict with the historical claims of a religion, then we have the perfect right to reject that religion which claims to be the truth for all mankind. However, one must be a bit careful because just because something has not yet been discovered by archaeologists, which confirms a historical account, does not necessarily mean that it did not happen, and evidence for it will not be uncovered by archaeologists in the near future. For example, the Bible clearly claims that the major Hittite empire once existed in the area of Canaan.

For a while, the evolutionists mocked creation scientists and the Bible, simply because archaeologists could not find the evidence for such an empire. However, it wasn't until just more recently that modern archaeologists actually discovered the obvious evidence for such a vast empire. I guess the evolutionists had to back up their truck as once again, the Bible proved true, even though it took a little time and searching by man. Perhaps that's one reason why Jesus said, *"Seek and you shall find"* (Matthew 7:7–8). However, on the other hand, no archaeological evidence has been found in the Americas which can clearly confirm the unique claims of the *Book of Mormon*.

For example, the *Book of Mormon* claims that the Americas were, in fact, settled by ancient Egyptians and Hebrews. However, not even one

Objection 41
Which Religion Is True Among Many?

single *authentic* Ancient Egyptian or Hebrew writing or archaeological object has been found by archaeologists which confirm their basic teaching on this issue!

Test #7: Testing a religion against the character of its founders

Any religion should also be tested against the well-known character of its *founder(s)*. When you think of it, like all our other tests, this too is only reasonable, especially if that founder (or founders) claims to have founded a faith or religion from the perfect eternal God who determines the eternal destiny of all mankind!

For example, if the founders of any religion maintain immoral character, let's be honest: no one should even take that religion seriously because it simply cannot be trusted! For example, when we read from reliable historical record that Mohammed, the founder of Islam, constantly raided caravans, murdered, and stole wealth from others, took the wives of others, mutilated others, and built up an army of cutthroats to achieve all these things, just to build up his own man-made religion by force, we should be able to safely rule out Islam as the one true faith right there on the spot! If a man claiming to have the truth and way of eternal life for the whole world can live immorally anyway they want like that, then that would be no different than a civil court judge killing, raping, and stealing and at the same time insisting that society trust him to administer justice!

My friend, the notion is absurdly insane! However, in stark contrast to Mohammad, there is no reliable historical record which bears witness to Christ or his apostles living immorally and doing any such immoral things as Mohammed did.

> If the founders of any religion maintain immoral character, let's be honest: no one should even take that religion seriously!

Test #8: Testing a religion against its own prophetic predictions of the future

It's plain and simple. As we covered in Objection #18 of part 1 of our series, the God who very intelligently created everything must ultimately be an eternal being. And this just makes sense with a God who offers mankind eternal life, for he could offer nothing of the sort if he himself were not eternal. But in order to be an eternal being, God would also have to be absolutely perfect in character in order to endure eternally. And in order to predict the future with accuracy, the one true God would have to be all-knowing, which, of course, would be part of his moral perfection. Therefore, if any religion falsely predicts the future, they simply could not speak for the perfect eternal God who is all-knowing and created all!

For example, as we will point out in further detail, the Jehovah's Witnesses have foolishly attempted and failed to predict the exact year of Christ's return on many occasions in our recent past. How then can they and their prophets speak for God and lay claim to the one true faith? The answer is they can't and should be ruled out just on this basis alone (aside from even many other very reasonable tests, which they also completely fail to pass).

Additionally, Joseph Smith, the founder of the Mormon religion, gave several false prophecies just within the Mormon book of *Doctrine and Covenants*, which simply did not come to pass. We cite more than one of those prophecies in Objection #50 when we discuss the Mormon religion. The reality is that false prophecies always come from a false prophet. And if the founder of a certain religion is himself a false prophet, then obviously, that entire religion is also false.

> The reality is that false prophecies always come from a false prophet. And if the founder of a certain religion is himself a false prophet, then that entire religion is also false.

Test #9: Testing a religion against the fruit it has produced

It is certainly true that every religion can be abused and truly misrepresented and probably has been. However, when a belief system itself (when not misrepresented) directly produces consistent obvious bad fruit, then that too should be a spiritual red flag.

For example, what about a belief system like the Theory of Evolution? What kind of fruit has it really produced since Charles Darwin's death? Many may not know it, but both Charles Darwin and Karl Marx lived in some real poverty and sickness with abnormal suicides and deaths in their families. Darwin himself married too close of a cousin, which

Objection 41
Which Religion Is True Among Many?

very possibly was a result of his beliefs in natural selection. As a result, at least one of his children suffered abnormalities.

Furthermore, history has shown that once God is taken out of the picture, men—especially those with power—become moral loose cannons, and they often leave a great wake of destruction behind them. Why? Because they obviously believe that they no longer have to be accountable to God if they do not even believe in him! Talk about no accountability or oversight! And considering the Theory of Evolution inevitably teaches no God and survival of the fittest, it's no wonder that merciless bloodshed has been a constant fruit which it has produced on both a small and large scale.

Of course, the Columbine High School shooting could be cited as one of many small-scale examples. The teenagers who did the shooting wore natural selection T-shirts and performed their merciless act on Hitler's birthday, who also strongly believed in evolution. Just an isolated freak coincidence? I think not.

In other words, if people really believe they are a direct descendant of the ape family, why should it surprise us if they act just like them? And what about the fruit evolution has produced on a bigger scale? To say the long-range effects of evolution manifesting after Charles Darwin's death had nothing to do with the great bloodshed caused by communist or socialist rulers who specifically took on Darwin's basic beliefs of evolution in the century following would make little sense considering the spiritual beliefs of man have always driven his political actions throughout history.

Like Charles Darwin, Karl Marx, the founder of Marxism (which is also a spiritual belief system), also rejected God of the Bible and believed in Darwinian evolution. Lenin, Stalin, Mussolini, Hirohito, Mao Zedong, and Hitler all believed not only in evolution but also in either communism or socialism, which beliefs have typically all rejected the God of the Bible. And what honestly were the fruits of all these men? The truth is, my friend, that collectively, our very recent history bears witness that all combined, they were responsible for the merciless deaths of well over 100 million souls!

Test #10: Testing a religion against divine power displayed

If a religion claims to have come from the one and only true God who is perfect, eternal, all-knowing, and all-powerful, then it is only reasonable for that religion to be backed by the divine power of its claims in some real ways. Even if a belief system just claims to represent reality for all mankind without mention of a perfect God, then should it not provide some real evidence of power or clout which exceeds that of mere human opinion or the very limited common ability of mankind? Otherwise, we can all just make up our own religion if nothing beyond weak human performance is required to validate it as the truth!

Because one mere human opinion is just as good as any other, if no uncommon power is displayed through that belief system, give me one good reason why we should let that belief system define reality for the rest of the human race? Examples of such divine power displayed to all mankind would include both miracles and many prophecies fulfilled which foretold the future with 100 percent accuracy. While the Holy Bible is, in fact, littered with both of these obvious displays of God's power throughout our reliable historical record, my friend, no other religion or belief system in the world has even come close to sufficiently displaying any real power on earth which would convince us it is from something other than mere human weakness just influenced by the demonic realm!

Conclusion

So, in conclusion, these ten basic tests are both effective and reasonable as a means to rule out all the false man-made religions of the world, which simply could not have originated from an eternal God who is perfect and does not contradict himself. Just as real honest evidence would be required for anyone claiming to be God (like Christ did), so also it is equally reasonable for the one true faith to provide the necessary and only reasonable evidence for its powerful claims as well. Ultimately, Bible-believing Christians do not just believe Jesus Christ is just who he claimed to be because of their own personal *lives have been changed much for the better* but also because biblical Christianity has always stood up to the very reasonable tests we've just discussed.

Objection 41
Which Religion Is True Among Many?

In other words, biblical Christianity is not an emotional blind faith. It is only a reasonable faith, which may indeed go beyond our reason in many respects (as all religions and belief systems must) but never against reason, like all false religions do. As it has been well said:

> The human heart simply cannot accept what the human mind rejects.

Now let us employ these various testing methods against the following different religions of the world and see just how they fare. Since all tests may not as prominently apply to one particular religion/belief system as well as they do others, we'll be testing each one with only those tests (that we've discussed) which apply the best to them. And while we are, of course, not able to test any religion/belief system thoroughly or completely (which would take volumes of work), the tests which we do apply should certainly be sufficient to expose whether or not that religion/belief system is worthy of our basic trust. And please also know that while there could be many more false religions which we discuss, we've just chosen to expose the main popular ones for the sake of keeping this work as short as possible.

Additionally, while we will test the following religions or belief systems and expose the fact that they *are not even close to what we would reasonably expect of the one true faith*, please once again understand that it's certainly *not the adherents* of any false religion which the true Church is against but rather just the *false teachings* within that false religion which deceive men away from the one and only true God and his eternal salvation.

Let's be honest: if the eternal salvation of men is at stake, are we not totally justified to reasonably test any religion/belief system which would have major influence upon it? Therefore, the only thing to be *against* are just the deceptions of those belief systems which hold men captive and endanger their opportunity for eternal life.

When testing any religion or belief system, it is a time to be objective, not taking anything personal, simply because God loves all men equally and does not wish that any should perish (2 Peter 3:9)! And if you are one who may be entangled in a false belief system or religion which we discuss, it is my sincere hope that by carefully exploring the following honest evidence, you would be finally set free to believe in the truth of the Bible, which offers all men the eternal life and fulfillment that only your one true perfect creator can provide.

While it may be clearly understood that many within the different conflicting religions of the world are born into them and thus emotionally attached to them, the bottom line is that our adherence to any belief system which professes to prescribe the only way of eternal life for all mankind must be founded upon something much more substantial than our emotional attachment! Because, ultimately, it must be realized that, really, no man can be *just* born into the spiritual truth or grandfathered into heaven through birth. Therefore, our chosen spiritual beliefs must be a personal choice for which we take personal responsibility to find the truth of reality based on sufficient honest evidence. Thus, the saying:

"We are not born winners, we are not born losers: but we are all born choosers."

OBJECTION 42

I'm A Humanist

A loving reminder: Before each false belief system we discuss, just so my loving intentions cannot be misunderstood, I will *once again* remind the reader that it's certainly *not the adherents* of any false belief system which the true Church is against but rather just the *false teachings* within them which deceive men away from the one and only true God and his eternal salvation (Ephesians 6:12). Therefore, my dear reader, please know that our discussion of these various different religions or belief systems is very much a *love* issue.

Defining humanism

Humanism itself is kind of a larger umbrella belief system which actually branches out into various different God denying belief systems like atheism, evolution, and agnosticism. But no matter what the humanistic belief system, it will ultimately steer men away from a belief in personal God and teach men to be self-reliant instead. And while self-reliance may sound good and appeal to many, it actually makes very little sense when you really pause to reasonably think about it. For what part did you play in order to be born into existence? And after death, we obviously lose any control we have in this life.

Therefore, how does sole self-reliance in between birth and death make any sense whatsoever? If you weren't the initiator of your life, how does it make any sense to be self-reliant after you were born? Equally, if we can't be guaranteed to have sole control of our lives in the afterlife, how does sole self-reliance before our afterlife make any sense?

Therefore, what only makes real decent sense is a strong dependence upon an intelligent creator who alone could have been the only one who brought the entire intelligent human race into existence in the first place and will also be the guardian of our soul after this life. Not to mention self-reliance really only works if you can promise yourself that you will be forever strong!

We refer to atheism, evolution, and agnosticism as belief systems (and not religions), simply because according to the technical definition of a religion, it must hold a belief in a God or gods, which humanistic belief systems typically reject. Another characteristic of overall humanism isn't just self-reliance or the denial of God, but is also the general denial of sin or moral wrongs as well.

So in this objection, we'll be mainly testing humanism against the well-known moral condition of man and the historical fruit it has often produced within the human race, and as you'll see just these *two tests alone* are quite sufficient to expose humanism as a belief system, which is clearly unworthy of our trust to give us the life and love we need.

> What only makes real decent sense is a strong dependence upon an intelligent creator who brought the entire intelligent human race into existence in the first place and will also be the guardian of our soul after this life.

Testing humanism against the true moral condition of man

If you walk down the street and randomly ask people if they believe they are a good person, many will quickly say they believe they are. And if we were to be honest, that's the reality we'd all prefer because after all, who wants to really admit they have a sin nature they battle with every day? But when you ask them if they ever lie, steal, lust, take God's name in vain (the God they don't believe in), gossip, or are selfish and unmerciful (all of which we already covered thoroughly in Objection #19), it is rather hard to be convinced that every man doesn't constantly struggle with a basic inborn sin nature, just as the Bible has always taught.

Objection 42
I'm A Humanist

So just what does that say about those humanistic belief systems which teach that there really is no such thing as sin or moral wrongs and that man is basically in good moral condition but is just imperfect?

Humanistic belief systems typically maintain that man himself is basically in good moral condition; he is just learning from his mistakes, and over time, is spiritually evolving into a better race. But if that's honestly true, then we would fully expect to see some evidence of that basic moral improvement after six millennia, would we not? And if you are an evolutionist who believes mankind is much older than six millennia, then we would really expect to see evidence of that basic moral improvement over millions of years! But statistically, is our world today really morally better than recorded history bears witness?

Most historians would say the morality of mankind has not improved much; in fact, our technologies have just served to expose our truly flawed nature even more. Humanists also often way overrate human potential through things like positive thinking. It's good to be positive, but first and foremost, should we not make sure we are connected to reality if we don't want to get hurt? There's a humanistic airhead saying which says, *"If you can imagine it or dream it, you can achieve it!"*

However, in stark contrast, the Bible teaches us that *"no man can have anything unless it is given to him from heaven"* (John 3:27). So which one *honestly* sounds a lot more like real life in the big city to you? If you can really achieve literally *anything* you can imagine or dream, how's that going for you so far in your life?!

> Most historians would say the morality of mankind has not improved much; in fact, our technologies have just served to expose our true nature even more.

The rapid decline of American morality

For some basic examples, just in the last sixty years ago or so in the US, it is pretty obvious that morality in general within our American culture has not at all *improved*. And it is doubtful that world morality as a whole is much different than America. Please note that the following moral changes *for the worst* within American society, which are also are largely prevalent around the world:

1. By June 17, 1963, our Supreme Court declared school-sponsored prayer and Bible readings unconstitutional.
2. On January 22, 1973, abortion was legalized by our government.
3. On June 26, 2015, same-sex marriage was legalized by our government.
4. More and more laws today are being passed to support transgenders who reject their God-given sex.
5. Not that long ago, gambling was also made legal in every convenience store, whereas it never was before that.
6. Many restaurants and movie theaters now both serve liquor, whereas prior to ffiteen years ago or so, this was just not the case.
7. Now we have wet houses in addition to recovery houses for alcoholics where they can go to just drink themselves to death instead of recover.
8. In addition to street drugs, mood-altering over-the-counter prescription drugs have exploded in sales in just the last twenty years or so. Even marijuana is now legal for some reasons. And God only knows what's coming next.
9. Even the food quality in our grocery stores has gotten much worse in the last sixty years; and, yes, that too is a moral issue, simply because it's just been greed that has fueled our man-made or contaminated food which has probably been the number one cause of death for Americans!
10. Along with driving under the influence of alcohol and drugs, cell phones now cause many motor vehicle accidents. Just a while ago, this, of course, was not the case.
11. Ever since the Internet, child pornography has just exploded. Today, it is a multibillion-dollar online industry with over 100,000 sites dedicated to the crime and is one of the fastest growing businesses in the world. And in some nations around the world, child pornography is even perfectly legal.
12. Most recent statistics just show an increase in violent crimes, which, of course, include terrorist bombings

which have literally exploded within the last twenty years. Before that, terrorist bombings were just not heard of as much.
13. And, of course, the film industry has not shown any moral improvements either.
14. Our prisons today are fuller than ever. If, in fact, mankind was somehow morally improving or evolving into a better race, this would certainly not be the case.
15. It is just commonplace for young couples now to live together for years without getting married, if they ever get married at all! But one must ask the very reasonable question: if they really love and trust each other, then why don't they really commit to each other by getting married? The obvious answer must be that they really don't know if their partner loves them and they really don't know if they can trust them! Thus, they don't feel safe enough to really commit. And all this, too, is a general reflection of our morality. Of course, we could go on and on, but hopefully, you get the point.

World wars

While author, Steve Pinker, who wrote *The Better Angels of Our Nature*, argues war in general is on the decline just because it has been seventy years since our last big World War (WWII), many others believe it is far too premature to state such a thing. According to Kelsey D. Atherton from *Popular Science*, in his article titled "Is War Really in Decline?" (September 2013), it is certainly premature to make such a call on permanent war-decline given our track record. In his opinion, we must wait at least 150 years (from the last major war) before any such claim could be concluded. And today's world is unique in the respect that, unlike WWII, we have major nuclear capabilities which could clearly wipe out the world's population quickly if nuclear war broke out, so a longer hesitancy to get into a third world war should just be selfishly expected!

If one bothers to look it up, today, there are still many major wars going on in our world as well as smaller violent conflicts involving many countries. And just in the last sixty years or so, nuclear war has uniquely threatened the very existence of the entire human race like nothing ever before it. So, during the last seventy years, it's certainly not like man has forgotten all about war! The truth is that no time before us has mankind been in this much danger of *self-destructing* because of our advanced weapon technologies.

Some New Age thinkers may suggest that because we have had no real nuclear or atomic bomb usage since WWII, it shows the human race is maturing. But many others believe given our quite violent track record *throughout all of human history*, it is just the calm before a much larger storm, and we are just preparing behind the scenes for the grand finale nuclear crescendo!

In light of the other growing conventional war conflicts, which have always existed and exist in the world today, one is rather more apt to conclude that the actual reason no nation has pushed any nuclear war head buttons so far is purely for selfish survival reasons and has nothing to do with moral improvement or maturity of the human race! So, then, just how have we evolved into a better race morally? We just need to be self-honest with the facts: the human race is simply *not morally improving overall* as history continues to unfold. The melody may have changed because of modern technologies, but we're still playing the same old sinful song, and our self-destructive human nature will be only magnified by technology.

It hasn't just been single societies like the Roman empire that have morally collapsed from within, for this has been happening with the whole human race on a grander scale, ever since our sin entered God's perfect creation. Only now, with our technologies, we are just able to cause our own destruction on a grander scale with much more efficiency. And I can assure you, this is nothing we should be shining our fingernails on our shirt about! And because of our fast-advancing technologies, which often just magnify and expound man's sin, Armageddon and the return of Christ is nearer than the unbelieving world begins to even realize.

Yes, atheism, evolution, agnosticism, and even belief systems like the New Age movement are all examples of those humanistic belief systems which tend to maintain that mankind is somehow morally evolving into a better race and that there really is no such thing as sin or moral rights and wrongs. In other words, the human race is

Objection 42
I'm A Humanist

just spiritually evolving by learning what works and what doesn't, and there just has to be some learning casualties along the way! However, if a dear close family member of someone in those belief systems got brutally murdered, and the murderer said to the judge that he was just spiritually evolving by learning what works and what doesn't, would that person (who doesn't believe in moral wrongs or sin) even begin to swallow all that phooey? Not likely, my friend, not likely!

You see, whenever people are on the wrong side of sin or moral failure, all of a sudden, they are full believers in it! But whenever convenient to suit their misguided spiritual beliefs, then they *very inconsistently* will reject the concept of moral failure.

According to the Bible, sin is just "the breaking of God's moral laws" (Romans 3:20). And if indeed there is no such thing as moral rights and wrongs, then we might as well not only burn down every church in the world but also every courthouse in the world because they too are the biggest supporters of nonreality!

Therefore, any belief system claiming that there is no such thing as moral rights or wrongs (or sin) should indeed be held suspect right away. Not only because they go against every church and courthouse of every society in the world, which has existed in human history, but also because they go against the very conscience of man throughout all human history, which has also always testified that there is indeed such a thing as moral rights and wrongs. How do you think churches and courthouses got built in the first place? By the collective consciences of mankind, which also bear witness to our loving creator who created the united conscience of man! And why does every man know it is wrong to steal, lie, commit adultery, etc., in his or her conscience?

Simply because when we are the victim of those things, we all know *in our conscience* it is wrong, just because of the pain it caused us! So for any belief system to insist that there is no such thing as moral wrongs is essentially insisting that there is no such thing as pain.

Of course, we'd all like to live in such a world right now, and it may be very appealing to just not believe in the sin nature which has always plagued mankind. But all such fantasy beliefs simply do not stand up to real-life events as billions throughout our history have testified! And to deny *any obvious reality* (like moral wrongs), which honestly registers in the collective conscience of humanity, is to once again be *dishonest*, which is just another moral wrong.

Thus, ironically, those who adamantly deny the reality of moral wrongs (or sin) in our world just end up plainly demonstrating the very realty they are attempting to deny through their dishonesty!

Like we've already mentioned, among those belief systems which have commonly denied the reality of sin or moral wrongs are Darwinian evolution, atheism, secular humanism, agnosticism, the New Age movement, and others. Therefore, we can safely rule out all such humanistic belief systems as the one true faith just on this massive important issue alone! Why? Because they simply do not honestly line up with the basic reality of man's true fallen moral condition which we all experience firsthand every day!

Let's be honest: if man was basically good, then the newspapers and TV news would basically reflect that reality! And if mankind was basically good, then the often used saying, "Try to see the good in others," would never have been born! And while this honestly narrows down our search for the one true religion, we should also at the same time recognize that biblical Christianity has always lined up perfectly with man's true moral condition as it has always maintained that all mankind was born into sin ever since the very first man and woman disobeyed God in the garden of Eden. Additionally, it has not only taught that mankind was born into sin but that the sin of the human race will actually compound over time and threaten our very survival, just before the return of Christ. And, so far, world morality and events are lining right up with those many biblical predictions quite nicely!

> Ironically, those who adamantly deny the reality of moral wrongs (or sin) in our world just end up plainly demonstrating the very realty they are attempting to deny through their dishonesty!

Testing humanism against the historical fruit it has produced

As we also touch upon in Objection #58, humanistic belief systems like Darwinian evolution and atheism have often produced bad fruit within the human race as it essentially gave birth and rise to both socialism and communism. And it doesn't just take Holocaust survivors to attest to that fact. The whole world has had its nose rubbed in the negative fruits of Darwinian evolution over the last 150 years and

Objection 42
I'm A Humanist

millions have perished at the hands of the socialistic and communistic regimes which have believed in it.

Are we saying all Darwinian evolution believers are violent communists or socialists? No. Are we saying that all atheists are violent? Certainly not because we are not so much even talking about specific people; but rather, we are talking about the basic historic repercussions of a whole belief system upon our entire world. And the particular humanistic belief system of Darwinian evolution and its teachings have, in fact, created an environment which fully *supports* violence. It really all just depends upon how devoted the adherents are to its survival of the fittest mentality, and it also depends upon how much political power a fervent evolutionist may possess to carry out their beliefs! So, because Darwinian evolution as a belief system certainly has lent itself to violence through its survival of the fittest mentality and its elimination of a moral God to be accountable to, it will then always have that same *violent potential* with godless men who possess much political power.

The Bible, on the other hand, teaches that we are all very accountable to a moral God who teaches us to love everyone, even our enemies! Nor does the Bible teach us that this short little natural life is all there is so we must murder our way up to the top of some imaginary success mountain as Hitler tried to do. Unlike Darwinian evolution, the Bible does not place the main emphasis on our physical survival during our short natural state but rather our spiritual survival during and after our natural state. And much emphasis is placed on our eternal life simply because it is truly the big picture in comparison. In fact, our eternal destiny is bigger in so much as outer space is bigger than your bedroom!

The Bible teaches us that as Christians, we are just here on earth in our natural state for a short visit (wherein our hearts love for God is tested) before we enter eternity with God. But true humanism really has no emphasis on an eternity with God, much less any moral accountability to him.

> Because Darwinian evolution certainly can lend itself to violence through its survival of the fittest mentality and its elimination of a moral God to be accountable to, it will then always have that same violent potential.

Do you see the major difference in teachings? One believes in an eternal loving creator to whom we are all accountable, and the other lacks any oversight whatsoever as all men do, just what seems right to them at the time, even if they have much political power over others. And since violent fruit is indeed quite harmful to man himself, Darwinian evolution should seriously lack the moral qualifications of any belief system which would attempt to gain the trust of the entire human race as the true explanation of life on earth.

Let's bring it all down to a smaller scale. If you were a Jew in Hitler's concentration camp, being severely abused and scheduled for death, and German officers at the same time tried to teach you and convince you that Hitler's brand of Darwinian evolution was the real explanation of life on earth, would you even begin to trust that they had a handle on the truth? Not likely at all, simply because even in our hearts and conscience, we all know that those who hold the truth must also be loving as well! Because every human being actually needs love in order to survive, the two (love and truth) must always be connected and not divorced from each other. As it has been accurately said:

> Truth without love is deficient truth...and love without truth is deficient love.

And we can see that the Bible has always agreed with this basic reality as verses like 1 Corinthians 13:6 testify that God's true love always *"rejoices in the truth."* But, again, if you were an American prisoner of war in the Japanese prison camps of WWII, being tortured against the basic humanitarian rules of war, and the one torturing you tried to convince you of his brand of evolution, would you even begin to trust that they had a handle on the truth? Not likely!

Let's face it: if Jesus and his apostles went around killing and torturing everybody in an attempt to establish a socialism or communism regime like Hitler, Stalin, and the Japanese did during WWII (instead of loving and healing them), biblical Christianity would never have even gotten off the ground! And the only reason communism or socialism historically got as far as it did was largely through shear brute force and dishonest stealth, which certainly doesn't give it much credibility at all since we all know that such tactics take no real character at all!

Objection 42
I'm A Humanist

Yes, it is more than interesting to see just what moral fruit Darwinian evolution did produce when men in great political power (like Hitler, Stalin, Mussolini, Mao Zedong, Hirohito, Lenin) had the chance to express their evolutionary beliefs through that power. However, it seems many of those within our younger generations today who may be drawn to seriously believe in the theory of Darwinian evolution are truly ignorant and totally fail to connect all the bloodshed of socialism and communism of our last century with the Theory of Evolution!

But the evolutionist may ask, what about the crusaders who waged war against the Muslims in the name of Christ? As we point out in our Objection #64 of our series, those who may not know real history on the subject of the Crusaders' Holy Wars may indeed be rather ignorant of those facts as well! For first of all, since Christ himself (along with his disciples) never led men into religious or political wars of any kind (like the crusaders) in order to take back the holy land from the Romans, we must conclude that the *Catholic* crusaders, while they may have used the name of Christ for their bloody Crusades to take back the holy lands, were not even living biblical Christianity when waging such political wars. And if the historical truth were told, the popes of the Catholic religion back then were just abusing the Bible to wage their very misguided political wars in a greedy attempt to gain more land (especially the holy land), which wasn't even theirs in the first place! In fact, when one realizes that it was only the Roman Catholic religion (which we easily expose as a cult in Objection #49) and not even the true Church which launched the holy war crusades, then their blatant abuse of true biblical Christianity during those Crusades begins to be clearly seen.

It is more than interesting to see just what moral fruit Darwinian evolution did produce when men in great political power (like Hitler, Stalin, Mussolini, Mao Zedong, Hirohito, Lenin) had the chance to express their evolutionary beliefs through that power.

You see, anyone can abuse the true faith, but that should never discredit that faith in the eyes of those honest if that faith simply does not at all teach the abuse being displayed! As we expound more upon the Crusades in Objection #64 in part 4 of our series, the Holy Wars were more of a political action with a misguided religious stamp upon them. And the popes who put Christ's name to their military actions were, of course, not following Christ in their crusades, even though they may have used Christ's name and the Bible to launch them. However, quite to the contrary of *abusing their evolutionary beliefs*, Hitler, Stalin, Mussolini, Mao Zedong, Horashio, and Lenin were all playing quite fair within the bounds of their evolutionary beliefs because they were just being good evolutionists who were loyally carrying out their own survival of the fittest mentality. And that, my friend, is the big difference between the two!

Conclusion

So, in basic review of humanism as a belief system, we not only see that it often denies the true moral condition of sinful man but has also often produced much bad violent fruit through Darwinian evolution, which removes a moral God whom we are all morally accountable to. Thus, just through the failure of these two basic tests, we should then be able to easily see that humanism in general certainly lacks the moral qualifications of any belief system which should attempt to gain the trust of the entire human race as the real truth which is connected to reality. However, just as Jesus proved his divinity to the honest soul many times over when he walked the earth (as we already covered in Part 2 of our series), so too is his word completely trustworthy which foretells the awesome eternity which God has for all those who love him. As Revelation 21:3–4 clearly teaches:

> *"[B]ehold, the dwelling place of God is with men, and he will live with them, and they shall be his people, and God himself shall be with them, and be their God. And God shall wipe away all tears from their eyes; and there shall be no more death, neither sorrow, nor crying, neither shall there be any more pain: for the former things are passed away."*

But the Bible teaches us plainly that *only through Christ* can we obtain God's eternal life (John 14:6). I myself was raised with humanism to a large degree. But it wasn't long before my own strength, wisdom, understanding, etc. proved quite insufficient to solve my own problems.

At age eighteen, I gave Jesus a real chance, and after forty years of being a Christian, I can personally testify that it was God's love which ultimately changed my life for the better. But if I had never

Objection 42
I'm A Humanist

given Christ a fair chance to even reveal himself to me, then I know I would have never gotten the love, healing, and truth I needed.

If you are one who is tired of running from God and you, too, want to personally experience his awesome unconditional healing love for you, I invite you to just take that first small step of faith by sincerely praying the prayer of salvation located at the end of this book. Even if you've been a humanist for years, you can still break away from that obvious false belief system today which threatens your true salvation through Christ. And don't be concerned with what your family members may think of you because, simply put, they will not be you're judge on judgment day! This decision is between you and God (your creator) alone. No matter what your past is like, God loves you and sincerely wants you to be a part of his awesome eternal kingdom!

Jesus said, "I am the resurrection and the life. He who believes in me, will live even though he dies; and whoever lives and believes in me will never die." (John 11:25–26)

OBJECTION 43
I Believe in Hinduism

A loving reminder: Before each false belief system we discuss, just so my loving intentions cannot be misunderstood, I will *once again* remind the reader that it's certainly *not the adherents* of any false religion or belief system which the true Church is against but rather just the *false teachings* within them which deceive men away from the one and only true God and his eternal salvation (Ephesians 6:12). Therefore, my dear reader, please know that our discussion of these various different religions or belief systems is very much a *love* issue.

Defining Hinduism

Hindu is simply a Persian word which means: "The people and culture of the Indus River region." Even though our list is undoubtedly incomplete, some of the main beliefs of Hinduism are typically the following:

1. *The belief in Brahman*: Hinduism itself is basically a pantheistic religion which maintains that everything is God and God is everything. And, strangely enough, at some point in the history of their religion, Hindus chose to call their God (made up of everything) "Brahman." This includes everything from inner space to everything in outer space. No matter whether its planetary bodies,

Objection 43
I Believe in Hinduism

people, animals, plant life, or the subatomic world, it all collectively makes up what they call Brahman. Brahman is totally impersonal, indefinable, and indescribable. However, because Hindus also worship up to 330 million other lesser gods as well, called avatars, it would also seem that Hinduism embraces polytheism (a belief in many individual gods) to some degree as well. However, because according to Hindu beliefs, even all these lesser gods are all just manifestations of Brahman which is made up of everything; their religion as a whole would probably be best classified as a pantheistic religion rather than a polytheistic religion.

2. *The belief that man is one with God because man is God*: There is no distinction between creation and creator within Hinduism. All is worshiped as God. Even the historical Jesus who uniquely displayed all the divine attributes of God Almighty in his many undeniable miracles while living a sinless life is just thrown into the big Brahman mix and is no different than the smallest dirt, speck, or atom!

3. *The belief that man's primary problem is his ignorance that he is one with Brahman*: According to the Hindu religion, the whole reason our prisons are full and the world is at war isn't because mankind wrestles with a sin nature inherited from Adam and Eve. It's simply because we are all just ignorant that we are one with Brahman! But, of course, one must ask the reasonable question: If all mankind is truly part of God and already one with God like Hindus insist, then why don't we already realize it? And whatever answer Hindus would give us, why on earth should we believe them? And what accounts for all of man's bad moral choices? Hindus also believe that once man realizes he is one with Brahman, he loses all selfish individuality like a drop of water loses its individuality in an ocean. Hindus believe that once selfish individuality is extinguished, all evil is essentially extinguished along with it.

But, again, one must ask the reasonable question: If it's just a matter of such a simple realization, then why has the world always been such a moral mess? And, honestly, why do Hindus themselves struggle with bad morality, just as much as the rest of humanity, if they possess the only true religion by which man can morally improve? And because Hindus themselves have never been morally superior to the rest of mankind (due to their realization they are one with Brahman), it would certainly seem that such a solution to the moral failure of all mankind proves to be all too simple, even for the Hindu!

> Why do Hindus themselves struggle with bad morality, just as much as the rest of humanity, if they possess the only true religion by which man can morally improve?

4. *Hinduism teaches the obscure belief called reincarnation*: Hinduism essentially teaches that when man dies, he just comes back as another person, animal, plant, or something else (maybe even a rock, worm, or demon). In fact, the obscure belief of reincarnation probably originated within the Hindu religion. And according to this belief, what you become in the next life all depends on the choices you make in your present life. All these personal choice consequences are known as karma.

But, again, one must ask the honest question: If reincarnation were really true, how could all nonlife objects or even all the lower forms of life (like insects or even animals) possibly make good moral karma choices in order to be promoted in their cycle of reincarnation? Evidently, there's much more going on inside of worms than scientists have realized! Did you know that worms can make moral choices because they have a conscience? Neither did I! Hah!

And how could one be demoted to a rock in their next life (by making bad moral choices) if that specific rock they are demoted to has already been there thousands of years before they were demoted to it? Did someone else become that same exact rock before they were demoted? If so, the precise timing of other things and/or creatures becoming that same exact rock (and all other rocks, which must include every grain of sand!) could not really have any overlap or lapse

Objection 43
I Believe in Hinduism

time between all the promotions and demotions; otherwise, the rock itself would be nonexistent. When you just think about it, the whole thing really becomes rather ridiculous when you try to reasonably work out the theory of reincarnation!

And if one is demoted to become a demon in the next life because of bad moral choices in their present life, who was that same exact demon before they were demoted? And if men just take turns becoming the same exact demon because of their bad moral choices in this life, then again, there could be absolutely no lapsed time in between bad men becoming that demon or better men being promoted from that demon; otherwise, the demon itself would be nonexistent. The exact timing would have to be absolutely precise on every object, animal, and thing; otherwise, nothing would exist!

But because all men have free wills (according to karma), the timing on what men become could certainly not be precise. And if grasshoppers could make bad or good moral choices, then they (along with all other insects) would also have to have both a *free will* and a *conscience* as well. As you can hopefully see, none of it really makes much sense at all the more you dare to reasonably think it out! Not to mention, there is not one shred of *scientific evidence* for such a fantastic process which survives only in the imagination of those who believe in *reincarnation*. However, if Hindu gurus wanted to control the populace with this whole idea of reincarnation, it would only work all the better if the concept could have no real proof to back it up, simply because then, their fantastic beliefs could never be challenged!

And, unfortunately, that's just what we find in all the false religions: their leaders just expect the populace to follow them quite blindly. And this way, their leaders never really have to take responsibility by providing the honest evidence which should back their belief system. Nevertheless, according to the karma within Hindu reincarnation, what happens in your future lives (plural) is all determined by your actions now. Nothing results from environment, others, angels, or even a monotheistic God. All the consequences of acts undertaken in this and earlier lifetimes will be manifested in one's next life.

In other words, if you are a good Hindu, you'll be promoted in your next life (and if you're fortunate, you'll become one of the avatar lesser gods which inhabit the cow!). But if you are a bad Hindu, you'll be demoted in the next life, and you could even be turned into a worm or demon, depending upon all your actions in this life!

But in Hinduism, *the ultimate goal* is, of course, to be the best Hindu they can be in order to be eventually promoted (through the process of reincarnation) into the godhood of Brahman and finally escape the constant cycle of life, death, and rebirth which they call reincarnation. He who breaks free from this long cycle breaks free from all suffering, pain, and earthly existence. Thus, a Hindu's goal is to be absorbed into the universal oneness of Brahman (like a drop of water in an ocean) where one loses all individuality and self-identity. Sounds fun and rewarding huh?

To be released from all self-identity is a liberation Hindus refer to as Moksha and is achieved through works, devotion (which is just more works), and the gaining of knowledge (which is just more works). This blissful liberation called Moksha at the end of reincarnation's process for those who are good Hindus is the closest thing to the Christian understanding of heaven which Hinduism teaches, which certainly doesn't seem very close to it at all! In ancient Hinduism, typically, women could not even achieve Moksha, only men. I wonder who decided that wonderful reality? I can assure you, it wasn't a Hindu woman! In stark contrast to *ancient Hinduism*, women within biblical Christianity have always had the very same *eternal destination rights* as do men.

> If reincarnation were really true, how could all the lower forms of life (like a rocks, insects, or even animals) possibly make good moral karma choices in order to be promoted in their cycle of reincarnation?

The origin of Hinduism

Unlike most religions, historians are really unsure as to just *when* Hinduism as a religion actually started. This, of course, does not automatically prove that Hinduism goes all the way back to the beginning of mankind or that it is even the oldest religion. It just means that the exact start of Hinduism has not yet been confirmed by historians as it is quite old and *sadly lacks such a reliable historical record*

Objection 43
I Believe in Hinduism

which would verify even its basic origin date. However, since the word *Hindu* itself is a Persian word, it is probably safe to say it is at least as old as the Persian empire which dominated the world from roughly 538 to 333 BC. But many historians would even date it to be as early as 2000 BC, which is around the time of Abraham, the father of the nation of Israel. However, there is very little historical evidence which would confirm Hinduism as much older than that. In fact, a strong piece of evidence which would lead us to believe Hinduism *is not older than the time of Abraham* is that the name of its god, Brahman, was very likely taken from the name of Abraham in the Bible.

Another variation of Brahman in Hindu writings is Brahma, which is essentially Abraham with the first letter A moved to the back side of the word. Coincidence? Not very likely, simply because older Hindu writings not only specifically mention the biblical Abraham but also his wife, Sarah, as well as Noah (of Noah's flood), even though the spellings of their names are not the same as our English spellings. Thus, if, in fact, the very pantheistic God of Hinduism obtained its name from just an alteration of the biblical Abraham's name, then it would indeed make sense to believe their title Brahman was *manufactured* at least after the biblical man, Abraham, himself was well known. And if the very title of the Hindu God, Brahman, must be younger than the biblical man Abraham, it is certainly not unreasonable to believe that the beginnings of the Hindu religion were basically constructed by man sometime after the biblical Abraham was well known in the land because of how God miraculously worked through him to begin the nation of Israel.

Those who would insist that Hinduism is the oldest religion in the world may also ignorantly assume that biblical Christianity started with Abraham who is the Father of the nation of Israel. However, if one is going to believe the Bible which teaches us that Abraham was the father of the nation of Israel, then they should also believe all of the Bible which teaches us that the very roots of biblical New Testament Christianity go all the way back to the very first man, Adam, in the creation week of Genesis. The fact that New Testament Christianity goes all the way back to the very first man Adam in the creation week of Genesis is easily confirmed by verses, such as Genesis 3:15, which foretells Christ's defeat of Satan on the cross nearly 4,000 years before it happened.

Furthermore, even if we were to give Hinduism the benefit of the doubt and actually say it is older than the man Abraham of the Bible (around 2000 BC), it still wouldn't be older than false religions like Satanism, which technically must go all the way back to the garden of Eden when Satan first deceived Eve into sin.

Either way, going by the reliable historical record of the Old Testament (*reliable* historical records which the writings of Hinduism greatly lack), Hinduism is certainly not the oldest religion known to man, even though Hindus or New Agers might insist that it is. In addition to all the evidence which points to the fact that Hinduism is nowhere near as old as biblical Christianity, probably the biggest clue is its *oldest Hindu text* (the *Rigveda*), which only dates back to about 1500 BC. However, no matter just exactly when Hinduism technically started, because of the *reliable* historical records which the writings of Hinduism greatly lack, historians are also at a loss as to establishing any specific founder of it as well. And, thus, one cannot even test Hinduism against the moral character of its founder(s).

> In addition to all the evidence which points to the fact that Hinduism is nowhere near as old as biblical Christianity, the oldest Hindu text (the Rigveda) only dates back to about 1500 BC.

Testing Hinduism against the true moral condition of man

While Hinduism teaches that man is basically good and has unlimited potential, it at the same time fully acknowledges all the evil committed by mankind in the regressing process of reincarnation. Hinduism even goes so far as to teach that if any man should slay a cow (which they believe to be very sacred because the 330 million avatar gods which inhabit it), he or she would actually become a demon in the next life! Of course, the problem with this is that throughout more than one time in history, Hindus themselves have actually resorted to the slaughter of their own sacred cows in order to survive during times of famine, even though it is absolutely forbidden to do so according to their Hindu beliefs. I guess that's where at least some of the demons have come from according to their own beliefs!

Objection 43
I Believe in Hinduism

Also, according to Hindu beliefs, the Hindus themselves are supposed to evolve into *selflessness* when eventually absorbed into the Brahman through the good process of reincarnation. However, historically, the Hindus of India and/or other nations have undoubtedly struggled with selfishness, just as much as the rest of the human race which doesn't even believe in Hinduism. So, quite honestly, what good has Hinduism been for the Hindu anyway?

Not only historically, but even today, Hindu women have been belittled and mistreated in a variety of ways, which keeps them from being equal to Hindu men. And we are not at all talking about something like their status of authority in the family unit. According to Hindu history, kidnapping, slavery, and rape of their women has been a constant problem. Even though their women may be treated better today, evidently, they still have *a way to go* to achieve moral equality with Hindu men.

In the history of Hinduism, it was just the norm for Hindu men of high social status of ancient times to visit prostitutes on a regular basis while at the same time insist that their wives (plural because they also believed in polygamy) be strictly confined to their home and never be in the company of a strange man without a family member present. Talk about major hypocrisy, right? Even today, Hindu spiritual masters (or gurus) can have free premarital sex with women if it's in accordance with their particular teachings. But, personally, I've not heard of many guru Hindu women who can do the same! And even though the whole thing is obviously immoral, it also shows much prejudice against their women and basic hypocrisy within their belief system.

In stark contrast with how Hindu women have been treated, biblical Christianity has always treated its women with respect and has never taught any abuse of women whatsoever. In fact, one can even today go online and research the top ten cultures around the world for women's rights, and you will also find that they are predominately Bible-believing Christian cultures!

Additionally, in the past, even when Hindu nations have suffered famines, many Hindus have literally starved to death while they let their sacred cows live in their midst, just because of their religious beliefs. So, either way, during times of real famine, Hindu cultures have been rather forced to be immoral. If they ate their cows, they were immoral according to the Hindus themselves. And if they starved to death while letting their cows live, then according to the Western world, they were being immoral. If valuing the life of a cow over that of a person is not a moral flaw, then just what is a moral flaw?

My friend, if someone had to choose between you or a cow dying, and they chose to let the cow live, what would you honestly think of their morality and/or religion which caused them to choose thus? Either way, their belief that mankind is basically good makes little sense with not only their own historical Hindu customs and scriptures, but also just the normal human evil we constantly witness in the non-Hindu world as well. Thus, it is only fair to say that Hinduism also fails as the one true faith when tested against the true moral condition of man.

> If valuing the life of a cow over that of a person is not a moral flaw, then what is?

Testing Hinduism against self-contradictions

The religious/social beliefs of Hinduism have evolved (have actually constantly changed) over a long time period, which is actually typical of most false religions. Thus, what was morally true for ancient Hindus is no longer true for modern-day Hindus in many different facets of Hinduism (their harsher treatment of Hindu women being just one example). In this basic respect, their whole religion is rather self-contradicting, simply because it is always fluid and ever-changing to what the Hindus themselves think best as time goes on. I guess this basic dynamic characteristic only makes sense if there is no morally perfect supreme authority/creator to be accountable to, and man himself is just as much God as anyone or anything else.

Nevertheless, if Hindus can just change their own religion to their own liking any time they please, why have a religion at all as man can do whatever he pleases quite nicely without the front of a big complicated religion like Hinduism? Either way, though, when man just makes up the rules as he goes along, even our conscience should tell us that good morality is being thrown under the bus; or should we say under the cow!

If Hindus themselves are God according to their own religion, then should it surprise us that they can just change Hinduism to their own liking as they go? And if there isn't an all-knowing perfect creator

Objection 43
I Believe in Hinduism

God (monotheism) behind Hinduism, it also just makes sense that Hinduism must have started very imperfectly through the imperfect constructs of men and just needed constant moral tweaking as time rolled down through the centuries. But, of course, the whole problem with this is that as soon as the truth contradicts itself (like the Hindu religion has hundreds of times because of its many changes), it can no longer be considered the reliable truth to those honest! Everything is rather meaningless if one can just change their own morality to their own liking as they go in life as anyone can easily do that because it takes absolutely no character at all to do it!

The Hindu religion as a whole, of course, claims to follow all their teachings within their own religious law books. Nevertheless, Hinduism, even today more than ever, continues to be a pluralistic religion which has built within it many variations and exceptions to the rule. In fact, what may be true for one group of modern-day Hindus may not be true for all modern-day Hindus. Therefore, we find that Hinduism is not only self-contradicting as a whole when comparing ancient Hinduism with modern Hinduism, but even within only its modern teachings, it is also quite self-contradicting as well.

The problem with Hinduism is that one could argue from every angle to support different beliefs, all depending upon how a person views things. And all this personal relativity, which has to bring self-contradiction within the Hindu religion, should certainly not surprise us when, in fact, the Hindu scriptures as a whole also contradict themselves constantly. It is at least *easier* to understand how the written works of some religions, which are separated by thousands of years, could end up contradicting each other. But many plain unsolvable contradictions are even found within individual Hindu texts which are not even separated by much time at all.

Within Hindu texts, there are not only logical and conceptual contradictions but also many factual contradictions as well. And, thus, the very loose Hindu conception of their own scriptures is largely explained when we realize that Hindus approach their scriptures in quite the same poetic/nonliteral spirit as we might approach Dante or Milton. While their main value and regard for Hindu scripture may be of an artistic/poetic nature, the whole question of whether they be an accurate communication of reliable truth seems rather irrelevant to the general Hindu mindset. In fact, much to the contrary of admitting any discredit toward the obvious contradictions within Hindu scripture *(which claims to be the truth for all the world)*, Hindus actually tend to embrace all their contradictions and openly declare that both sides of their contradictions are of equal authority and spiritual value! In other words, within the religion of Hinduism, most anything goes—just don't kill a cow! What a mess, huh? And what gives a Hindu guru any authority to have even created such a mess anyway?

In fact, within Hindu scripture as a whole, it is rather difficult to say just what philosophical opinion *would not* be welcomed with open arms. Contradictions just seem to add to the spiritual excitement of it all! However, we all know that quite reasonably and logically, it is rather impossible for both sides of an unsolvable contradiction to be true and, therefore, of equal spiritual value. Just because some guru might deem it so certainly should not make it true for those sincerely wanting the truth. In fact, those in any court of law who would suggest such a thing would either be declared incompetent, insane, or dishonest! And if Hindu's even tried to adopt their "anything goes" mentality into the practical rational aspects of even their own lives, which directly affected their personal well-being, their family lives would come to a screeching halt real quick!

For example, they expect their banker to be mathematically accurate without personal relativism, just as they expect that anyone doing surgery on them would be a qualified surgeon and not someone who is just qualified through personal relativism! They also would expect the pilot who's flying the plane they are in to land only on the narrow runway which is made for planes and not anywhere they open-mindedly want to through personal relativism. The list, of course, goes on, but hopefully, you see the hypocrisy between their spiritual beliefs and their rational life! And when one considers that the very eternal salvation of men may be at stake through the embracing of such ridiculous beliefs, openly teaching that any unsolvable contradiction is just fine and actually a mark of true spirituality should be completely unacceptable to the honest soul who sincerely seeks the reliable truth which gives men life and not harm. One of the biggest mistakes man can make is believing that our spiritual beliefs do not need any rational reasonable evidence to support them, just because they are spiritual in nature and must go well beyond our reason at some point!

Objection 43
I Believe in Hinduism

> Strangely, Hindus actually tend to embrace all their contradictions and openly declare that both sides of their contradictions are of equal authority and spiritual value!

Even what Hindus teach about Christ doesn't add up

Many Hindus suggest that all what Christ taught in the New Testament he actually learned in India from age thirteen to twenty-nine. However, since Christ's teachings throughout the New Testament are nothing like that of pantheistic Hinduism, then we are rather forced to conclude that he either forgot completely what he learned in India or completely modified it beyond any recognition! In fact, there is almost no overlap of beliefs between New Testament Christianity and Hinduism. Other Hindus even suggest that Jesus Christ, along with Rama, Krishna, and many other Hindu gods was just another incarnation of their God, Brahman. However, the obvious inconsistency of Christ's teachings with that of pantheistic Hinduism also destroys such an idea, especially since Christ never mentioned the Hindu god, Brahman, by name even once! And, finally, since Jesus himself clearly claimed to be the one and only true creator God and way of salvation for all mankind (John 10:30–33, 11:25–26, 14:6; Acts 4:12), he certainly could not at the same time be just one of many ways to God as Hindus often believe and teach. Thus, all in all, Hinduism easily fails this very reasonable test against *self-contradictions* as well.

> Since Jesus himself clearly claimed to be the one and only true God and way of salvation for all mankind, he certainly could not at the same time be just one of many ways to God as Hindus often believe and teach.

Testing Hinduism against the well-known facts of science

As we've already pointed out in our Objection #2 in Part 1 of our series, the very impersonal nature of the pantheistic god, Brahman, must be the very first strike against Hinduism as a religion. For when addressing man's existence from a just a rational or scientific standpoint alone, just the basic scientific law of cause and effect would indeed seem to forbid any nonpersonal or non-intelligent force behind it all, like Brahman. Science has long discovered and recognized that no effect can be *greater than* its cause. In other words, the cause of something is always greater than the effect of that cause, and I don't believe true science has yet found an exception to this basic law of science. And when we rationally apply this same basic law of cause and effect to man's existence, it would then be only reasonable to believe that whoever brought the human race into existence is also superior to us in our own *personal* nature as our cause.

For example, if all mankind (characterized with intelligence and creativity) has always been *personal* in nature, needing close relationships which require love and communication, it would only be reasonable to believe our cause (*whoever* it was) would also have to be fully characterized by all of these very same things as well. With just this basic scientific understanding, then, our cause must certainly be a person who is like us desiring relationships, etc., rather than mere chance or some impersonal force, which, of course, is not a person at all. And unlike the impersonal pantheism of Hinduism, only monotheism can make any sense at all with this basic scientific law of cause and effect and the very personal world we all live in which is literally filled with billions of *persons* who have always been *personal* in nature. Thus, on this point alone, Hinduism as an impersonal belief system would be at variance with one of our most proven laws of science.

Also, as we've already briefly mentioned, according to long-standing Hindu creation myth, a great sea turtle swimming across a cosmic sea (in outer space) has four elephants standing upon its slanted shell which in turn have the whole earth resting upon their backs. Knowing that any myth itself is fictitious in nature and untrue, the question quickly arises: why would any serious religion which portrays itself as the one true explanation of all reality (both spiritual and physical) even have such a false mythological explanation of how the earth is held up? Unless, of course, Hindus actually believed this myth to be true for the last 2,500 years before modern science could prove it to be mere foolish human imagination!

It is true that many obvious myths within religions may have certain spiritual lessons built into them so that those belonging to that religion can somehow grow spiritually from them. But other than the fact that

Objection 43
I Believe in Hinduism

Hindus have historically regarded the turtle to be a symbol for God because of its long life (which is rather absurd if God must inevitably be both perfect and eternal), what possible spiritual lesson could a cosmic sea turtle holding up the earth via four elephants give the Hindu?

Nevertheless, this whole sea turtle myth (and other silly Hindu myths) is not exactly something which gives the Hindu religion much credibility if one is really searching for the reliable truth to base their eternity on. And many may actually reject Hinduism for such rational reasons, simply because they know well that the human heart cannot accept what the mind rejects! And if Hindus in the past have truly believed this sea turtle myth to be reality, it just discredits their whole religion all the more as it at the same time seriously pretends to be the final explanation of all realities, both physical and spiritual.

But if, in fact, it has always just been a fictitious myth in the mind of all past Hindus, then that, too, does not give the Hindu religion any more credibility either simply because all it has for any kind of an explanation as to how our earth is held up is one such fictitious fairy tale which really serves no apparent good purpose. Of course, the scientific absurdity of the Hindu sea turtle/elephant explanation of how the earth is held up should be rather obvious to anyone seriously looking for the reliable truth.

In stark contrast, however, the Holy Bible has always been scientifically accurate in its explanation of what holds up the earth. It, of course, does not tell us everything there is to know about outer space and the planetary bodies, but what it does reveal has certainly proven to be scientifically accurate. Job 26:7, Psalm 19:4–6, and Isaiah 40:22 all not only teach the scientific reality that the earth is spherical in shape (some Hindu myths even have a flat earth supported by elephants and a sea turtle) but that nothing physical supports it because God hung it *upon nothing* physical in outer space (which we now scientifically know to be the gravitational force of our sun). Let's just briefly discuss these three quite telling verses of God's Word:

> "He (God) *stretcheth out the north over the empty place and hangeth the earth upon nothing.*" (Job 26:7)

Most Bible scholars date the book of Job to have been written around the time of Abraham (2000 BC). The *empty place* (Hebrew word *tohu*) undoubtedly refers to the newly created earth which was *without form* (Genesis 1:2, which uses the same Hebrew word *tohu*) in the beginning of its creation. As the earth received its spherical form during its creation, its *north* direction was also defined and *stretched out* when the gravitational force systems from other planetary bodies like our sun caused it to rotate and/orbit.

Here in Job 26:7 (written roughly 4,000 years ago), God not only reveals to us that the earth is rotating and/orbiting (as God stretched out the earth's *north* direction) but that it was suspended by *nothing* physical which is what modern science has discovered to be the mysterious force of gravity, namely the gravitational force of our sun. The Holy Bible once again proves its divine authorship as Job 26:7 was written at least 3,500 years before Sir Isaac Newton scientifically identified this gravitational force!

> *It is He (God) that sitteth upon the circle (Hebrew word for circle means sphere) of the earth, and the inhabitants thereof are as grasshoppers; that stretcheth out the heavens as curtain, and spreadeth them out as a tent to dwell in.* (Isaiah 40:22)

As we said, Proverbs 8:27, Job 26:10, and Isaiah 40:22 all clearly refer to the spherical shape of the earth when looking at the Hebrew words used. The scientific European world emerging from the Dark Ages used to seriously believe that the world was flat. But if they had just believed God's Word, they could have saved themselves the humility of believing sailors could actually sail over the earth's edge!

Additionally, roughly 2,700 years ago, God also revealed that the universe was indeed expanding (a more recent discovery of modern science) as Isaiah 40:22 also teaches us that God *"stretcheth out the heavens as curtain, and spreadeth them out."* Job 9:8, Psalm 104:2, Isaiah 42:5, 4:24, 51:13, and Jeremiah 10:12 all also make clear references to God stretching out or spreading out the heavens. Let's look at yet another verse of God's Word which also confirms the scientific accuracy of the Bible:

> *[T]he sun, which is as a bridegroom coming out of his chamber, and rejoiceth as a strong man to run a race. His going forth is from the end of the heaven, and his circuit unto the ends of it: and there is nothing hid from the heat thereof.* (Psalms 19:4–6)

Objection 43
I Believe in Hinduism

This verse is not teaching that our sun orbits a fixed earth as some skeptics may try to assert, simply because it does not even mention the earth, much less teach that the earth stays in a fixed position. It simply teaches that our sun has its own circuit around the earth and other planetary bodies. Of course, modern science has not only discovered that the earth rotates around the sun but that at the same time, the sun goes around the earth in its much larger orbit. And since no one yet knows just where the stationary center of the universe is, motion of all planetary bodies is relative motion to one's position.

Therefore, surveyors, navigators, and astronomers most all have found that the best point to assume as the zero point of motion is the surface of the earth at the location of the observer. And King David here in Psalm 19 also takes this same scientific approach when referring to the sun's motion relative to the earth. But at the same time, King David's statement is also correct for any other fixed point since the sun and our Milky Way galaxy do actually move throughout the universe. Not only has modern science confirmed God's Word when it discovered the sun moves in a gigantic circuit around the center of the Milky Way galaxy but that the Milky Way galaxy itself also moves in respect to other galaxies.

In other words, within God's creation, everybody gets to dance, and what a beautiful life-giving dance it is for us humans on earth! Additionally, when this verse in Psalm 19:6 teaches us that *nothing is hid from the heat* of the sun, it's not unscientifically referring to all of outer space and all planetary bodies; it's just referring to the fact that nothing is hidden from the sun's heat within its own *circuit* which it just mentioned in the very same sentence.

Thus, many centuries (and even millenniums) before modern science even discovered it, the Bible has always clearly taught that:
1. The earth is spherical in shape.
2. That the earth rotates on its axis while also orbiting around the sun which suspends it by unseen gravitational forces.
3. That the sun even has its own larger circuit within its own galaxy.

Can you see how radically different that is from the mythical nonsense of some cosmic sea turtle carrying four elephants which in turn bear the weight of our earth? In fact, many other false man-made religions *only* have similar bizarre and very unscientific explanations for our physical universe. But no religion on earth even comes remotely close to the scientific accuracy of the Holy Bible which has always been leagues ahead of man's scientific discoveries from the very start. Could that be because the creator of our universe actually wrote the Holy Bible through his many different prophets which all happen to miraculously agree with each other? I think it very well could be, simply because when one honestly thinks about it, that's the only explanation which makes any sense at all! Nevertheless, we can see that Hinduism also fails this very reasonable scientific test as well.

> No religion on earth even comes remotely close to the scientific accuracy of the Holy Bible, which has always been leagues ahead of man's scientific discoveries from the very start.

Testing Hinduism against its prophetic predictions of the future

While the Hindu scriptures are basically found in three different sources (the *Vedas*, the *Mahabharata*, and the *Bhagavad Gita*), the entire collection of diverse Hindu scriptures is so immense that a person could spend a lifetime sorting through its thousands of pages. Even the most orthodox portions of Hindu scripture are many times larger than the Bible. In fact, if Hindus had an organization like the Gideons, they would have to donate an entire small library of books to each hotel room rather than a single volume like the Bible! Most find that the body of Hindu scriptures is so large, so complicated, so difficult to understand, so full of contradictions, and so various that they don't even want to try and wade through the jungle of it all to even authenticate its supposed spiritual value. And the fact that it is so immense and so complex is largely what enables the Hindu defense of it, simply because most do not even want to take on the task of trying to expose all its contradictions with reality. But thank God, such an immense task is not even necessary just to expose the religion as a whole to be false and unworthy of our trust!

Though Bible students rarely master the three original languages of the Bible (Greek, Hebrew, and Aramaic), sufficient lexicon aides exist so the original meaning of the text can be clearly understood without

Objection 43
I Believe in Hinduism

basic confusion. However, Hindu students trying to understand Hindu scriptures completely lack this advantage since the Vedas were delivered from an impersonal source. English translations are available for the primary Hindu scriptures, but even the best translations are quite difficult to understand. On the other hand, most English translations of the Bible are on the reading level of a sixth- to twelfth-grader. But this is certainly not the case with the Vedas, which even educated scholars find difficult to understand! In fact, even the language of the *Rigveda* (Archaic Sanskirt) is a dead language and quite inaccessible to most Hindus. Other Hindu scriptures are written in classical Sanskirt, Prakrit, Tamil, and other regional dialects, making them very difficult to even understand. And even if all the language difficulty barriers are overcome, Hindu texts are still hard to understand, not to mention Hindu scripture plainly contradicts itself constantly.

Additionally, Hindus have no final authority which is objective as Hindus generally regard subjective religious experiences to be a higher knowledge than that of their written texts. Furthermore, Hindu scriptures actually contain very little that is noble, just, pure, virtuous, or praiseworthy. Different Hindu scriptures present completely different paths to their idea of salvation, and the Vedas contain *no predictive prophecies* and record *no miracles* which would confirm that their religion either in part or as a whole came from even a reliable divine source (or even gods who have progressed within the cycle of reincarnation). So, for all these reasons, one learns that Hindu scripture is actually of little spiritual value to not only the outside world but even the Hindu!

On the other hand, the Holy Bible is authentic, authoritative, and is a well-proven revelation of the one true God, not only through the fulfillment of its many predictive prophecies but also through the reliable historic record of its many miracles and the real eyewitnesses of Christ doing those miracles within the real geological places of the Middle East which anyone can even visit today. Within the Holy Bible, a single simple theme is expanded throughout, which is the redemption of man through Christ, the true Jewish Messiah. The moral laws within are more reasonable than that of any other religious system, and to date, the Holy Bible has been found to be without error and unsolvable contradictions by serious scholars. And probably not last, and certainly not least, biblical Christianity offers a brighter hope and a far better eternal future to any soul than does any other religious or humanistic belief system known to man.

In a real sense, Hinduism also fails the test of divine revelation through fulfilled prophecy as it really has no real predictive prophecies which have clearly been fulfilled throughout history to even confirm that it is a reliable source of spiritual truth.

> Different Hindu scriptures present completely different paths to salvation, and the Vedas contain no predictive prophecies and record no miracles which would confirm that their religion came from even a divine source.

Testing Hinduism against the fruit it has produced

The obvious immoralities approved of and even taught by Hindu scripture range from gross prejudices and rigid social hierarchies to rape, murder, and all manner of sexual immoralities. But again, that is not a problem for Hinduism which just embraces the obvious immorality clearly taught within Hindu scripture and actually tries to make it a sign of spirituality rather than calling it for what it truly is, which is a moral wrong! For example, there are many references to sexual roles within Hindu religious rituals.

In the *Kama Sutra* of Vatsayayana (known to Hindus as the sex manual), it clearly celebrates sexual love as Kama is the Hindu god of love. In addition to its *explicit* information for use between husbands and wives, there are also whole portions of scripture devoted to the instructions on how to get the wives of other people as well as prostitutes. In fact, even the most orthodox of Hindu scripture is marked with approved violence and sexual perversions. Because we cannot make such an accusation without backing it up, please excuse our references of the following Hindu scriptures which are not only highly immoral but downright disgusting. For example, in the Hindu Brihadaranyaka Upanishad (6.4.9, 21), it clearly condones rape as it states:

> *Surely a woman who has changed her clothes at the end of her menstrual period is the most auspicious of women. When she has changed her clothes at the end of her menstrual period, therefore, one*

Objection 43
I Believe in Hinduism

should approach that splendid woman and invite her to have sex. Should she refuse to consent, he should bribe her. If she still refuses, he should beat her with a stick or with his fists and overpower her, saying: I will take away the splendor from you with my virility and splendor.

Another portion in the Shatapatha Brahmana (13.5.2.1–10), which crudely teaches bestiality (human sex with animals), outdoes the immorality which we just cited as it teaches women to have sex with horses during certain Hindu rituals. And examples such as these could go on and on. And to add to the list of gross immoralities within Vedic scripture, even human sacrifice is taught (see Aitaraya Brahmana 7.13–18)—as if pornography, bestiality, rape, racism, and obvious inequalities of the sexes were not enough!

For an example of Hinduism's support of fornication, if a woman is having a difficult time having a child within her marriage, she can go to a spiritual guru, and he can attempt to father her child if it's within the teachings of that particular guru to do so! While the Bible-believing Christian is reasonably abhorred by such socially acceptable fornication because it is a moral wrong based in the conscience of man and commandments of God, Hinduism is actually just the opposite, teaching that certain kinds of fornication/adultery are divine and actually one's spiritual duty toward God! While such contradicting moral values may indeed be quite confusing to the Western Christian, it may indeed give us some real insight as to just *why* so many misguided souls have actually been *attracted to Hinduism!*

As we've already pointed out, most all false religions appeal to the sin nature within man in a variety of ways, which usually boils down to offering sex, drugs, or money. Much to the contrary of Hindu scriptures, while the Holy Bible may indeed cite many immoral behaviors, it always does so in order to teach us *how not to live* because such behaviors inevitably bring on the destruction of man and the judgment of God. But you'll never find it condoning or approving any such immoral behaviors as does the Hindu scriptures, and it most certainly would never teach that they are any sign of true spirituality!

> While such contradicting moral values may indeed be quite confusing to the Western Christian, it may indeed give us some real insight as to just why

so many misguided souls have been attracted to Hinduism!

Other kinds of bad fruit within Hinduism

As we've already mentioned, the cow is considered sacred in Hinduism. But that's not all that's considered sacred, for anything that comes out of the cow is also considered sacred too. Its urine is sacred, its manure is sacred, and its milk is sacred. Sound ridiculous? I hope so! Even the dust of the cow hoofprints are studied by Hindus and supposedly have real meaning in Hinduism. Because Hindus believe that 330 million avatar lesser gods indwell only the domestic cow, festivals honoring Krishna priests actually shape the cow dung into images of their god, Krishna, the god of mercy and childhood.

We must always remember that the demonic world which ultimately hatches all false religions in order to deceive men away from the one true God and his salvation really hates mankind and is always trying to degrade us! And shaping cow dung into images of their god, Krishna, is just another prime example of that degradation! Because it is actually forbidden to slaughter cows in India, India itself probably has more cows than most other nations in the world. However, as we have already mentioned, because Hindus value the life of a cow over that of even a person during times of famine, many Hindus have actually starved to death as a result. If this also isn't obvious bad fruit produced by Hinduism, then what is it?

Even though India itself has been ravaged with starvation in many places, the cow has always been able to eat as much as it wants, unless, of course, Hindus break their own teachings and slaughter their cows to avoid starvation, which we've already told you they've also done on occasion throughout history.

In Hindu India, cows are pretty much allowed to roam anywhere, anytime. If you can believe it, even retirement homes have been set up in India for aging cows! Murderers sometimes get off with a lighter sentence than those who kill a cow. This, too, is all just more bad fruit which Hinduism continues to display. Hindu theology teaches eighty-six reincarnations are necessary to transform the soul of a devil into the soul of a cow and one more to become human. But according to Hindu beliefs, if a human kills a cow, through their imaginary process of reincarnation, it sends the soul of that person all the way back to the form of a demon again.

I guess, then, according to Hindu belief, most of the demonic world must have come from Americans slaughtering all the cows we do! If you're a typical American beef lover who supports the slaughter of cows for food, better enjoy your humanity now because according to Hindu beliefs, you'll literally be a demon in the next life! And if you've worked in any kind of a slaughterhouse or grocery store in the meat section, you'll undoubtedly be a demon in your next life as well. And just to add to their fantasies, at the moment of a cow's death, Hindus absurdly believe that if they hold the tail, the cow will guide them safely to the next life. Sounds like something you want to stake your eternal destiny on? Not me, my friend, not me!

But we must remember that the Hindu religion was designed to be fluid (ever-changing into whatever Hindus desire), and thus, really anything goes. Many Hindus say that they would rather die themselves than harm a cow and be demoted to a demon in the next life. However, as we've already mentioned, past Hindus have resorted to the slaughter of their cows just to avoid starvation — those poor devils! This obscure and ridiculous cow worship in Hinduism dates back to at least AD 465 AD, but like many other things within Hinduism, no one seems to know just when exactly it started within Hinduism or just who actually started it. And why was the cow chosen and not some other valuable domestic animal like horses? As you can see, none of it really makes much sense. And, quite obviously, Hinduism should also miserably fail this reasonable test in the heart and mind of the honest soul just as it has produced much of the bad fruit within past and present Hindu societies which we've already discussed.

> Hindu theology teaches eighty-six reincarnations are necessary to transform the soul of a devil into the soul of a cow and one more to become human.

Testing Hinduism against its divine power demonstrated

Hindus may claim some supernatural activity within the history of their religion, but if there has been any, it has undoubtedly been of demonic origin (like Satanism) as it does not even come close to the supernatural power which Christ, his apostles, and even the Old

Testament patriarchs clearly demonstrated openly on earth in front of many historical witnesses. Gurus walking on some bed of hot coals does just not qualify for any supernatural power which would be comparable to Christ's miracles. Besides, Christ did good to mankind with every one of the miracles he did.

But just what good does it do anyone if a guru walks on a bed of hot coals, which could even be by demonic aid? We all know supernatural life-giving power would speak much louder than words for anyone claiming that their religion is the one true faith. But for some reason, Hinduism, along with all the false religions in the world, continues to just expect the world to believe in their false gods blindly without those gods having to show any substantial supernatural evidence that they are anything more than fictitious false deities contrived in the minds of controlling men full of various immoral lusts.

And Hinduism's claim that all the Hindu avatar gods (inhabiting the cow) are part of their one and only God called Brahman is certainly no exception. Are we just supposed to blindly take their word for such a fantastic idea? *Honestly*, where is any honest evidence or supernatural power which backs up their fantastic claims? And where is any honest evidence that 330 million avatar gods inhabit the cow and not a horse or some other animal? Or that avatar gods are even real? Is such a fantastic thing true, just because Hindu gurus have said so? You might as well say that whole invisible cities full of people reside in the wings of dragonflies!

While such a ridiculous notion may not be able to be proven false, since there is absolutely no sound evidence for it, it certainly should not be trusted as true either! Even all spiritual realities which go beyond our reasoning should never be divorced from honest evidence in this rational world we can observe which would back them. Of course, all spiritual beliefs will go beyond our reasoning at some point as they must, but like those within biblical Christianity, we should always be able to ground them with much honest evidence in this observed world, which soundly connects them to reality.

For example, the reason I believe in the future city of New Jerusalem which the Bible tells us of is because Jesus and the apostles all validated all such teachings of theirs through the miraculous power of God over and over again! Not to mention, the Bible does, in fact, pass

Objection 43
I Believe in Hinduism

all reasonable tests which we can apply to it, whether those tests be scientific, historical, etc. In other words, my friend, our spiritual beliefs should never be founded upon blind faith!

Spiritual beliefs laying claim on reality are much like floating icebergs. Yes, we cannot see much of a floating iceberg because most of it is below the surface of the water. But if it truly is an iceberg, and you want everyone else to believe it is an iceberg, then you should be able to at least see a tip of the iceberg in order to justify your claim that there is a real massive iceberg there. In other words, just because we are talking about the spiritual realm doesn't mean the rational realm should not connect to it in many ways! The rational realm should always connect to it if, indeed, it is the trustworthy spiritual truth.

However, amazingly enough, you'll find that all false religions just expect you to believe in their iceberg, even though they cannot even reasonably show you even the tip of it sticking out of the water! They just want you to believe them blindly while they are disconnected from any real power (beyond human weakness) or honest rational evidence. But since our creator obviously gave us a mind and five senses to use in our discovery of truth, such an expectation from false religions is certainly beyond unreasonable!

If any Hindu throughout history thoroughly demonstrated the power of God (as did Christ and his apostles) while teaching that 330 million avatar gods inhabited the cow, then I, too, would believe in avatars! But, my friend, no *reliable historical record* from any other religion (other than biblical Christianity) even comes close to recording any such major miracles that would convince us of something beyond what mere weak mortals can contrive with the help of the demonic realm.

Hinduism also teaches us that literally everything is God. But where is any real rational evidence for such a fantastic claim? Again, are we just supposed to blindly take their word for it while they completely escape their responsibility to provide reasonable evidence backed by supernatural power for all their fantastic claims? Hinduism even claims that we humans are God; but again, where's any proof of such a ridiculous claim when the human race has always just struggled not to self-destruct?

Hindus may very well claim that there is no such thing as a creator who is distinct from his creation. But, again, why should anyone believe them if their religion has never been backed by any real power which would exceed that of men dabbling in the demonic realm? On the other hand, when Christ and his apostles all walked the earth, they fully demonstrated the power of God through major supernatural miracles hundreds of times over in front of many public eyewitnesses. And since those many miracles all consistently helped and loved men in some way, we know they were not of demonic origin. And as we've already discussed at length in part two of our series, the Bible itself is laced with over 2,000 future-predicting prophecies which have already been fulfilled, all proving Jesus is just who he claimed to be and that the Bible was also divinely authored! And as we've already mentioned, this awesome divine power displayed *is something unique to biblical Christianity alone.* As the saying goes:

> Jesus did not at all expect the world to follow him blindly. He publicly healed the blind to prove his deity!

My point is simple and clear. It's quite unreasonable for any religion to expect the world to follow them blindly and just take their word for it without power clearly demonstrated, which would exceed that of mere humans or the demonic realm, especially when it directly affects the eternal salvation of all men! Even though Hinduism's idea of heaven/salvation may be quite different than the Jewish/Christian view, it nevertheless still expects the whole world to just believe in their whole pantheistic spiritual reality which obviously lacks the very reasonable divine power to back up their fantastic claims. However, much to the contrary of all the false religions in the world, Jesus Christ certainly did not expect the world to follow him blindly without the reasonable divine power displayed to back up his claims. As we've already mentioned in Objection #36, Jesus Christ powerfully satisfied all of the following reasonable divine attributes which we would fully expect of God:

1. He made an utterly unique entrance into human history.
2. He was without sin, living a morally perfect life under the observation of all witnesses around him (not to mention

Objection 43
I Believe in Hinduism

his own family members who lived right with him).
3. He manifested his supernatural presence in the form of major supernatural acts, namely large undeniable miracles.
4. He spoke the greatest words ever spoken.
5. He actually enabled humanity to become like himself.
6. He truly satisfied the spiritual hunger in humanity.
7. He proved he had power over humanity's most pervasive and feared enemy: death.
8. He made an utterly unique exit from human history.
9. He had a powerful permanent and universal influence upon all mankind which would stand far above the influence of anyone else.

It's quite unreasonable for any religion to expect the world to follow them blindly and just take their word for it, especially when it directly effects the eternal salvation of all men!

But since when did any Hindu god prove their deity to the whole world as Jesus plainly did many times over through all these reasonable divine qualifications? In fact, no Hindu god (or gods) has even manifested themselves in any kind of a real supernatural way for the whole world to see as Christ clearly did! Hindus may have made many statues of their many different gods and insisted that they were god, just because a statue of that so-called god was made by men. But not one of their gods (which includes Brahman) has ever shown themselves to be a real living god with the reasonable proof of divine power for mankind to see like Jesus plainly did as he walked among men right here on earth, performing many miracles in the sight of men.

In other words, Brahman only exists in the deceived imaginations of Hindus, simply because there is no real proof or evidence that would convince us otherwise! Yes, there are plenty of statues of Christ. But the big difference is that Christ was a real living historical figure!

My friend, this cannot be said of any other statue of any other so-called god of any other so-called true belief system in the world! When did Vishnu, Krishna, Rama, or any other Hindu god ever come alive among men and prove their deity through any divine power for the whole world to plainly witness? All we have in Hinduism is wooden/

stone statues of their Hindu gods which completely lack the reasonable divine evidence that they are anything but a dead lifeless man-made object! The Holy Bible, on the other hand, is 99.5 percent reliable as a historical document, something which certainly cannot be said of any Hindu texts!

The truth is that most Hindu's are just raised in Hinduism, and they probably have never even thought to insist upon the very reasonable supernatural evidence required to validate all the deity claims within Hinduism. In other words, even though there is absolutely no evidence that Hindu beliefs go beyond that of mere human imaginations and misguided men dabbling in the demonic realm, perhaps Hindus themselves have never thought to even question their beliefs because of their strong family ties to Hinduism. They have just blindly taken some guru's word for it, and then, in turn, expect the world to take their word for it.

But when you think about it, any misguided soul within any false religion can do that! Any religion can manufacture wood or stone statues in commemoration of the gods they believe to be real. But that obviously does not make them real because every religion in the world has completely different gods which they insist are the only true gods. And very logically then, there must be many false gods as well as false statues. It is so easy for a religion to just say that their god is God or that their gods are even real. But let's have some real honest evidence for such a large claim, shall we?

The truth is that only Jesus Christ satisfied these amazing but reasonable God qualifications when he walked among men on earth living a sinless life and powerfully demonstrating his divinity many times over in the very face of humanity.

Any religion can even create written stories of supernatural activity, but as we have already mentioned in Part 2 of our series, the Holy Bible proves its divine authorship through thousands of fulfilled prophecies which ultimately center around the fact that Jesus Christ is the one true God. And all these past prophecies coming true within the Bible can easily be historically verified through our historical records. And the fact that this very same Jesus (whom most all fulfilled Bible prophecy centers around) also proved his deity many times over on earth by living a sinless life and powerfully demonstrating his divine power in the very face of humanity is something which no religion on earth even comes close to for divine power demonstrated. And, certainly, no ancient Hindu writings reveal this kind of massive divine power demonstrated with any kind of prophetic/historical proof.

When comparing the divine power demonstrated between the Holy Bible *and any other ancient religious text*, it's kind of like putting a greyhound dog in a race with a walking stick insect! My friend, there's absolutely no contest whatsoever! The simple truth is that no other religion or belief system isn't even in the same ballpark with biblical Christianity! No, as it concerns divine power demonstrated, biblical Christianity stands quite alone from all the other religions in the world, including Hinduism.

Conclusion

In view of the fact that we've just discussed a partial summary of the obvious failings of Hinduism, it certainly should be quite apparent that Hinduism itself is sufficiently exposed as a man-made and deeply flawed system of belief. And considering many other religions in the world are historically based directly from Hinduism, then it certainly should at the same time strongly discredit them as well. Hare Krishna, Buddhism, Zen, TM (Transcendental Meditation), Shintoism, Baha'i, Scientology, the Masonic lodge, and the New Age movement are all examples of additional very flawed man-made religions which have taken *much of their basic beliefs* from Hinduism which foundationally predates them.

Sadly, Hinduism is the third largest religion in the world today which claims roughly 900 million souls! My friend, if you happen to be a Hindu, please do not at all be personally offended by the simple facts of Hinduism which we've just presented here. Either what has been conveyed is fairly representative of Hinduism (or Hindu belief) or it isn't.

As we said from the beginning, we are just exposing the obvious moral failings of *any false religion* which would pull men away from the one true God and his eternal salvation with love as our ultimate motive, simply because we believe all men have the right to know about their one true creator and the eternal salvation he freely offers us. Please just let these simple truths find home in your heart that you may see once and for all that the belief system of Hinduism is seriously flawed and is simply not worthy of your trust, especially as it concerns your eternal destiny!

However, Jesus Christ not only backed up all his authoritative claims with the awesome power of fulfilled prophecy and miracles, but he also lived a sinless life and fully demonstrated his love for you by taking the punishment for all your sins upon himself when he died on a Roman cross nearly 2,000 years ago. All you have to do is truly believe it, and you will be right with God and obtain his everlasting life, just as he promised all men.

The afterlife promises of Hinduism are not only vague but seriously lacking in any real hope when compared to the awesome detailed eternal blessings of biblical Christianity. Just as Jesus proved his divinity to the honest soul many times over when he walked the earth, so too is his Word completely trustworthy which foretells the awesome eternity which God has for all those who love him. As Revelation 21:3–4 clearly teaches:

> *"[B]ehold, the dwelling place of God is with men, and he will live with them, and they shall be his people, and God himself shall be with them, and be their God. And God shall wipe away all tears from their eyes; and there shall be no more death, neither sorrow, nor crying, neither shall there be any more pain: for the former things are passed away."*

But the Bible teaches us plainly that only through Christ can we obtain God's eternal life. As Jesus plainly taught within John 14:6, *"I am the way and the truth and the life. No one comes to the Father except through me."*

If you are one who has practiced Hinduism and can easily see the lack of real honest evidence, power, and morality within it and would like to give the real biblical Jesus a chance to reveal himself to you as your one true creator, I invite you to just take that first small step of faith by sincerely praying the prayer of salvation located at the end of this book. Even if you've been a Hindu for years, you can still break away from that obvious false religion today which threatens your true salvation through Christ. And don't be concerned with what your family members may think of you because, simply put, they will not be you're judge on judgment day! This decision is between you and God

Objection 43
I Believe in Hinduism

(your creator) alone. No matter what your past is like, God loves you and sincerely wants you to be a part of his awesome eternal kingdom!

Jesus said, "I am the resurrection and the life. He who believes in me, will live even though he dies; and whoever lives and believes in me will never die." (John 11:25–26)

OBJECTION 44
I Believe in Buddhism

A loving reminder: Before each false belief system we discuss, just so my loving intentions cannot be misunderstood, I will *once again* remind the reader that it's certainly *not the adherents* of any false religion or belief system which the true Church is against but rather just the *false teachings* within them which deceive men away from the one and only true God and his eternal salvation (Ephesians 6:12). Therefore, my dear reader, please know that our discussion of these various different religions or belief systems is very much a *love* issue.

Defining Buddhism

Unlike religions which are concerned with a God and an afterlife, Buddhism has always been mainly concerned with just the solution to the sufferings of all mankind during and after this life. Being born into a time when Hinduism was already quite prevalent, Buddha himself actually tried Hinduism and rejected it in his later youth. However, because one can easily see some real basic similarities between both Hinduism and Buddhism, it leads us to believe Buddha did not reject Hinduism altogether and that to a large degree, Buddhism was, in fact, somewhat developed out of Hinduism. In fact, Buddhism is pretty much the same pantheistic song with just a different humanistic melody. They both embrace the teaching of karma (the consequences of acts undertaken

Objection 44
I Believe in Buddhism

in this life will be felt in the next one) and reincarnation (man dies and keeps coming back as something or someone else in another life until he has evolved to godhood). And they also both teach Samsara and Illusion.

However, while Hinduism teaches that everything is the impersonal god, Brahman, Buddha himself refused to even deny or affirm the existence of God. In fact, original Buddhism did not even involve faith, worship, prayer, praise, or forgiveness of sins. This is why Buddhism itself really cannot even be considered a religion because it simply does not acknowledge a God or gods. It is more accurately defined as a human philosophy (such as the teachings of Confucius) which is just characterized with pantheism, polytheism, and idolatry.

However, while he refused to deny or affirm the existence of God, Buddha himself at least had the reasonable sense to deny that he himself was divine (we must give credit where it is due)! Therefore, Buddhism is essentially Hinduism which has a few more morals, no caste system, and no focus on the pantheistic Hindu god, Brahman. Some of the basic teachings of Buddha are as follows:

>*First noble truth*: Both pleasure and pain in life are considered sufferings.
>*Second noble truth*: Suffering is caused by all cravings or the desire to have things different than they are.
>*Third noble truth*: Suffering has an end.
>*Fourth noble truth*: This noble truth offers the means to the end of all suffering through the eight-fold path and the middle way. The eight-fold path (often depicted as a wheel with eight spokes) includes: right views, right intention, right speech, right action, right occupation, right endeavor, right mindfulness, and right concentration. The middle way is itself the rejection of all extremes of thought, emotion, action, and lifestyle.

The origin of Buddhism

The founder of Buddhism is Siddhartha Gautama, a young man native to our present-day Nepal. While it is technically uncertain, most historians date Buddha's life from about 536 BC to about 483 BC. As the teachings of this young man spread, eventually, he became known as Buddha, which supposedly means "enlightened one." Buddha himself was the son of a very wealthy king and queen whose wishes were that he was to be protected from all problems and suffering of any kind. Later, however, his curious nature led him out of his safe palace where he was suddenly exposed to the sufferings of real life as he encountered those with diseases, etc. Buddha was so shocked by the sufferings he witnessed that he was obsessed with finding a solution for all the sufferings of mankind. And, essentially, that's how Buddhism got started. Today, its theme still revolves around Buddha's solution to all sufferings of man.

Testing Buddhism against the true moral condition of man

Buddhism maintains that a person's actions, thoughts, etc., can be skillful, wholesome, or not beneficial. But since Buddhism rejects the reality of a perfect eternal divine being who created us, then, of course, there can be no sin which is the breaking of his perfect moral standards. But Buddhism does teach there is such a thing as evil deeds for which the doer is solely responsible in his next reincarnated lives. So because Buddhists have just removed our creator from the equation of life, they then just call it evil, not sin.

But the real question is, if Buddhism has removed a monotheistic God from the equation of life, who then is the final authority who actually determines for the entire human race which deeds or thoughts are wholesome or beneficial and which are not? And just who determines then what evil is and what is not? Buddha? You? Me? Why if we all are quite imperfect, to say the least, and we have no real moral clout beyond one another? Hmm…seems like a bit of a conundrum to me.

Thus, we are back to relative morality which is like everyone playing the same board game by any rules they think best. It is true that mankind as a whole has always generally agreed on what is morally wrong within our collective consciences (like murder, rape, unjust wars, etc.). And this speaks to the fact that we all have a common creator who must have built his own morality into our very conscience which he created all men with (just like a board game only comes with one set of rules from its creator). But at the same time, it is also true that some men choose not to follow their God given consciences, and thus deviate greatly from what we all know to be morally right (just like some may try to deviate from the rules while playing a board game). So, again, in the case of disagreements among even Buddhists, who determines morality if our very own creator is rejected?

Objection 44
I Believe in Buddhism

If Buddhism has removed a monotheistic God from the equation of life, who then is the final authority who actually determines morality for the entire human race?

Man determining his own morality is like a student grading their own papers. It is just wrong, not to mention meaningless. It is only our creator who has the authority and clout to define all of morality for the entire human race because:

1. It is only he who is morally perfect and eternal.
2. It is only he who brought mankind into existence.
3. It is only he who knows how we function the best as his own creation.
4. It is only he that created us all with the same conscience that testifies of his same moral standards.

So, when Buddhists throw out the only trustworthy final authority compass to determine all morality for the human race, it is much like throwing the umpire out of a baseball game. Confusion, division, and frustration can only follow. For example, if one Buddhist believes something is an evil or not beneficial, and another Buddhist does not agree, then who's to determine which is correct? Only it is far worse because real life is not just a ball game, and our perfect creator is not just some imperfect umpire in some game! And if the eternal destinies of men are at stake in what we choose to believe, then the issue of morality and who determines it is quite serious indeed. Even employees have learned that if they do not have a single authority for a boss to follow, confusion, division, frustration, and hurt will be the end result. Similarly, we all need the single authority of our one and only true creator to not only unite us but to define safe reality for us.

When *any religion* throws our own creator out of life, when all life only comes from him, it makes about as much sense as a paratrooper expecting to live without a parachute after he has jumped! If our only source of life is permanently abandoned, then all we have left is death, and there is simply no way to get life out of death. And, amazingly enough, those in false religions who have thrown our one and only creator out of their lives also arrogantly claim to know the spiritual truth for everyone else! Talk about the blind trying to lead others through a minefield! So why should anyone follow a Buddhist (or anyone else) when, in fact, they have gone against their own God-given conscience and thrown out their very own creator who is their only source of life? What exactly qualifies any Buddhist to declare to the rest of the world that Buddhism is the one true belief system if, in fact, their morality and weak humanity is really no different than anyone else's?

Again, if the Buddhist cannot show or demonstrate to others any real power in Buddhism beyond the mere weakness of men who are influenced by the demonic realm, why should anyone take their word for anything?

Since God has given all men a conscience which very clearly bears witness to himself and his moral standards, and Christ fully demonstrated his unique divinity in all power by living a sinless life and doing many divine miracles before many witnesses over a three-year period of time, then that is the kind of power that would earn our trust for his basic authority to teach us about something so important as our afterlife. And just because of the power, love, and divine clout Christ openly displayed to all humanity, it is certainly then a moral wrong for mankind to reject him.

Buddhists may flatly deny the reality that Jesus is our creator, but since Christ provided all the reasonable divine proofs for his claims, and no Buddhist ever has even come close to doing the same, who then should we believe? The truth is that when we are just looking through the eyeglasses of our own dark sin nature to determine truth, there is simply no way to arrive at the truth any more than a broken compass can lead someone true north out of a dense fog.

Like Hinduism, Buddhism also believes in reincarnation which typically maintains that the human race has already shown themselves to be basically good because of all the good deeds they had to do in their past lives in order to even become human. This is not to say that humans cannot commit evil and even regress in their process of reincarnation; however, to even be human already shows basic goodness in the process of reincarnation. However, the reality of all men being born with a sin nature long before they are even old enough to learn how to make good or bad moral choices simply cannot be harmonized with the whole process of reincarnation, which is only determined by good or bad moral choices. And, ironically, because Buddhism rebelliously rejects

Objection 44
I Believe in Buddhism

the reality of God our creator, his perfect moral standards, as well as the obvious reality of man's incurable inborn *sin* apart from our creator, it just confirms all the more the very reality of the sin which it refuses to acknowledge.

Thus, because it maintains that man is basically good and does not have an inborn sin nature, we must conclude that Buddhism, too, as a belief system utterly fails when tested against the true moral condition of man.

> Ironically because Buddhism rebelliously rejects the reality of God our creator, as well as the reality of man's inborn sin, it just confirms all the more the very reality of the sin which it refuses to acknowledge.

Testing Buddhism against self-contradictions

There are many self-contradictions within Buddhism, but we will just cite those which should be sufficient. Like we've already mentioned, while Buddha himself refused to deny or affirm the existence of God, he at least had the reasonable sense to deny that he himself was divine. However, in contradiction to Buddha himself, *many* of his followers have historically believed that he was divine! So right there, we find a major contradiction of beliefs within Buddhism today which is not really some small issue within a given belief system! In fact, this issue is so basic it transforms Buddhism out of the realm of mere human philosophy into a religion (with a god). Some Buddhists today still believe Buddha to be divine, while others side with Buddha himself and deny that he was divine. But either way, you can still be a qualified Buddhist!

Supposedly, Buddha also taught that one can lead a pure life without imposing commandments and using the fear of punishment. But at the same time, he taught that every evil deed done by a person will be fully paid for in their following lives within the process of reincarnation. Here, again, we see a major contradiction as the real truth is that Buddha had many specific ordinances to live by (whether one calls them commandments is rather irrelevant), and there was a definite fear of punishment built into his karma/reincarnation belief system if one should violate those ordinances. And, of course, the very same could be said of Hinduism.

And just like the false self-conflicting Hindu religion, Buddhism today has a traditional conservative branch and a more liberal branch. The conservative branch is referred to as Theravada, and the liberal branch is referred to as Mahayana. Because these two groups within Buddhism contradict each other in even some *basic* beliefs (like whether or not Buddha was divine), then such *basic* differences should be an indication that Buddhism as a whole certainly cannot be the one true reliable faith.

While both conservative and liberal Buddhists may believe that man's ultimate goal is to be released from the suffering within the cycle of reincarnation, which they call Nirvana, conservatives take no position on whether they will even be conscious during their entire eternal state afterwards. However, liberals do believe that they will be at least conscious throughout their eternal state. This, too, should not be considered a small difference of beliefs. When differences within a belief system are minor, it generally does not threaten the credibility of that belief system. However, when they are major, like who's God, or is there a conscious afterlife, then it certainly should threaten the credibility of that belief system!

But no matter whether or not one is a conservative or a liberal within Buddhism, neither one has much of a real tangible idea of a *good afterlife*. The bliss they hope for when they finally get out of the cycle of death and rebirth is rather unexplainable, even if it is attainable. And believing in any belief system (like Hinduism, Buddhism, and the New Age movement), which really offers no tangible idea of one's eternal destiny, makes about as much sense as going to the airport and asking for an airplane ticket and not requesting a specific destination for that ticket!

Biblical Christianity, on the other hand, is just the opposite as the Holy Bible goes into all kinds of real good detail when describing the literal heaven, New Jerusalem, and the new earth, which are to be the awesome eternal homes of all Bible-believing Christians who simply believe in what Christ did for them on the cross. The following is just a partial basic list of all the awesome blessings which await the true believer in Christ:

Objection 44
I Believe in Buddhism

Just some of the main promises of God for all true believers in Christ

1. *All believers in Christ will live with Christ:* First and most important of all, all believers in Christ will get to live right with Christ, our creator, in New Jerusalem, which is on the new earth for all eternity (Revelation chapter 21).
2. *All believers in Christ will escape eternal punishment in hell:* All true believers in Christ will escape eternal punishment in hell, simply because they truly believe Christ already took the punishment for their sins on the cross and satisfied God's perfect justice (John 3:35–36).
3. *All believers in Christ will escape the coming seven-year tribulation period:* God's promise is to supernaturally remove all believers in Christ off the earth and bring them to the third heavens (where God resides) just before the seven-year tribulation of Revelation begins (Luke 21:34–36; 1 Thessalonians 4:16–18; Romans 8:11). This event is referred to as the rapture resurrection of the Church which will literally happen in the blink of an eye (1 Corinthians 15:51–52).
4. *All believers in Christ will receive a resurrected eternal body:* During that brief moment when raptured, all believers in Christ will receive their perfected eternal bodies which will literally last forever (Philippians 3:20–21). In their new bodies, all believers in Christ will be in their prime, probably about the age of thirty, and any of the effects which sin has had on them will be gone, whether it is just general aging or any other effects of sin (like scars, deformities, disease, etc.; Revelation 21:4). Everyone will have perfect eyesight, hearing, and perfectly good teeth and hair. All the effects of sin will be completely gone! Believers in Christ during their eternal state will likely be able to walk through walls (like Christ did in his resurrected state), be invisible, and travel at the speed of thought!
5. *All believers in Christ will receive eternal rewards:* Right after the rapture resurrection, all believers in Christ will receive their eternal rewards (Luke 14:14; 1 Peter 5:4). Even if they gave someone a glass of water, they will still receive an

eternal reward for it (Matthew 10:42)!
6. *All believers in Christ will live within New Jerusalem*, a city made by God himself which has the immense square dimensions of 1,380 miles tall, wide and long (John 14:1–3; Revelation 21:16)!
7. *All believers in Christ during their eternal state will all help Christ rule and reign in his new kingdom*, which begins right after the seven-year tribulation is over (Revelation 20:4).
8. *All Believers in Christ will never suffer any pain ever again throughout all of eternity* (Romans 8:18; Revelation 20:4).
9. *And even with all this, believers in Christ haven't even a clue as to all the blessings of God which await them as God clearly promises in* 1 Corinthians 2:9: *"As it is written, eye has not seen, nor ear heard, neither has it entered into the heart of man the things which God has prepared for those who love him."*

And last, but not least, just the way Buddhism even began is self-contradictory. Buddha just up and left his young wife and child about to be born in order to find a solution to human suffering? My friend, it doesn't take a Philadelphia lawyer to figure out that something is very wrong if one causes great suffering to those closest to him all under the pretense of finding a solution to human suffering! How can anyone purposely be a part of the problem of human suffering and at the same time pretend to seek a solution for it? And please keep in mind that Buddha never even went back to his wife (aside from just few and far between visits), even after he was supposedly enlightened! Thus, overall, we find that Buddhism quickly fails when tested against self-contradictions.

> Believing in any belief system which really offers no tangible idea of one's eternal destiny makes about as much sense as going to the airport and asking for an airplane ticket and not requesting a specific destination for that ticket!

Objection 44
I Believe in Buddhism

Testing Buddhism against the well-known facts of science

The fact that both Hinduism and Buddhism largely rely upon very unscientific teachings such as reincarnation should be another red flag for those seriously looking for the reliable trustworthy truth. Again, are we just supposed to take their word for it that the whole fantastic age-long process of reincarnation is even real? Where's any real proof for it? Let's be *honest*: in the field of science, there is about as much proof for the process of reincarnation as there is for all lesser forms of life (like rocks, insects, birds, fish, and animals) having a conscience and the capability of making moral choices in order to be promoted or demoted to their supposed next life in the process of reincarnation. Thus, it would seem there is only sound evidence against it and none obviously for it. And let's face it: religions like Hinduism, Buddhism, and even the New Age movement all largely stand/or fall apart depending upon whether this very improvable process of reincarnation is even true!

The bottom line is Hinduism, Buddhism, and the New Age movement all greatly lack any scientific backing for most of their basic claims. It is certainly true that all religions (even biblical Christianity) have basic beliefs which transcend the natural sciences. But that's exactly why strong *supernatural* evidence for a given belief system is absolutely essential to give credibility to those beliefs which extend beyond the natural sciences. If some Hindu, Buddhist, or New Age religious leader teaching reincarnation claimed to be our creator (instead of Jesus) and then actually backed it up with a sinless life, many major miracles and fulfilled prophecies which flatly prove his divinity, I might actually believe in reincarnation! But as it is with many other teachings other than their teaching of reincarnation, both Hinduism and Buddhism just expect us to take their word for it quite blindly while they completely escape their responsibility to provide any reasonable honest evidence, which not only includes scientific or historic evidence but also supernatural evidence!

Yes, Jesus, his apostles, and the Old Testament prophets all taught us many spiritual realities which cannot be proven in and of themselves as well. But the difference is that all these men proved that they were undeniably connected to our one true God and creator because of all the divine power that flowed through them in the form of prophecies and miracles! But in Hinduism and Buddhism, we certainly have no such men to assure us we are even being taught the truth as it concerns those spiritual realities which cannot be proven in and of themselves.

Additionally, much of biblical Christianity can be confirmed through the sciences. But because almost no facet of Hinduism or Buddhism can be confirmed through any well-established scientific discoveries, this too is a red flag, especially since their pantheistic teachings must include the entire science world as well! Even if a Hindu or Buddhist would rely upon the theory of Darwinian evolution for their explanation of what is, as we've already shown in our very first objections, the Theory of Evolution is still waiting for its basic scientific backing after 200-plus years of modern scientific investigation!

There are no intermediate life-forms which are obvious within our fossil record when there should very reasonably be just as many of those (if not more) as there are fossils for fully formed life-forms! In fact, no *kind* of animal does not even want to naturally crossbreed with another *kind* of animal. If macroevolution from one kind to another were really true on any level, these two *very basic realities* would certainly not be the case. And even if the Buddhist, Hindu, or New Ager may say they reject the theory of Darwinian evolution, but at the same time still believe we all evolved from lower forms of life through reincarnation, there is even less scientific proof for this process. Thus, Buddhism also fails when tested against science as well.

> It is certainly true that all religions have basic beliefs which transcend the natural sciences. But that's exactly why strong supernatural evidence is absolutely essential to give credibility to those beliefs.

Testing Buddhism against the character of its founder

We are told that Buddha and his wife, Yasodhara, had an arranged marriage by Buddha's parents when Buddha was only about sixteen years of age. And we are also told that at about age twenty-nine, Buddha (against even his parent's wishes) just up and left his wife and only son (Rahula) because he was determined to find a solution to all human suffering. But, really, how much sense does it make to deliberately cause the closest people in one's life great suffering of this kind all in

Objection 44
I Believe in Buddhism

the name of finding a solution to human suffering? That makes about as much sense as a man burning his own house down right before he strikes out to become a firefighter! We are told that his wife, Yasodhara, was absolutely devastated (and overcome with grief) by his sudden departure, just before his son was born, and rightly so. Wouldn't any wife? We are also told that Buddha did not come back but to *just visit* his wife and son until seven years later!

As much as Buddhists may try to make Buddha's sudden departure from his family look like some big moral humanitarian mission, I think it's quite obvious there was something more going on in young Buddha's life at the time when he forsook his wife and son to find a solution to all human suffering. It is much easier to believe that he was a very human young father who was probably not only very overwhelmed with all the royal expectations which came from his controlling father but also, with all his imminent responsibilities as a first-time father. Let's face it: Buddha was certainly not the first young father in the human race to leave his wife and first child nor was he probably the first prince to run from his oncoming royal responsibilities!

Therefore, Buddha himself had two very big common reasons to try to escape his responsibilities. After all, if he was so shocked just by seeing the human suffering which he encountered, it is certainly not hard to believe this *very sheltered* young man was also afraid of the heavy commitment involved with raising his new son and pleasing his wife, mother, and father. And instead of being honest with himself and his wife within his claustrophobic condition, he probably just found it much easier to run and believe he was actually leaving his wife and son for some grander and nobler cause, namely to find a solution to all human suffering. Buddhists try to defend Buddha's character at this point by saying that times were different back then in Buddha's culture, and men could do such things without it being a moral wrong. But obviously, since his wife was devastated, she felt quite different about it.

Let's all be honest here (and not continue to live Buddha's lie with him): Because human love and loyalty between a man and wife has always been the same for everyone in every culture of human history, we can't begin to believe such a cultural excuse concerning the very basics of marital love. Suddenly leaving one's wife just before your first child is born (without a *truly moral* explanation) is a nasty moral wrong in any culture during any time in history! You can't make a corpse look any better just by trying to put a dress on it!

Other loyal Buddhists will try to justify Buddha's actions here by asserting that his departure was okay, simply because his wife and son lacked for nothing as they were royalty in his father's care. But really, that doesn't work either because everyone knows that in every culture, marriage is first and foremost about trust and a healthy love relationship, not just material provision.

The point that she happened to be taken care of (no thanks to Buddha) is rather irrelevant to the central love relationship of marriage. Your spouse is supposed to be your best trustworthy friend and the closest person in your life in any culture! Besides, even if his wife and son weren't going to be taken care of, Buddha still would have left because obviously, in his mind, he had to leave in order to find his solution to human suffering. However, the fact that young Buddha knew his wife would be taken care of by his father was all part of the strong temptation for him to up and run from his own responsibilities as a father. His father spoiling him and protecting him from the harsher realities of life was undoubtedly a big part of Buddha's problem from the start.

Other Buddhists attempt to defend Buddha's character by coming up with the excuse that he wasn't yet enlightened when he left his wife and son. But that doesn't work either because then why didn't he ever return to his role as a father and husband, even after his enlightenment and finding out that true liberation lies within and not anywhere in the external world?

Evidently, we are told that because Buddha was enlightened by the time he did return to *just visit* his wife (seven years after he left) that all "I, me, mine, and myself" was gone from Buddha's own character; thus, the enlightened Buddha made absolutely no distinctions between his wife, his son, and a stranger in their midst as supposedly he loved everyone the same. But what a bunch of hogwash! For someone who was *supposedly* rid of self, Buddha was just more full of himself than ever because he completely escaped his responsibility to love his wife and son uniquely more than a complete stranger! Wow.

If you are a married Buddhist, how would you really feel if your spouse just up and left you and after seven years, finally returned

Objection 44
I Believe in Buddhism

home (with no communication), and treated you no different than any stranger? And instead of any kind of an apology, Buddha had the deluded audacity to act like it was his life's biggest achievement and made a whole religion out of it? I say, how icky and even demonic!

Strangely enough, and probably just because his wife and son wanted the closest relationship with him that they could have, they too adopted his bizarre beliefs and decided to live his lie with him! What a desperate and insecure reaction to their pain! Nevertheless, the selfless Buddha never did go back to his role as a husband and father. And, hypocritically enough, Buddha had at least two other wives other than Yasodhara (that we know of) by the names of Gopa and Mrigaja.

To not see that this whole thing called Buddhism got its start from a rather big moral mess is to be rather blind indeed, simply because life all boils down to just what Christ himself taught, and that is *"Love others the way you would have them love you"* (Matthew 7:12).

How many wives do you honestly think would knowingly sign up for such heartless unlove, abandonment, and betrayal? Not many, my friend, not many. If you happen to be a married Buddhist who defends the obviously flawed character of Buddha when he left his wife and child and just took on more wives, please try to do so with your own spouse and just see the results. I think those results would be less than desirable. Honesty here is once again key to recognizing the truth.

> For someone who was supposedly rid of self, Buddha was just more full of himself than ever because he completely escaped his responsibility to love his wife and son more than a complete stranger!

What about the Apostle Peter who was married before he became Christ's disciple?

But one might say, what about the Apostle Peter who left his wife to become one of Christ's disciples? First of all, it is a common misconception that Peter actually left his wife to become Christ's disciple. The evidence which we have from God's Word actually points to the fact that Peter stayed in his husband role to his wife the rest of his life and did not at all cut off his husband-wife relationship, just because he became Christ's disciple. For example, we know Peter was still in a healthy relationship with his wife in the beginning of his discipleship with Christ, simply because Christ came to Peter's house, and while there, Christ miraculously healed Peter's mother-in-law from a fever (Matthew 8:14–15). In fact, Matthew 8:16 even says that many more who were sick and even demon-possessed came to Peter's house (that night while Christ was there), and Peter's house was actually used for Christ's ministry at the time.

Then yet in another verse of God's Word, we find that not only Peter but some of the other apostles who were also married actually took their wives right along with them in their traveling ministries (please see 1 Corinthians 9:5). Not all of Christ's disciples were celibate: this, too, is a common misconception, even though Bible-ignorant Hollywood may have portrayed things to be that way in some of their films!

What about passages like Matthew 10:35–37?

In Matthew 10:35–37, Jesus said to his disciples:

"Do not suppose that I have come to bring peace to the earth. I did not come to bring peace but a sword. For I have come to turn a man against his father, a daughter against her mother, a daughter-in-law against her mother-in-law, and a man's enemies will be the members of his own household. Anyone who loves his father or mother more than me is not worthy of me."

The whole context of this passage isn't that we shouldn't love our family members or that we should abandon them like Buddha did; otherwise, the rest of Christ's teachings (which were echoed by his apostles) to love our family would certainly make no sense at all (see Matthew 15:3–6, Ephesians 5:25–29; 1 Corinthians 7:3–5, 10–13, 27; 1 Timothy 3:1–5, 12).

The *true context* in Matthew 10:35–37 is just to love God *more* than our human family. And he's saying that our highest love for God in this respect will actually be tested to the point of causing division in our family if our family does not want to acknowledge or follow Christ. And when Jesus said that he came to bring *a sword*, he wasn't referring to a literal sword to cause literal war on earth because even the one time his disciple, Peter, tried to use a literal sword, Jesus seriously upbraided him for it (Matthew 26:51–54). Jesus was only talking about the spiritual division in the hearts of all men which would be caused by the spiritual sword of his own Word (Ephesians 6:17) when men failed to love God the most.

According to the Bible, if family members all loved God in their lives the way they should, there would be no division even in the family, simply because all family members would be on the same spiritual page of loving God the most (Matthew 12:49–50). But, of course, Jesus knew that all men would not love God like they should and prophetically foretold the spiritual division that would come as a result. In other words, Jesus came to test all mankind's heart love for God in this basic respect, and this was a very necessary test of heart before he would choose to share his eternal life with us! But in the name of some higher spirituality manufactured by Buddha himself, it would certainly seem he sacrificed his basic love for his family. However, the Bible teaches us to love both God and our family, even though it may teach men to love God more than their family when it comes to family being at variance with God.

The Apostle Paul probably said it best in 1 Corinthians 13:1–3 when it comes to man sacrificing his love for his fellow man (especially family members) in the name of their *supposed* spirituality:

> *"If I speak with the tongues of men and of angels, and have not love (Greek word for love here is a real tangible love), I am resounding gong or a clanging symbol. If I have the gift of prophecy and can fathom all mysteries and all knowledge, and if I have faith that can move mountains, but have not love, I am nothing. If I give all I possess to the poor and surrender my body to the flames, but have not love, I gain nothing."*

And if Buddha's whole religion started with his sacrifice of the very basic love he should have had for his wife and son, this should certainly be a major red flag in the heart of any honest soul looking for the reliable and trustworthy truth.

Testing Buddhism against its prophetic predictions of the future

Much like Hinduism, Buddhism as a belief system cannot even be confirmed through the fulfillment of predictive prophecies, simply because it really has none. We must remember that Buddhism rejects any idea of a monotheistic God who would even attempt to reveal himself through predictive prophecies. Therefore, it only makes sense that the writings of Buddhism (which are chiefly about the life of Buddha who did not even claim to be divine) would contain no real predictive prophecies. Thus, Buddhism completely lacks this kind of power (of fulfilled prophecy) to substantiate its claim to be the universal truth for all mankind (not to mention Buddha, of course, did not live a sinless life nor do any supernatural miracles which would convince us of anything beyond mere human weakness influenced by the demonic realm).

And while this may not necessarily be a failure, per se, of this particular test, we would reasonably expect Buddhism to substantiate its incredible definition of reality for the whole human race through *some kind* of real power beyond mere human ability and opinion if, in fact, it has no predictive prophecies or good life-giving supernatural power. But even in this basic respect, it certainly disappoints us.

> We would reasonably expect Buddhism to substantiate its incredible definition of reality for the whole human race through some kind of real power, but even in this basic respect, it certainly disappoints us.

Testing Buddhism against the fruit it has produced

Like all false religions, the worst fruit Buddhism produces is that in the name of goodness and the alleviation of all pain, it actually deceives men into eternal suffering in hell according to the Bible! And considering Buddhism's main boast is specifically to alleviate the sufferings of all mankind, this makes it even more deceptive and is its worst failure as a trustworthy belief system. As Jesus clearly stated in John 3:35–36, *"Whoever believes in the Son (referring to himself) has eternal life, but whoever rejects the Son will not see life, for God's wrath remains on him."*

Many other verses of God's Word also make it clear that all men who permanently reject Christ and the punishment he took on the cross for their sins must then suffer the just punishment for all their own sins in hell for all eternity (2 Thessalonians 1:8–9; Matthew 25:46; Mark

Objection 44
I Believe in Buddhism

9:43–44). That's why in Matthew 7:15–17, Jesus said:

"Beware of false prophets, which come to you in sheep's clothing but inside are ravening wolves. Ye shall know them by their fruits. Do men gather grapes from thorns or figs from thistles? Even so, every good tree brings forth good fruit; but a corrupt tree brings forth evil fruit."

Considering Buddhism started with Buddha forsaking his young family, how can we honestly conclude that this was not bad fruit (which Buddha never admitted to or even changed, which also makes him obviously dishonest)? Evidently, Buddha also taught that if one who is married reached the enlightened stage of Anagami, all sexual desire for one's spouse completely disappears for good. But considering we are told that Buddha had at least two other wives (after he was enlightened), it would certainly seem that Buddha had a rather difficult time reaching the stage of Anagami himself! And even if this was to be the true spiritual goal of all married men, what sense would that really make after they just got married?

Since such a goal achieved would seriously curb the human population, how could it possibly be something which would produce good fruit for the entire human race? If it is good for some, it should be good for all. But if *all* men achieved such a state, it would obviously bring the human race to extinction. So how can such a goal even be considered spiritual? On the other hand, God within the Holy Bible always clearly teaches all mankind to *"be fruitful and multiply and fill the whole earth"* (Genesis 1:28, 9:1, 7), which has obviously proven to be far more realistic and healthy for the existence of the human race.

Testing Buddhism against its divine power demonstrated

Like Hinduism, Buddhism greatly lacks the supernatural power of both predictive prophecies that have been fulfilled as well as any miracles that have been performed. Additionally, according to all reliable historical records we possess, Jesus also lived a sinless life. But, of course, this cannot be said of Buddha who up and permanently left his wife and child. Thus, there really is no real supernatural power demonstrated within Buddhism which would convince us it was founded upon anything but mere human weakness influenced by the demonic realm.

And while this may just be the privilege of a belief system which denies a monotheistic creator who is all-powerful and all-knowing, Buddhism nevertheless completely fails to substantiate its definition of reality for the whole human race through *any kind* of real power which would cause us to trust in it as the one true faith. Evidently, Buddha, too, just expected the world to follow his teachings of karma, reincarnation, and his noble truths with blind faith. Hmm...sounds rather unreasonable, don't you think?

On the other hand, when Christ and his apostles all walked the earth, they fully demonstrated the power of God through major supernatural miracles hundreds of times over in front of many public eyewitnesses, alleviating the major sufferings of many people through those many miracles. And they never taught anything like reincarnation once. Nor did they even teach that mankind's main goal is to avoid *all* human suffering which has certainly been far more realistic for the human race so far!

Additionally, the Bible itself is laced with over 2,000 future-predicting prophecies which have already been fulfilled, all proving Jesus is just who he claimed to be! And as we've already mentioned, all this awesome divine power displayed is something unique to biblical Christianity alone. As the saying goes: "Jesus did not at all expect the world to follow him blindly...he publicly healed the blind to prove his deity!" But when did Buddha ever heal the blind, change the weather, walk on water, or raise from the dead? The historical truth is that he was just as human as you and I!

> But when did Buddha ever heal the blind, change the weather, or raise from the dead? The historical truth is that he was just as human as you and I!

Conclusion

While dynamic estimates are tough to pin down with too much accuracy, roughly 500 million people worldwide claim to belong to the Buddhist religion. But since we've already shown that Buddhism and Hinduism (which Buddhism is largely based from) fails the reasonable tests that can be applied to them, this then is another sad number of people who have really been deceived.

Objection 44
I Believe in Buddhism

If you happen to be a Buddhist, please consider the honest evidence within this objection which plainly confirms Buddhism as false and simply not worthy of your trust. And since the reality which Buddha attempted to prescribe for the rest of the human race completely lacks the power to substantiate his claims of reincarnation and other beliefs, it would truly be unreasonable for you or anyone to just take his word for it. We certainly don't mean to suggest that Buddha did not have *any* truth; it just means that the partial truth he gave you (if it was the truth) cannot not make you right with your one and only true creator and give you the eternal life which only he can grant.

However, since Jesus Christ did back up all his authoritative claims with a sinless life, the awesome power of fulfilled prophecy, and performed miracles in front of many historic witnesses, you can fully trust just what he said to be the truth of your very own creator. And just as Jesus proved his divinity to the honest soul many times over when he walked the earth, so too is his Word completely trustworthy which foretells the awesome *painless* eternity which God has for all those who love him. As Revelation 21:3–4 clearly teaches:

> *"[B]ehold, the dwelling place of God is with men, and he will live with them, and they shall be his people, and God himself shall be with them, and be their God. And God shall wipe away all tears from their eyes; and there shall be no more death, neither sorrow, nor crying, neither shall there be any more pain: for the former things are passed away."*

But the Bible teaches us plainly that *only through Christ* can we obtain God's eternal life (John 14:6). If you are presently a Buddhist but know in your heart that you too need your one and only true creator, and you desire to be right with him and have his eternal life, I invite you to just take that first small step of faith by sincerely praying the prayer of salvation located at the end of this book. Even if you've been a Buddhist for years, you can still break away from that obvious false belief system today which threatens your true salvation through Christ. And don't be concerned with what your family members may think of you because, simply put, they will not be you're judge on judgment day! This decision is between you and God (your creator) alone. No matter what your past is like, God loves you and sincerely wants you to be a part of his awesome eternal kingdom!

Jesus said, "I am the resurrection and the life. He who believes in me, will live even though he dies; and whoever lives and believes in me will never die." (John 11:25–26)

OBJECTION 45

I Believe in the New Age Movement

A loving reminder: Before each false belief system we discuss, just so my loving intentions cannot be misunderstood, I will *once again* remind the reader that it's certainly *not the adherents* of any false belief system which the true Church is against but rather just the *false teachings* within them which deceive men away from the one and only true God and his eternal salvation (Ephesians 6:12). Therefore, my dear reader, please know that our discussion of these various different religions or belief systems is very much a *love* issue.

Defining the New Age movement

While many of today's New Age movement believers may refuse to even categorize themselves as New Age believers, nonetheless, it still seems to be the general title used for their particular set of spiritual beliefs when one searches either the encyclopedia or internet. Even though there are admittedly few religions in the world which have the great diversity of beliefs within it that the New Age movement has, we still find plenty of shared basic beliefs which would actually *categorize* those within the New Age Movement.

One can, of course, call the New Age movement anything they would like; nevertheless, for sane conversation, one must settle for some title which represents the set of beliefs which New Agers themselves have uniquely ascribed themselves to. Of course, the following is just a basic description of the common spiritual beliefs within what is known as the New Age movement which exists today. And because of the widespread diversity of New Age beliefs, our basic list should not, of course, be considered exhaustive or all-inclusive for all New Age believers.

Some typical basic beliefs within the New Age movement

1. Often, New Agers refuse to be categorized or defined by any certain sets of beliefs or even *morals,* for that matter. New Agers typically also reject labels or the specific use of even certain terms as they are all seen as tools to categorize, which they view as the actual *cause* of divisions within the human race. However, for sane meaningful conversation among themselves, even New Agers must settle for all their own terms and labels; they may be just different terms and different labels and that is about all.

However, from the time the New Age movement has been recognized in modern times, more than once, New Agers have changed many of their own terms and labels, and even today, New Agers may disagree among themselves on which terms and labels to use for their particular beliefs. But even though terms and labels come and go within the New Age movement, the basic concept of their main beliefs which they are describing are nevertheless quite often the same.

2. Just like the Hinduism religion it is actually based from, the New Age movement typically adopts a *pantheistic* form of divinity which permeates all of the universe but is certainly not limited to just our universe. To the New Ager, God is literally everything, and everything is literally God. Thus, they believe humans, plants, animals, dirt, or anything else we find in nature to be god. New Age pantheism is actually quite different than monotheism (belief in one supreme creator God), polytheism (the belief in many different gods), or atheism (the complete rejection of God and/or all gods) and is, in reality, quite incompatible with all of them. New Agers today may even dogmatically refuse to call their religious belief system a religion at all, but since they technically do believe in a *form*

Objection 45
I Believe in the New Age Movement

of divinity, the New Age movement can fairly be classified or defined as a religion according to the real definition of the term. While New Agers may reject monotheism (the belief in one single supreme being), they often do believe in monism, which means oneness, as their ultimate goal is to become one with the universe, tapping into its power, etc.

3. Typically, their all-encompassing form of divinity would also include human beings themselves, as well as a wide variety of nonhuman beings (which they consider semidivine) such as angels and masters (UFOs) with whom they can communicate, typically through a form of channeling. And because their holistic form of divinity would include even themselves, there is commonly also a strong emphasis upon the spiritual authority of self.

4. Since New Agers typically view history as divided up into a series of different ages, a common New Age belief is that mankind once lived in an age of great technological advancement and spiritual wisdom but has now entered a period of spiritual degeneracy which will be victoriously rectified through the establishment of a coming New Age or the Age of Aquarius.

5. Within the New Age movement, there is also typically a strong focus on physical healing through various forms of alternative medicine, special diets like the Paleo diet, yoga, positive thinking, biofeedback techniques, etc.

6. The New Age movement also has a strong emphasis on New Age science and actively seeks to unite science with their idea of spirituality. The belief in various forms of astrology (a random interpretation of the stars which determines one's personality, compatibility with others, etc.) is also common within the New Age movement.

7. Interestingly enough, it has also been noted that those who make up the collective New Age movement today are typically middle- and upper-class citizens; but, of course, that does not technically have to be the case.

8. Because of its refusal to be categorized, the New Age

movement is not only more diverse and vague than most religions, but its adherents also often emphasize that all the different religions of the world with their conflicting basic doctrines can even be finally united within the New Age movement. We've all seen the "Coexist" bumper stickers which are often on the cars of those who believe in the New Age movement to some degree. However, while such bumper stickers might certainly sound good, one can't help but notice that such bumper stickers just have not been realistic throughout all of recorded human history so far if by "coexist" they mean we can all belong to a one world New Age religion without moral compromise! And the fact that there are certainly more different conflicting religions in the world today which also refuse to be a part of the New Age Movement also tells us that the New Age "coexist" beliefs are failing miserably.

9. Those in the New Age religion are also typically against violence in any form. Again, such beliefs certainly may sound good but also start to lose their realistic clout when it comes to peaceful mankind having to put down real tyrants in the world, like Hitler. On the other hand, while Christ certainly told us to domestically love our enemies, the New Testament also makes it clear that God did establish good governments in the world to put down evil if absolutely necessary to keep it from spreading and destroying all mankind (Romans 13:1–5). I wonder if the New Agers would have liked being under his authority if Hitler had actually won!

New Age pantheism is actually quite different than monotheism, polytheism, or atheism and is in reality quite incompatible with all of them.

The origin of the New Age Movement

While it is commonly thought that today's New Age movement developed in the Western world during the 1960s and 1970s, roots to the New Age belief system can easily be traced as far back as the age of enlightenment during the sixteenth century and even far beyond

Objection 45
I Believe in the New Age Movement

that back to the very similar religion of Hinduism. And the fact that the modern New Age movement is ultimately based from Hinduism shouldn't exactly give it much credibility as we've already confirmed that Hinduism itself utterly fails many reasonable tests which prove it to be false and unreliable as the one true faith. For if the very roots of a tree are rotten, then how can the trunk or branches of that same tree be healthy?

However, in its more recent history, we can certainly pinpoint more than one historical figure which fueled many of the unique spiritual beliefs which we find in the modern New Age movement today. In fact, many New Agers today tend to be rather ignorant that many prominent esoteric thinkers, such as Helena Blavatsky (the Madam Blavatsky who helped spearhead the spiritual beliefs of Hitler's SS), really did help found and form the modern New Age Movement which we see in the world today.

Another prominent esoteric thinker of our recent history who helped fuel the specific spiritual beliefs of today's New Age movement would be the Swedish eighteenth-century so-called *Christian* mystic, Emanuel Swedenborg, who professed to not only have the ability to communicate with the angels but also the demonic realm as well! Two more prominent esoteric thinkers of our recent history who helped fuel the specific spiritual beliefs of today's New Age movement would be psychiatrists and/or psychoanalysts Freud and Carl Jung. However, it should be noted that even they both disagreed with each other to a large extent in even their *basic beliefs*. In fact, most all the esoteric thinker types which helped found the modern-day New Age movement would have disagreed with each other on many of the *basics* within their belief systems.

However, such basic diversification among themselves remains a hallmark trait of New Age believers today. Somehow, contradicting truths are just not a problem for the New Ager. In fact, the more diversification, the better, and everybody is welcome! But one must certainly ask the fair question: Is supposed unity with the sacrifice of truth even true healthy unity?

Yet another prominent esoteric thinker of our recent history who helped fuel the specific spiritual beliefs of today's New Age Movement would be the German physician and hypnotist, Franz Mesmer, who taught animal magnetism, a supposed force running through the human body. Modern New Agers today typically believe in some kind of a similar force which permeates all our physical universe. Such a force is even promoted through Hollywood movies such as *Star Wars*, which coined the phrase "May the Force be with you." But, of course, we Bible-believing Christians who know that there is only one God and creator of all also know that New Agers who would use such a phrase are just ignorantly violating the biblical preexisting phrase, "May God be with you."

Interestingly enough, it is quite common for many false religions (such as the modern-day New Age movement) to reject the main teachings of the Bible while at the same time borrow terms and even scriptures from the Holy Bible for their own New Age religion building purposes.

True, many New Agers may not even be conscious of this habit of borrowing terms and scriptures from biblical Christianity, but we must remember that all false religions are ultimately hatched from the demonic realm which would certainly want to do so in order to sound credible and be more deceptive. But, reasonably, if their false religion is really the one true faith, why on earth do they even need to borrow any scriptures or terms from the Holy Bible in the first place? I can assure you that biblical Christianity certainly does not borrow anything from the New Age movement just to appear more credible!

Nevertheless, there are, of course, many more esoteric thinkers of our recent history who helped fuel the obscure spiritual beliefs of today's New Age movement, but sufficient is our short list which proves that the modern New Age movement did not at all just start in the 1960s or 1970s.

> Many false religions which reject the main correct doctrines of the Bible often hypocritically use what scriptures they can from the Bible, just so they can deceive and appear more credible.

Objection 45
I Believe in the New Age Movement

Testing the New Age movement against the true moral condition of man

Like many false religions, the New Age movement tends to reject the belief in man's sin or moral wrongs which are just the violation of the perfect moral standards of our eternal creator. Since they totally reject any belief in a monotheistic creator God, it only makes sense that they also reject any idea of breaking his moral standards. Respectively, then, they must insist that all spiritual truth and morality is subjective or relative to one's own perspective. However, while such a relative morality position may be maintained out of one side of their mouth, even all New Agers must admit out of the other side of their mouths that all the moral failures of others which would directly affect them personally would certainly not be relative to anyone's personal perspective.

For example, if someone came up to a New Ager and shot them with a gun, I'm quite sure that New Ager would consider it a definite moral failure which is simply *not relative to anyone's perspective*! Nevertheless, the New Age religion continues to encourage each of its participants to just experiment within the moral jungle of this world and experience the results in order to establish their own personal morals on their journey toward oneness with the universe. In other words, for the New Ager, true morality comes from within each of us (whatever we think is right at the time) and not from without (like from our parents, God, or his Word, the Bible).

As we've already indicated in our Objection #22, there are, of course, many basic problems with this whole idea of subjective truth and morality which should be obvious to the honest soul. For example, if within their idea of spirituality, there really is no absolute moral truths which apply to everyone (as Bible-believing Christians believe), then why would New Agers always object to someone murdering their family members? What if the murderer really did not see that murder was wrong from his or her perspective? Sounds absurd? What about all the shooters who have thought themselves justified after a shooting spree? Similarly, why would they always object to someone stealing from them? Why would they always object to the women in their family getting abused? The list, of course, could go on for some time, but, hopefully, you get the point.

What they truly believe about morality is not at all consistent and thus ends up being rather dishonest! If even honesty itself is truly subjective to the New Ager, then why do all New Agers fully expect their spouses to be honest with them and be completely faithful to them? Why then do all New Agers fully expect their bankers to handle their money with complete honesty? Why would they fully expect their pilot to be sober in the plane they are flying in? Or why do they fully expect the doctor doing surgery on them to not be at all subjective as to just how they perform their surgery? Again, the list, of course, goes on…but you get the point that all New Agers are rather forced to be inconsistent (some would say hypocritical) with their own beliefs about *subjective truth and morality*.

For example, a New Ager may believe that homosexuality, cross-dressing, drunkenness, and fornication are all okay but at the same time believe incest, rape, bestiality, and adultery are morally not okay. But why? Just because they might believe it to be so? Are we to just take their word for it? What real authority do New Agers have to determine what's morally right and what's not? It may be perfectly okay for New Agers to truly believe man is his own god and determines his own morality until someone comes up and violates them in some real way. Then all of a sudden, morality is not so subjective or relative after all.

If I believe morality is relative like New Agers typically maintain, then why can't I go around stealing from New Agers? That right there, my friend, is the obvious problem with relative morality! It doesn't have to follow Christ's golden rule or even the Ten Commandments, for that matter. And if just some moral standards are subjective and some not subjective, then who determines just which ones are subjective and which ones are absolute moral standards for everyone? You? Me? The New Agers? Christians? But why? Why does *any imperfect man* have the authority to determine morality for themselves or other very imperfect men?

And if none of us have the authority to determine morality because of all of our great moral imperfections, and at the same time, we reject our own very qualified creator who alone has the authority to determine morality for his own creation, then it should be perfectly okay for anyone to shoot anyone anytime they feel like it! Why not if morality is truly subjective?

Objection 45
I Believe in the New Age Movement

As you can see, once the subjective morality door is opened, really anything goes, and no one should be able to complain about the horrible results if they truly believe in subjective morality. And when any religion such as the New Age movement rejects the absolute truths of their very own perfect creator, which have always been upheld by our churches, civil court systems, and the collective conscience of mankind throughout most all recorded human history, just when it is in their personal favor to do so, they just further prove that mankind himself is plagued with the gross immorality which they attempt to deny. And because the New Age movement typically rejects the idea that man is plagued with sin or immorality, it would certainly seem that the New Age movement fails this basic test and proves to be a false religion just on this basis alone.

> It may be perfectly okay for New Agers to truly believe man is his own god and determines his own morality until someone comes up and violates them in some way.

Testing the New Age movement against self-contradictions

Ironically, the New Age movement, which is one of the most diverse in its teachings, actually heralds itself as the catalyst of true unity for all the conflicting religions of the world. But when one honestly thinks about it, how can any religion possibly unify all the diverse religions in the world with the greatest degree of disunity within their own religion?

Let's be honest: the only way such unity could be achieved among all the diverse religions of the world would be if all men belonging to them were willing to *completely compromise* all their basic beliefs! Therefore, basic compromise must really be the prerequisite to the supposed New Age world unity. Such a unity plan not only makes no sense whatsoever but also has never begun to work in the history of the human race! In fact, human history has proven over and over that true unity (or even love for that matter) can never be accomplished through the compromise of truth!

We must remember that Satan is the master of deception and behind the hatching of all false religions (1 Timothy 4:1–2). And what could be more deceptive than to portray true unity as something which can actually be achieved through basic compromise? It's about as unreasonable as evolutionists insisting that all the order we see in our natural world actually came out of disorder, a special reality science has never been privileged to observe. And, similarly, world unity with the compromise of truth is also a special reality which the world has never been privileged to observe!

Admittedly, the modern New Age movement claims to represent a spirituality without borders, defined doctrines, or defined morality, which is inclusive of all other religions and pluralistic. But, again, is not boasting of spiritual unity without defined doctrines and morality a bit like a city boasting of no traffic accidents without any defined traffic laws? It is not only self-contradicting and extremely unrealistic but grossly hypocritical and morally dangerous!

> The New Age religion boasting of spiritual unity without defined doctrines and morality is much like a city boasting of no traffic accidents without any defined traffic laws!

However, if the real issue is that the New Age movement just wants to believe whatever they want without any moral restraints because they are basically in rebellion against their one and only true creator, then their whole fluid and morally elusive belief system begins to make some real sense, even though it is still quite appalling to the honest soul. The truth is, if civil world governments even attempted to unify their countries with the self-contradicting reasoning of the modern New Age movement, mankind would have self-destructed long ago! Such self-contradicting reasoning would never begin to work in the real practical world and only works in the New Age pretend spiritual world.

Along with 2,000 of its prophecies already fulfilled throughout history, the Bible also predicts that the soon coming one-world government ruled by the Antichrist will foolishly attempt such a self-contradicting world religion with the obvious compromise of truth. But it should be equally exposed that also according to the Bible, that same coming one-world government ruled by the Antichrist will only last three and a half miserable years! Hmm...suppose there just might be a connection between its gross compromise of truth and its extremely short duration?

Objection 45
I Believe in the New Age Movement

But, also according to the Bible, the Antichrist himself will actually destroy the one-world religion he and his False Prophet has created right after it has served his selfish purpose of gaining control of the world (Revelation 17:12–16). But because a one-world religion will be instigated by the Antichrist and his false prophet just before Christ returns, many Bible scholars and Christians fully suspect that the New Age movement will be a large part of it, simply because it is uniquely one of the only religions in the world which foolishly even attempts to unify all the contradicting religions in the world into one big happy religious family. Thus, in this basic sense, the New Age movement is probably more self-contradicting and dangerous than any other false religion in the world, simply because really anything goes within it!

Other gross inconsistencies of the New Age movement include:

1. If according to New Age belief, Jesus was just one of many enlightened men who successfully tapped into the power of the universe to heal hundreds of people in his short three-year ministry, then why did he constantly lie and claim to be God and the only way to God (John 8:57–58, 10:30–33, 14:6)? Is constant lying the New Ager's idea of true enlightenment?

2. If Jesus was truly an enlightened man as the New Age movement believes, then in his great enlightenment, did he then speak the truth when he constantly taught that all those who reject the punishment that he took for their sins on the cross must then take their own punishment for their own sins in eternal hell (John 3:16–18; Matthew 25:41–45)? If Jesus and his apostles all constantly lied about this basic truth of the Gospel, then why would New Agers consider them to be at all enlightened? Just which part of Christ's teachings, then, are considered enlightened according to New Agers? And which are not? And why? Do we all then just get to pick and choose between Christ's teachings?

3. If some New Agers try to even deny that Christ was a real historical figure, then at the same time, they are then also forced to believe that all the Christian and non-Christian historic testimonies which testify of his real

existence (only some of which we covered in Objection #35) are completely fictitious and contrived by a massive collaborate band of deceiving liars. But since there is no such evidence for all such historical testimonies of Christ's existence being completely just contrived by some collaborate band of deceiving liars, then we are left with the conclusion that those who aggressively insist that Christ was not a real historical figure are really the ones who are dishonestly spinning a web of deception, simply because they are likely threatened by the fact that Christ is not only a real historical figure but also just who he claimed to be: God Almighty whom they will have to be accountable to someday.

In addition, all non-Christians (who refused to believe Christ was who he claimed to be) who historically did testify of Christ's actual existence would all have to have a good motive for lying and saying Christ existed when, in fact, he really didn't. But since such antagonistic unbelieving non-Christians would be much more apt to deny the existence of someone they didn't want to believe in, then such a good motive to affirm Christ's existence would simply not be there! But if some New Agers are genuinely threatened by the fact that Christ was indeed a real historical figure who could be just who he claimed to be, then because that same Christ confronts their sin, we can easily see a good motive for them to deny his existence despite all the honest historical evidence for it.

Also, if New Agers would insist that all historical testimonies which affirm Christ's actual existence are historically unreliable, then at the same time, they must pronounce such a verdict upon all our historical records which are not even as reliable as those many biblical and nonbiblical documents which plainly testify of Christ.

4. If extraterrestrials or aliens are really real and have actually interacted with our planet through UFOs, then why do we have no solid scientific evidence for it available to the public, even with all our modern technologies? And why don't our historical records even mention extraterrestrials or aliens prior to the last hundred years or so when the Theory of Evolution was basically popularized? For the

last 6,000 years, before the Theory of Evolution was popularized by Charles Darwin, were all the aliens just too shy to show themselves? And even during the last hundred years or so, all we have for real proof of aliens is Hollywood and hearsay! That certainly seems rather unlikely.

It is actually much more believable to believe that all such superhuman phenomenon has come from the demonic realm, passing themselves off as aliens with the simple objective to deceive mankind into the Theory of Evolution and away from our one true creator and the eternal life he offers all men. After all, just what would aliens have to hide if they are far superior to us? And if they can't interact with us because they would alter the course of the human race if they did so, then why, according to New Agers, have there been so many sightings of them? And how could they possibly hurt us more than we are already hurting ourselves by revealing themselves to us when we are just barely surviving our own war technologies and nuclear capabilities as it is? How could any alien species endanger us more (by interacting with us) than we are already endangering ourselves?

As we've already discussed in our Objection #10 of Part 1 of our series, the whole idea that aliens are purposely hiding from us just because they don't want to alter our perfect destiny makes very little sense indeed when you just look at the very bloody history of the human race!

And even if one awkwardly forces it to somehow make *some* sense, then why have they already shown themselves to us via many UFO sightings if, in fact, they shouldn't at all interact with us in the first place? Again, none of it makes any sense, and this, too, is a self-contradiction. However, if the Bible is correct and all supposed UFO sightings are really manufactured by the demonic world to get men to believe in the false doctrine of evolution and deceive them away from our one true creator God and his eternal salvation, then the *very elusive nature* of these supposed aliens is much more understandable! If someone is mysteriously hiding from us without ever manifesting themselves plainly, it only makes good sense that they really have something to hide! And according to the Bible, demons certainly do!

5. But New Agers certainly can't say the same of our creator who actually became one of us and fully revealed himself to us in the person of Christ through hundreds of miracles, a sinless life, and hundreds of fulfilled prophecies which fully proved his divinity!

If New Agers (especially the ring leaders of the movement) are truly enlightened, then why must their answers to the above questions be so inconsistent with their own New Age belief system? There are many more inconsistencies or self-contradictions within the New Age movement which we could cite, but sufficient are those we exposed to show that the whole New Age movement is not only at variance with itself but also sound reasoning and reality. We must, therefore, honestly conclude that it utterly fails this basic test as well.

Testing the New Age movement against its prophetic predictions of the future

New Agers easily claim the that the human race is evolving and morally improving. And they not only believe that the human race is morally improving but that it will continue to do so through their religion which will dominate the world and finally solve its unity problems, putting an end to hatred, murder, war, etc. While such a notion certainly *sounds noble* and is undoubtedly attractive to many, is it honestly even in alignment with the entire history of mankind? And if not, is our human nature suddenly going to change for the better after 6,000 years just because New Agers wish it to be so? And if the New Age religion is the real truth, and the New Age religion has just grown into the responsible position of solving the world's problems, then why has the unity of the world just gotten worse in the last few centuries?

On the other hand, the Bible itself has predicted just the opposite of *true and lasting world unity* just before Christ returns. And even though it, too, predicts that there will be a one-world religion and a one-world government, it predicts that both will be a very *temporary fake unity* controlled by that wicked man called the Antichrist (who is literally possessed by Satan) and the moral condition of the world will just plummet before and during his short and very ruthless bloody reign. Then, after that, it predicts that Christ will return and defeat the Antichrist and finally establish his everlasting peaceful reign on

Objection 45
I Believe in the New Age Movement

earth after God has thoroughly shown the human race that man simply cannot solve his own moral problems through mere humanistic effort.

The big lesson? We actually need our creator! And we don't need him just because God is on some big power trip because it would actually be impossible for an eternal being to be prideful as he would have to be morally perfect to even be eternal. Therefore, we actually need our creator because we came from him, and it is just the simple truth of the matter. And, of course, this only makes good sense when one thinks about it at all. And since simple logic tells us that both of these conflicting views of our very near future cannot be correct, which view is truly supported by the honest evidence of our world today and what mankind has always experienced?

If the New Age view of world unity and moral improvement is correct, we would certainly see some real basic evidence for it ever since the New Age religion came on the scene (going back to the roots of the New Age Movement, which is at the very least the enlightenment period of the 1600s). However, if the Holy Bible is correct, then there should be evidence of moral decline within the human race from the 1600s up to today. Now let's let the evidence speak for itself to see which basic prediction is honestly in line with reality.

1. If our world was morally improving, we'd undoubtedly see *less opposing religions* in the world and not more. If you ask anyone on the street if there are less or more opposing religions in the world today than there was even 200 years ago, they would undoubtedly agree with the basic history of religions in any encyclopedia set and say there are certainly many more different conflicting religions today than in any other time in the recorded history of man! If, in fact, just in the last hundred years or so, the number of obvious false religions in the world has just exploded into the thousands, then that reality obviously could not be attributed to something like our very gradual 2 percent population growth.

But no matter just *why* we've had an explosion of false religions in the last hundred years or so, the fact is that false religions have increased like never before in man's history! And if New Agers see religious unity as evidence of moral improvement (which is only reasonable), then they simply cannot claim mankind is attaining true moral improvement on that basis considering the massive explosion of *opposing religions* in the last hundred years or so. In fact, even things like the number of nations and languages are ultimately an indication of *basic increasing world disunity* as today, there are also more *languages* and *nations* today than ever before in recorded human history!

> If our world was morally improving, and being more united because of it, we'd undoubtedly see less opposing religions in the world and not more.

> 2. If our world was morally improving, we'd also clearly see less wars going on in the world today. New Agers typically insist that such is the case just because our invention of nuclear war may have created a *slight* lull in the warmongering storm of humanity just in the last seventy years. However, it is difficult to prove that this slight lull in war is truly because the human race is morally evolving toward some world utopia, and not actually because the human race is just terrified of self-extermination through nuclear warfare! In other words, there is a big difference between moral improvement and raw fear of extinction! And we must also keep in mind some other factors as well.

Since the war graph has always greatly fluctuated in the short run of human history, to grab an isolated seventy years anywhere on the whole graph and try to prove the overall moral improvement of the human race with it is truly misrepresenting the bigger picture of an overall increase in wars within the human race.

Not to mention, it is even truly debatable that during the last seventy years, man has seen more peace on earth, even in light of the fact that democratic forms of government have been more prevalent. In fact, depending upon your source, some sources indicate that democracy has not at all proven to decrease the overall warfare of mankind. And just because the world has held off using our relatively new nuclear capabilities, that certainly doesn't at all mean we will continue to do so! In fact, since most every weapon man has devised for warfare against his fellow man he has ended up using quite extensively, it would make much more sense to believe that it's not so much a matter of *if* but just

Objection 45
I Believe in the New Age Movement

when we will use our nuclear capabilities. And *when* we do engage in nuclear warfare, that will undoubtedly change the war graph within all of human history to a much more negative degree. And interestingly enough, the book of Revelation gives us some real indication that man will definitely use his nuclear capabilities during the seven-year tribulation which it describes.

It's certainly good for all men to *desire* and *work toward* total peace on earth and be an optimist in this way. Bible-believing Christians totally believe in doing that. But first and foremost, we must be a realist before we have the right to be an optimist. One must not only look at the bloody 6,000-year history of the human race but also how very far we are from man creating any kind of a man-made peace on earth right now! The honest truth is that just more and more nations are obtaining nuclear capabilities, not less, and it is way too premature for New Agers to celebrate even the beginning of a man-made utopia on earth.

If an alcoholic just managed to not get drunk as often as usual for selfish reasons but kept building up his private stash of liquor, just in case he needed a drink, would you even begin to believe he was well on his way to complete recovery? Hopefully, you wouldn't, and neither would I! And this is the real boat we are in as far as national wars today are concerned if New Agers were to be just *honest with the facts*.

While both New Agers and Bible-believing Christians believe that a world utopia is coming, the main difference is that Christians believe our perfect eternal creator will have to step back into human history to accomplish such a massive task, and New Agers believe mankind himself can somehow accomplish this major miracle, even though he has never come close to doing so in the 6,000 years of recorded human history! And since every single prophetic prediction of Christ's first coming within the Holy Bible came true (which involve hundreds of prophecies that were given hundreds of years in advance), then why should anyone doubt the sure fulfillment of all Bible prophecies which clearly teach us that Christ's Second Coming will be absolutely necessary to fix this fallen world which is ultimately rebelling against him? However, in great contrast, New Agers have no supernaturally fulfilled prophecies to back up their wishful claims!

> If an alcoholic managed to not get drunk as often as usual but kept building up his private stash of

liquor just in case he needed a drink, would you even begin to believe he was well on his way to complete recovery?

3. If our world was morally improving, we'd also clearly see world economics improving. What? You mean morality is connected to economics? Yes! Typically, a large gap between the wealthy and the poor with very few middle-class incomes in between has never been a sign of *good morality* in any nation. In the US, such a widening gap is not really capitalism as some have asserted. It is just the abuse of capitalism! And because the gap between the wealthy and the poor keeps getting larger, many are even looking toward some form of socialism to level the playing field and close that widening gap between the wealthy and poor.

However, socialism just trades our freedom for security, and that has never been a good trade throughout man's history. The building major national debts we see in the world are also a sign of greed. To reduce it to a simple example, it is no different than when kids playing together refuse to share their toys. Morally, one might just as well call economic inflation greed and selfishness because in all reality, that's really what it is! Is there really less greed and selfishness in our world today? The answer to that question is certainly not an obvious yes! Most economists would say we are heading for financial disaster for a number of reasons. And if mankind was truly morally improving and evolving into a better race, once again, this would not be the case. Again, New Agers just have to be *honest* about this basic reality as well.

4. If our world was morally improving, we'd also clearly see our prisons slowly becoming more and more empty. But is this *honestly* what we all see happening worldwide? I don't think so! The prisons today are just as full as they have always been. Since prisons are a fair indicator of domestic crimes, we can safely conclude that our domestic crimes haven't decreased much either. But why can't New Agers see such plain truths right in front of their nose? Again, basic honesty is a prerequisite to believing the truth.

Objection 45
I Believe in the New Age Movement

If our world was morally improving, we'd also clearly see our prisons slowly becoming more and more empty. But as it is, we are seeing just the opposite.

5. If our world was morally improving, we'd also clearly see our world environment and ecology getting *better*. But what part of "better" don't New Agers understand? I know many are trying to do our environment good, but even with all we are doing, is our planet contamination basically getting worse or better? They now say there is more plastic in the oceans than fish! They also say there are hundreds of square miles of dead zones in the ocean where no sea life thrives anymore. And, of course, we all know our list could go on and on about environmental problems. If the New Agers can honestly say that our planet is getting better overall despite all our green efforts, then I would be first to agree with them that it's a sign of moral improvement. But if they can't, then they must cry uncle and admit that it is a sign of humanity being irresponsible with planet earth (and thus moral decline) because, my friend, they *honestly* can't have it both ways!

As the human race has experienced over the last 6,000 years, morality in general rarely just stays the same. Either we are morally improving in all these categories (and many others we have not mentioned) or we are morally declining. And we have just shown that just these five different basic barometers of human morality still indicate that human nature has just not at all improved with time. In fact, more people on earth, coupled with advancing technologies, just seem to have sped up and compounded our moral decline.

For a real example, one hundred years ago, we did not have nuclear warheads, but today, for the first time in recorded human history, we now have the capability to destroy the entire human race along with our entire planet! Wow! We sure have come a long way! If all these things are not obvious in your face signs of moral decline within the human race, what on earth could possibly convince you? All that is required is a little basic *honesty* with these many facts. As it has been said:

"The world is full of renegade lost souls who can only imagine false realities because the truth of God finds no home in their hearts. They trade honesty for insanity and freedom for security and do not care who they hurt in the process, even themselves. They insist on unity without truth...and world peace without true unity. For a good and moral world, they strive in vain because they know not that they are utterly blind and destitute without their creator."

Testing the New Age movement against the divine power it has demonstrated

The New Age movement basically teaches that all men (especially the New Agers themselves) have unlimited human potential via tapping into the vast powers of the universe. However, if, in fact, all New Agers have unlimited human potential by tapping into the vast powers of the universe, then why have the New Agers themselves been so miserably unsuccessful throughout human history in displaying this unlimited human potential? Whether one looks at New Age leaders back in recent human history or at the modern New Age movement ring leaders today, why haven't we seen this *unlimited human potential* achieved through their tapping into the vast powers of the universe?

Where is all this unlimited human potential flowing through the lives of people like Shirley McClain, Echart Tollie, and many other past and present New Age ring leaders? The truth is they live within the very limited constraints of weak humanity just like everyone else we know! Just where is this unique power which would even begin to validate the New Age movement as the one true belief system?

The truth is that New Agers are only pulling fighter jets out of swamps with their supposed mind control in Hollywood movies such as *Star Wars*! Are we just to take their word for such power derived from the universe? Are they not actually responsible to back up what they teach with some basic real evidence which would convince us of their superior spiritual beliefs? However, in stark contrast, when Christ and his apostles all walked the earth, we have very reliable historical record which should certainly convince us that they fully demonstrated the real power of God through major supernatural miracles hundreds of times over in front of many public eyewitnesses in order to back up their claims.

Objection 45
I Believe in the New Age Movement

Additionally, the Bible itself is laced with over 2,000 future-predicting prophecies which have already been fulfilled and historians cannot deny, all proving Jesus is just who he claimed to be. And as we've already mentioned, this awesome divine power displayed is something unique to biblical Christianity *alone*. Did Zeus, Thor, or any other so-called gods of any other religion come down to earth and openly display the power of their divinity in front of the human race as Christ did? No. No one has personally met any other so-called god (or gods) of any other religion throughout all of recorded human history, much less witness anything like the divine power which Christ and his apostles displayed. As the saying goes: Jesus was wise enough to not expect the world to follow him blindly. He publicly healed the blind to prove his divinity!

> Why haven't we even seen this unlimited human potential achieved through the vast powers of the universe in the lives of modern New Age movement ring leaders today?

If according to the New Agers, Christ and his apostles were just very successful in tapping into the powers of the universe because of the many mighty miracles they did, then why didn't they openly teach that they got their power from the universe as New Agers may believe? And why did they instead teach that they got it from the one and only monotheistic creator who New Agers completely reject? If they were all enlightened enough to raise the dead, then why weren't they enlightened enough to even tell us the simple truth of where they got their power?

Christ and all his apostles did tell us plainly where they got their power from. But New Agers just refuse to believe Christ and all the united historic testimonies of his apostles simply because the reality of Christ confronts their sin. But, again, where is all this vast power of the universe which supposedly flows through those enlightened New Agers which clearly sets them apart from the rest of humanity which does not at all believe in the New Age movement?

The power of the force taught in movies like Star Wars just stays in Hollywood. How convenient. But how utterly fake! Why should anyone stake their eternal destiny on such fake realities? If Christ and his apostles expected the world to believe in the Bible through similar fake promotions which never actually manifested in the real world, let's be honest, Christianity would have never gotten off the ground, and the world would not be full of New Testament churches today! Shirley McClain, Echart Tollie, and other New Agers can claim they are gods who are just increasing in the power of the universe all they want, but the truth is that they are all just getting weaker as they age like the rest of the world who is honest enough to admit it! The truth is that all the honest evidence points to the reality that it is our eternal monotheistic creator alone who has the only real power to change the course of this fallen world which has been corrupted by our sin.

What is the real problem behind the world's disunity?

Perhaps one of the main mistakes which the New Age movement makes is that it contends that defined spiritual beliefs, doctrines, and morals are themselves the actual problem behind the world's disunity. However, when you think about it, wouldn't that be as silly as believing defined traffic laws are the cause of all traffic accidents; therefore, we must do away with all traffic laws? But, really, what sense does that make to the honest soul? While getting rid of all traffic laws may appeal greatly to some motorists, the idea is of course just as absurd as throwing out all the absolute moral truths of the Bible, just because none of us can keep them perfectly. Does an archer throw away his target, just because he has a hard time hitting the bull's-eye? You see, the problem in this world has never been the biblical truths of God or his good moral standards. The problem is sin in the heart of man which continues to rebel against our perfect creator and his moral truths.

Because we know that the main cause of traffic accidents is either apathy or rebellion towards the existing traffic laws, which are just put into place *for our good*; we also know the main cause of spiritual disunity in our world is either apathy or rebellion towards the already existing moral standards of God plainly given to us in his word for our good (like the Ten Commandments). And this alone is what has caused all the disunity in the world, whether we are talking about all the different conflicting religions in the world or all the national wars! However, there still remains only one true faith, simply because there is only one true God and creator of all behind that one true faith. And

Objection 45
I Believe in the New Age Movement

only when man finally admits and surrenders to the fact that Christ our creator (who literally proved his divinity) is himself the only hope of world unity, then and only then will the world be finally unified!

> Perhaps one of the main mistakes which the New Age movement makes is that it contends that defined spiritual beliefs, doctrines, and morals are themselves the actual problem behind the world's disunity.

However, instead of being a part of the only solution to the world's disunity problem, the New Age movement is actually feeding the problem of disunity by insisting the world can achieve love and peace without the absolute perfect moral standards of our one and only true creator that has plainly revealed himself to all mankind. In this sense, the New Age movement is much like people trying to play a board game, while they throw away the rules which originally came with the game and make up any rules they want. But, of course, the obvious problems with this approach to life (and playing a board game) is:

1. Since the players themselves did not even create the game they play, they technically do not even have the right to create their own rules as appealing as that may be for some players! And that's exactly why it is called "cheating" to change the rules during any game. Similarly, when New Agers create their own moral standards and reject God's, they essentially do the very same thing in the game of life, even though they really do not have the right to do so because, quite obviously, they are not the creator of life!

2. As soon as one would change the rules which the game originator had created to go with the game, then they are actually no longer even playing the real game, are they? For example, if one changes the rules of Monopoly to their own liking, then they are really no longer even playing Monopoly, are they? Well, the very same is true with those in life who rebel against the moral standards and defined doctrines of God's Word. They are not actually living the real life that God their creator intended them to live any more than they actually have the spiritual truth, simply

because they've changed it to their own liking. They may like their own rules better, but the only problem is that it is no longer the truth, which they have, and they are not really even living real life, even though they may think they are!

3. They may think that just because they've taken the liberty to make up their own rules: that it's impossible for them to *lose* in the game of life. But, really, there's no quicker way to lose a board game than to cheat and change the rules, and the very same is true for real life! Similarly, New Agers may think that it is impossible for world unity to fail if everyone just compromises and forgets about God's Word and his moral standards. But, really, there's no quicker way to destroy mankind and world unity than to compromise the moral standards of God simply because they've just thrown away the only hope of unity and true love, which this world has ever had. History has always shown us that the further away civil governments have gotten from the moral standards of God's Word, the more destructive they've become. My friend, history has confirmed this reality many times over!

The bottom line is there is a real difference between positive thinking and the dishonest denial of reality, and it would certainly seem that the New Age movement as a belief system has ultimately tried to make the world believe that the two are the very same thing! However, the sacrifice of God's biblical truth and moral compromise will never bring unity any more than the real reliable truth can contradict itself. And the only reason the New Age movement even has any appeal in today's world is because it appeals to those who really just want to be their own god by just living any way they want. But, of course, the main problem with that whole objective is that no human being to date has been able to create life and the job of being God is just not available! Some may view the New Age movement as mere self-indulgent silliness. But, unfortunately, it is far more dangerous as *there is far more to it* than astrology, crystals, weird workshops, and their very elastic brand of psychology.

Objection 45
I Believe in the New Age Movement

Moral compromise will never bring unity any more than the real truth can contradict itself.

While many New Age believers disagree with each other on many points, as a whole, interestingly enough, the one thing most all New Age spiritual leaders typically hold to is a *firm anti-Christian world view*. And according to God's Word, that is exactly what confirms the *demonic nature* of the New Age movement. In fact, many New Agers actually even believe that man's fall into sin as described in the beginning chapters of Genesis was really man's ascent into knowledge, assisted by Lucifer (the devil), whom they insanely hail as the bringer of light and wisdom. Many New Agers expect that by either acts of men or by acts of spirits, the earth will be cleansed of all those who refuse to morally evolve as they do through moral relativism.

Ironically, many in the New Age movement claim that there will soon be a one-world government and a one-world (morally compromised) religion to go with it which they believe will finally unify the world. Thus, according to Bible believing Christians, they will fall right into the deception of the Antichrist and his predicted False Prophet. And, most likely, many of them will also begin to believe that a big part of that unification process will be getting rid of anyone (like Bible-believing Christians or Jews) who simply refuse to compromise the absolute moral truths of God's Word. But very thankfully, they will not have the *global* political power to enforce their so-called spiritual convictions until after the Church of Christ is gone through the rapture!

However, even though the New Agers cannot yet obtain global political power to actually enforce their spiritual convictions on the world, is it just some mere coincidence that these inhuman one-world New Age objectives have also been clearly predicted by thirty some different prophets and apostles within the Bible over two thousand years ago? Or does it make much more sense to believe that the devil himself is just priming the lost world ahead of time through false religions like the New Age movement so the unbelieving world will actually welcome the Antichrist with open arms when he does soon reveal himself? Many New Agers do not probably even realize it, but according to Bible prophecy (which has never been wrong), they are just the devil's pawns playing right into his hands and plans to destroy mankind both physically and spiritually!

If the seven-year tribulation period (consistently predicted through both the Old and New Testaments in about 500 different prophecies) is a soon coming reality, then New Agers have the very worst of times to look forward to not only in this life but the next. According to the Bible, the coming seven-year tribulation period will be the worst time of God's judgment upon man's sin known in human history. The 10 percent or so of the world's population which manages to survive it will undoubtedly have more psychological problems than ten Vietnam vets put together. However, according to those same prophecies, the future for Bible-believing Christians in this life, and the next is extremely bright in comparison. Those Christians walking with Christ will, in fact, be taken off the earth via the rapture resurrection of the Church, and they will actually miss the entire time of the long predicted seven-year tribulation judgment which will fall on those Christ rejecting unbelievers who have chosen to rebel against God and his Word (see Luke 21:34–36; 1 Thessalonians 4:15–18; 1 Corinthians 15:51–53). Not to mention the eternal life of the true Christian which the Bible has clearly revealed with many details is awesome beyond all that man could ever hope for (Ephesians 3:30–21)!

> The devil himself is just priming the lost world ahead of time through false religions like the New Age movement so the unbelieving world will actually welcome the Antichrist when he reveals himself.

Conclusion

Statistics are always changing, and depending upon the source for one's statistic, presently, there are roughly 12 million Americans who could be considered active participants in the New Age movement and another 30 million who would seem to be interested in it. While Hindus and Buddhists certainly have some common ground with the New Age religion, for the purposes of statistics, we are keeping them separate, simply because they keep themselves separate in title and doctrine. So, considering 70 million is only 1 percent of seven billion, the number of New Age believers is *at most* far less than 1 percent of the world's total population.

Objection 45
I Believe in the New Age Movement

If you are presently involved in the New Age movement, I sincerely appeal to you right now, for someday, you and I will stand before our own creator and give account to him for either our reasonable surrender to him or our rebellious rejection of him. Yes, it is certainly true that we all have the perfect freedom to believe whatever spiritual beliefs we want to because our creator actually gave us that freedom which his true love certainly demands. However, that doesn't at all mean that the results will be at all to our liking should our choice of spiritual beliefs be wrong! If we reject our very own perfect creator who is himself the only source of our eternal life, then how can he possibly ever give us the very thing (eternal life) we are rejecting?

Sometimes a horse will actually be afraid of his own shadow, even though we all know a mere shadow could never hurt anyone or anything. And, sometimes, man can be afraid of his own creator, even though by definition, his very own *perfect* eternal creator could never hurt him in any way because he must also be perfect love just to even exist eternally! And the fact that our very own perfect creator can actually love and bless us far more and better than we could ever love and bless ourselves rarely occurs to those in rebellion against him!

Nevertheless, it's the reasonable truth of which all true Christians can also testify. However, for those in this world who keep rejecting their perfect creator and the great love he showed us on the cross, there is a simple and yet profound saying which depicts such rebellion:

> Constant rebellion against true love = insanity.

If you happen to be one who is caught in the deception of the New Age movement right now, you must realize that the devil is truly the enemy of your soul, and that's why he's tried so hard to stain the true loving reputation of the biblical Christ in this world and cause people to rebel against him. But, sadly, in such cases when people do rebel against Christ, all their rebellion is really just against a lie or some false portrayal of Christ which the demonic world has created to deceive men away from God. If you've been in rebellion against God for a long time, what if it is not at all even the real biblical Christ which you have even been rebelling against all these years but rather just an unbiblical false portrayal of Christ created by the demonic world to deceive you? Perhaps some false portrayals of the biblical Christ have even come from how some "professing Christians" you know have lived. But just like we've already mentioned in Objection #40, there are two basic realities to be aware of in such cases:

1. First of all, there are actually false Christians in the world who may claim to live for Christ but, in reality, do not because they actually live in some lifestyle of sin (see 1 Corinthians 6:9–10). But why let another person's hypocrisy deceive you away from the true biblical Jesus and rob you of eternal life? Trust me, because God is all-knowing and perfect, they won't get away with a thing! The Bible clearly teaches us that the hearts of all men are *"open and laid bare to the eyes of him with whom we have to do"* (Hebrews 4:13).
2. Secondly, even the Apostle Paul, one of the most spiritual men who walked the earth, said that it was the perfect Christ which he was preaching, not himself because he himself was still very imperfect and needed Christ's forgiveness. And if you were to honestly search your own soul, you'd have to admit that you too are also very imperfect. So if you were to reject the perfect biblical Christ, just because of the many imperfections you've seen in other even true Christians who are sincerely trying to follow Christ, then you'd just be falling into basic hypocrisy yourself because you are just as imperfect as those imperfect Christians you are using to run away from God.

The fact that our very own perfect creator can actually love and bless us far more and better than we could ever love and bless ourselves rarely occurs to those in rebellion against him.

Sincerely seek, and you will find

In truth, the only way you are going to get to know the true biblical Christ is by simply reading the New Testament yourself with sincere contemplation and meet the perfect Christ who would never hurt you in any way. If you have never sincerely sought to know the true Christ by reading the whole New Testament cover to cover, I would strongly encourage you to do so for your own sake. Does not Christ, your very own creator, deserve to have a fair trial in the courtroom of your conscience before you would reject him? But how can you actually give

Objection 45
I Believe in the New Age Movement

Christ a fair trial if you never even read the New Testament from start to finish one time sincerely seeking the truth? Then, if you still reject Christ, you will at least be rejecting the perfect biblical Christ and not just some false portrayal of him created by the demonic world or sinful man.

You see, the devil knows that Jesus Christ is your only source of real truth, love, and eternal life, simply because he is, in fact, your creator. And if you just give the real biblical Jesus a chance, he will certainly prove that to you! And just as Jesus proved his divinity to the honest soul many times over when he walked the earth in real divine power, so too is his Word completely trustworthy, which foretells the awesome eternity which God has for all those who love him. As Revelation 21:3–4 clearly teaches:

"Behold, the dwelling place of God is with men, and he will live with them, and they shall be his people, and God himself shall be with them, and be their God. And God shall wipe away all tears from their eyes; and there shall be no more death, neither sorrow, nor crying, neither shall there be any more pain: for the former things are passed away."

But the Bible teaches us plainly that *only through Christ* can we obtain God's eternal life (John 14:6). If you are one who has been part of the New Age movement and would like to give Christ a chance because you know in your heart that the New Age movement simply cannot give you the eternal hope and love you need, I invite you to just take that first small step of faith by sincerely praying the prayer of salvation located at the end of this book. Even if you've been a New Ager for years, you can still break away from that obvious false religion today, which threatens your true salvation through Christ. And don't be concerned with what your family members may think of you because, simply put, they will not be your judge on judgment day! This decision is between you and God (your creator) alone. No matter what your past is like, God loves you and sincerely wants you to be a part of his awesome eternal kingdom!

Jesus said, "I am the resurrection and the life. He who believes in me, will live even though he dies; and whoever lives and believes in me will never die." (John 11:25–26)

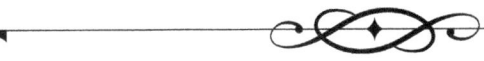

OBJECTION 46
I'm a Muslim

A loving reminder: Before each false belief system we discuss, just so my loving intentions cannot be misunderstood, I will *once again* remind the reader that it's certainly *not the adherents* of any false religion or belief system which the true Church is against but rather just the *false teachings* within them which deceive men away from the one and only true God and his eternal salvation (Ephesians 6:12). Therefore, my dear reader, please know that our discussion of these various different belief systems is very much a *love* issue.

The origin of Islam

Ironically enough, if you look into the history of Islam, there is much evidence that it was actually started by the Roman Catholic religion. In the magazine called *The Prophet* by Jack T. Chick, it goes through the history of Islam and how it all started with a Catholic Pope who actually sent out a Catholic nun to find an Arab and marry him in order to raise an army (fully funded by the Pope) whose purpose would be to get the holy land back for the Catholic religion. Well, that Arab was Mohammad (who did marry a Catholic nun), and the pope's plan was working for a while, but soon, Islam got so big that they rebelled against the Catholic religion instead of helping them militarily. While this is the true history of Islam as one *honestly* looks into it, most

Objection 46
I'm A Muslim

Muslims today probably do not even realize that their entire religion actually started as a front for the Catholic religion!

Of course, one must once again ask the very reasonable question in light of the late birth of Islam: If indeed Islam is really the one and only true faith, how did Allah, their God, ever expect the pre-Islam world to obtain all his vital spiritual truths and eternal salvation? Muslims claim that, spiritually, Islam actually evolved from New Testament Christianity and Judaism. But if it actually evolved from New Testament Christianity and Judaism, then why is Islam by name not once mentioned within the entire Holy Bible? And, additionally, why is Allah not once mentioned by name in the entire Holy Bible either? And if Islam actually evolved from New Testament Christianity, then why are the doctrines of New Testament Christianity so very different from that of Islam with almost *no common ground*?

As Proverbs 12:17 states, *"He who speaks the truth gives honest evidence."* And if Islam actually evolved from New Testament Christianity, then why didn't Christ or any of his apostles even mention the Muslim religion even once by name or its unique doctrines? It is easy for Muslims to claim that their religion actually evolved from New Testament Christianity and Judaism, but when even the basic deity and doctrines are most all very different, then such a fast claim should certainly be held suspect by those with the ability to be honest with themselves.

> If Islam is really the one and only true faith, how did Allah ever expect the pre-Islam world to obtain all his vital spiritual truths and eternal salvation?

Testing Islam against the true moral condition of man

Typically, Muslims believe mankind to be "basically good without an inborn sin nature from birth." However, since even Muslim children (as well as all other children) must always be taught to be good and never selfish, such a belief that man has no inborn sin nature from birth remains rather *unconvincing* to say the least. Additionally, since this overall Islamic belief of mankind being *basically good* goes directly against the widespread moral failure we all see in the entire history of the human race (which includes the Muslims), it should be easily denounced in the conscience of those at all familiar with human history. If killing everyone in the whole world who does not agree with Islam (as the Koran actually calls all Muslims to do; see verses like Sura 5:33 and Sura 9:5) is the Muslim's idea of man being *basically good* without an inborn sin nature, then I think we need to change the very definition of goodness just for the Muslims! As it concerns women in Islamic culture, the Koran in Sura 4:34 specifically states:

"Men are the managers of the affairs of women… Those (women) you fear may be rebellious, admonish, banish them to their couches and beat them."

You will never find a verse like that in the Holy Bible as God (of the Bible) loves all women whom he created and would never give such instructions! Yes, you will find stories of abuse in the Bible as examples of how *not to live*, but God, Jesus, or his apostles never teach us to abuse others in any way! In Objection #24, we do discuss the national right of Israel to put down godless evil peoples which threatened the morality of the world at the time (kind of like we had to do with Hitler), but that is an altogether different civil matter of national defense. However, despite many such moral failures portrayed by Muslim teachings in the Koran, Islam hypocritically still maintains that man is basically good without an inborn sin nature from birth. Thus, we must conclude that Islam easily fails this very reasonable test against man's true moral condition.

> Since even Muslim children must always be taught to be good and never selfish, such a belief that man has no inborn sin nature from birth remains rather unconvincing.

Testing Islam against self-contradictions

1. First of all, Muslims claim that the text of the Koran is written in perfect Arabic in every respect because Allah wrote it in heaven. The shorter encyclopedia of Islam states, *"To Muslims, the absolute perfection of the language of the Koran is an impregnable dogma."* Since whatever Allah does must be perfect, the Koran must be in perfect Arabic. This claim is found in Sura 12:2, 13:37, 41:41, 44.

However, the Koran is not at all written in perfect Arabic. It contains many grammatical errors, such as in Sura 2:177, 192; 3:59; 4:162; 5:69; 7:160; 13:28; 20:66; 63:10, etc. Further, the Koran contains sentences which are incomplete and not fully understandable without Muslim commentary aid. It contains foreign words, unfamiliar Arabic words, and words used out of their ordinary meanings. Adjectives and verbs are used without observance to gender and number. Pronouns which sometimes have no referent are illogically and ungrammatically applied. It also contains predicates in rhymed passages which are often remote from the subjects being discussed.

To sum up, there more than a hundred aberrations in the Koran which do not comply with the normal grammatical rules and structure of Arabs. All this being noted, there are obvious parts of the Koran which are not even written in Arabic at all, but over a hundred foreign words borrowed from many languages are instead applied. How then can all the Koran be written in perfect Arabic?

Also, did a God, called Allah, really write the Koran in heaven on tablets of stone as the Muslims claim? Muslims claim that the Koran was handed down from heaven and that Muhammad cannot be viewed as its human author. But according to the encyclopedia of Islam, the Arabic of the Koran is in the dialect and vocabulary of someone who was specifically a member of the Quraysh tribe living in the city of Mecca; thus Muhammad's fingerprints are coincidentally all over the Koran. If the Koran was written in some kind of perfect heavenly Arabic by Allah himself, this would certainly not be the case of it being in the exact dialect of the Quraysh tribe living in the city of Mecca. The Koran, in its content, vocabulary, and dialect much more reflects its human author, Mohammad, rather than some perfect heavenly Allah. Furthermore, there are no supernaturally fulfilled prophecies within the Koran which would even convince us it was divinely written.

    2. Secondly, Muslims further claim that because the Koran is perfect, there are no variant readings, lost verses, or conflicting manuscripts on the text of the Koran. However, the truth of matter is that the text of the Koran does, in fact, have many conflicting words from different manuscripts. Scholars have noted over ninety pages of variant readings within the text of the Koran. For example, in Sura 2, scholars have noted over 140 conflicting and variant

readings in the text of the Koran. Even Muslim scholars now are starting to admit that there are conflicting and variant readings within the text of the Koran. Interestingly enough, permission for Western scholars to take pictures of early Kufic Codices in the Egyptian Library has been denied in the past, and access to certain codices have been denied. So just what do Muslims have to hide?

Also, some original verses of the Koran have clearly been lost. For example, the Sura Al-saff had 200 verses in the days of Ayesha, but by the time Uthman standardized the text of the Koran, it had only fifty-two verses left. Other verses elsewhere have also been lost. The many verses which were lost in Uthman's version is recognized by both western and Arabic scholars alike. Also, another way verses were lost from the original text of the Koran is that they were simply changed. Evidently, one follower of Muhammad, named Abdollah Sarh, would often make suggestions to Muhammad about rephrasing, adding to, or subtracting from the Suras. Evidently, Muhammad often did what Sarh suggested.

Then, later, Abdollah actually ended up renouncing Islam altogether based on his own claim that the revelations, if they were from God, could not just be changed at the suggestion of a scribe such as himself! Then, later, Muhammad murdered Abdollah, for he knew too much and opened his mouth too often. Let's face it: if Jesus ever did such a thing with one of his disciples, nobody honest would ever have believed in biblical Christianity!

3. Thirdly, Muslims claim in general that the original manuscript of the Koran which Muhammad himself gathered and constructed is most definitely still in existence, and all Korans come from that one single original manuscript. But as to the common claim that the original manuscript of the Koran is still in existence, scholars have easily found out that there was no single manuscript of the Koran. By the time Muhammad died, he had not compiled any single complete text of the Koran. This, too, is common knowledge among Western scholars.

4. Fourthly, Muslims claim that because the Koran was written by Allah himself, no mortal man can translate it

into another language. The claim that the Koran cannot be translated is easily refuted by Western scholars, just because of the many translations of the Koran which exist today!

5. Fifth, Muslims claim that no one can write any perfect literature like that found in the Koran (Sura 10:37). When Muslims claim that no one can write any perfect literature like that found in the Koran, it is rather humorous considering the supposed elegant literature of the Koran is rather poor indeed when compared with many other writings of many other nations. Thus, in conclusion, all the above facts reveal that these Muslim claims are indeed fictitious and false, and with the scholarly world attending, they would certainly not stand up in any honest court of law. Therefore, after being reasonably tested against its own claims, the Muslim faith must reasonably be disqualified as the one true faith, just because of its many *trust-breaking* contradictions alone.

Abdollah ended up renouncing Islam altogether because he knew if the revelations were from God, they could not just be changed at his suggestion… then Mohammad murdered him!

Testing Islam against the well known facts of science

1. In Bakhari, vol. IV, no. 543, in *The Hadith*, it states: Narrated Adu Huraira:

"The prophet said, Allah created Adam, making him 60 cubits (90 feet tall)." My friend anyone who would seriously believe such nonsense, and expect the rest of the world to believe it, is being quite unreasonable indeed! Obviously Islam here is at great odds with biology basics—and, of course scientific reality."

2. Additionally, we read an even stranger doctrine in Muslim Vol. 1, no. 462 which states:

"The Devil spends the night in the interior of the nose."

And The Hadith: Bakhari Vol. IV, no. 516, which states:

"Satan stays in the upper part of the nose all night."

Not only is this obscure belief quite unscientific, but spiritually, such a belief is also rather absurd, unless Satan is omnipresent and can actually be in all Muslim noses at the same time! According to the Bible, demonic beings may rarely possess an entire person, but historically, no one has ever witnessed any demonic being just indwelling a single body part like the nose! Again, anyone can see that such nonsense could never have been inspired by any perfect deity as their Allah claims to be. Someone could also claim demonic beings indwell the little toes of all mankind, but since there is no real evidence for such a fantastic claim, it just discredits and degrades he who would believe such a ridiculous thing.

3. In *The Hadith*, it also seriously teaches that people should avoid lifting their eyes towards the sky while supplicating in prayer; otherwise, their eyes would be snatched away. This, too, is unscientific nonsense which, once again, just exposes the fact that *The Hadith* certainly could not have been inspired by any perfect deity.

4. In Muslim Vol. III, no. 5113 DCCCLXII (and also nos. 5114–5120), it teaches that non-Muslims literally have seven intestines, and Muslims have only one intestine. Obviously, this defies scientific reality as well and just further exposes that the prophet who wrote it was false and inspired by the demonic world instead of our true creator. And while there are many more such unscientific beliefs within Muslim holy books, just the ones we've cited should be plenty sufficient enough to expose Islam as false for the honest soul.

> Spiritually, such a belief is also rather absurd, unless Satan is omnipresent and can actually be in all Muslim noses at the same time!

Testing Islam against the well-known character of its founder

As we've already mentioned, if one can test a religion or belief system against the well-known character of its *founder(s)*, they should do so. When you think of it, this is only reasonable, especially if that founder (or founders) claims to have found a faith or religion from a perfect God which determines the eternal destiny for the entire human race!

Objection 46
I'm A Muslim

For example, Mohammad is the founder of the Islamic religion. But really, what does our well-known history bring to light of Mohammad's basic moral character? Though Muslims tend to paint a peace-loving picture for Mohammad, the truth is that obvious historical records show that he violently raided Jewish caravans and plundered them, constantly stealing both women and wealth. He murdered personal friends like Abdollah who threatened his cruel regime. And he started holy wars with many other peoples and enforced conversion to Islam through the sword.

As we've already cited in Objection #35, this is also plainly taught in the Koran itself (see Sura 5:33 and 9:5). But how does this compare to Christ and how he and his disciples walked the earth, teaching us to even love our enemies (Matthew 5:44)?

The one time Christ's disciple, Peter, even tried to defend Christ with a sword, Jesus rebuked him sharply and then instantly healed the man which Peter hurt (see Luke 22:49–51; Matthew 26:51–54). In fact, Christ and his disciples all allowed themselves to be martyred instead of ever resorting to violence to even defend themselves. Nor did they ever teach anything like putting to death all those who did not believe in Christ! The bottom line is that Mohammad cut hands off (Sura 5:33), and Jesus only restored human hands (Luke 6:6–10). How much more polar opposite could they be in moral character? Now that we've shed some real light on the moral character of Islam's founder and easily proved him unworthy of our trust, we'll now discuss the historical moral fruit Islam has produced as a religion.

> The bottom line is that Mohammad cut hands off (Sura 5:33), and Jesus only restored human hands (Luke 6:6–10). How much more polar opposite could they be in moral character?

Testing Islam against its prophetic predictions of the future

Muslims claim that their Koran (and even tradition books) has numerous predictive prophecies which have been fulfilled. But upon investigation of their claim, one will only find a handful of obscure and vague predictions which really do not at all confirm divine inspiration because of their obvious inaccuracies or their incomplete and vague nature.

For example, one such alleged prophecy within the Koran is that the Koran itself will endure forever. However, such an incomplete prediction certainly cannot qualify as divinely fulfilled prophecy since it remains to be seen just how long the Koran endures! In another alleged prophecy fulfilled, the Koran states concerning the Pharaoh of the Exodus:

> *"This day shall we save thee in thy body, that thou mayest be a sign to those who come after thee."*

Historians have commonly believed the Pharaoh of the Exodus to be either Ramesses II or his son, Merneptah. And since their bodies were thought to be lost for a long time, but in recent years have been found, the Muslims quickly claimed that their discovered bodies were a divine fulfillment of this particular prophecy. However, there has been much debate among archaeologists as to just who was the Exodus pharaoh, and now many archaeologists do not believe that it was Ramesses II or his son who reigned in the New Egyptian kingdom (about 1250 BC) but rather the Exodus had to have happened earlier by about 200 years (1450 BC) in the Middle Egyptian kingdom. One strong piece of evidence that Ramesses II could not have been the Exodus pharaoh is a monument that Merneptah, his son, erected in honor of Ramesses II right after he died.

The monument explicitly lists Israel as one of many established nations in the land of Canaan, which, of course, would be impossible if Ramesses II was the Exodus pharaoh. There is also much evidence that Amenemhat III was the Egyptian pharaoh during the time of Joseph, which again lines up with an earlier exodus than traditionally assumed. A film titled *Exodus: Patterns of Evidence* investigates and makes such a conclusion based on solid evidence. And if this is essentially true, it would not only explain just why past archaeologists have not been able to find evidence of the Bible's Exodus in history during the reign of Ramesses II, but it would also of course completely nullify the Muslim prophecy.

At any rate, there are numerous other vague or incomplete Koran prophecies which lack any sure historical proof of fulfillment, and *unlike* those many within the Holy Bible, they cannot even be historically confirmed as divinely inspired.

OBJECTION 46
I'M A MUSLIM

Obvious false Muslim prophecies

There are many prophecies and/or promises in either the Koran or in Muslim traditional books which are obviously false upon simple investigation. We will just cite a couple:

1. Sura 30:2–4: "*The Roman empire has been defeated in a land close by. But they (even), after (this) defeat of theirs, will soon be victorious within a few years.*"

The problem is that according to Yusuf Ali, the Arabic word for a few years, *Bidh'un*, signifies a period of three to nine years. But according to historical record, the Roman victory did not come until about *fourteen years* later. The Persians defeated the Romans and captured Jerusalem in about AD 615, and the Roman counter offensive was not complete until AD 628.

2. Sura 48:27: "*Truly did Allah fulfill the vision for his messenger. Ye shall enter the sacred mosque, if Allah wills, with minds secure, head shaved, hair cut short, and without fear. For he knew what ye knew not, and he granted, besides this, a speedy victory.*"

This prophecy concerned Mohammad's promise to Muslims that they would enter Mecca. And according to available records on this prophecy, Mohammad's promise was for *the very same year* the promise was made. But since history shows that the Muslim pilgrimage to Mecca that year was, in fact, stopped by pagan Arabs, the prophecy was, of course, proven false. Though there are numerous other false prophecies which can be found in the Koran, there are also many other false promises made within the Muslim books of traditions. For example, in book 37, number 4281–4283, Mohammad claimed that the end of the world Antichrist (Dajjal) was to appear shortly after the Muslim conquest of Constantinople. However, Constantinople was taken over by Muslims in May of AD 1453, and their prophecy of Medina (Yathrib) being in ruins as well as the Antichrist's advent to take place seven months after the conquest of Constantinople just did not obviously happen.

Muslims could argue that their prophecy actually referred to future conquests, but still, such conquests remain to be seen, thus their prophecy still remains unfulfilled! In order to confirm prophecies as divinely authored as in the case with Bible prophecy, many of them must be accurately fulfilled without one single error, even if all are not yet fulfilled. However, we are not only hard-pressed to even find a single Muslim prophecy which has obviously been miraculously fulfilled, but quite unlike Bible prophecies fulfilled, many have been proven false as history unfolded.

Testing Islam against the historical fruit it has produced

When comparing the Muslim god, Allah, in the Koran with the God of the Bible, one will quickly discover they cannot be the same God with just different names, simply because the character and commandments of both clearly conflict with each other. According to the New Testament and its eyewitnesses, Jesus Christ lived a morally perfect and sinless life (2 Corinthians 5:21; 1 Peter 2:22). He didn't rob or murder anyone, and there were many antagonistic witnesses around him, which would have made historical record of it if he had. In fact, if he had done so, it surely would have been brought up during his Roman trial before his crucifixion!

Quite to the contrary, all throughout the New Testament, we find that Jesus and his disciples only fed people, healed people, and raised them from the dead. However, on the other hand, when we look at the historical life of the Muslim prophet Muhammad and his followers, we find that they often murdered, maimed, and robbed many people in the name of Allah, *just to build their religion*. As the saying goes: Nobody should be impressed with moral compromise, simply because anyone can do that!

In the New Testament, Jesus teaches Christians to *"Love their enemies,"* that they may *"be sons of their Father in Heaven"* (Matthew 5:44). But the following references in the Koran call all Muslims to convert the world through murder:

1. In Sura 9:5, the Koran directly commands Muslims to fight and slay the pagans (those who are not Muslim) wherever ye find them, and seize them, beleaguer them, and lie in wait for them in every stratagem of war.
2. Again, in Sura 5:33, it directly calls all Muslims to

Objection 46
I'm A Muslim

kill anyone who would resist Islam by saying: *"Their punishment is...execution, or crucifixion, or the cutting off of hands and feet...or exile from the land."*

3. Sura 8:60–65 also calls all Muslims to violence.

Not only does the Koran call all Muslims to murder those who refuse to become Muslim but also calls all Muslims to murder those who leave Islam for any reason! For example, in Sura 4:89, it states: "Allah commands that any person who leaves Islam or encourages others to do so, should be seized and slain." Altogether, there are about a hundred such different verses in the Koran calling all Muslims to murder all non-Muslims whether they've never been a Muslim or are leaving Islam!

So does Allah sound like a loving God to you? Or much more realistically like a demonic being which inspired the Koran to be written through the false prophet, Mohammad, who was completely living for himself? Based on the *honest evidence*, you must of course draw your own conclusions. What about all the peace-loving Muslims today which actually are greater in number than the violent ones?

Well, even though it is admirable that they are not murderers like their fellow "brethren," we must conclude that since they are not obeying the actual teachings within their own Koran, they should honestly be considered just poor Muslims or backslidden Muslims! And, no doubt, the violent Muslims consider them to be such as well if they are all to follow the clear teachings of the Koran.

> When we look at the historical life of Muhammad and his followers, we find that they often murdered, maimed, and robbed many people in the name of Allah just to build their religion.

Is Muslim violence just war or murder?

But why couldn't it be said that Mohammad was just acting in military defense of his own nation and that Muslims today are just doing the same? For a couple of good reasons. First of all, Mohammad was the founder of the Muslim religion, and his violent actions were religiously based: he wasn't working for just an Arab civil government. Secondly, we must remember that civil governments were put into place to keep law and/order and put down evil (Romans 13:4), not promote it just because someone else doesn't spiritually believe the way they do.

Additionally, Mohammad committed evil acts which no moral civil government should enforce. He killed the innocent which were not even a military threat, just so he could plunder them and take their wives. He even killed both women and children during his warmongering as well. And in his brutality, he maimed and murdered his victims. These are all things civil governments *should never do* as they clearly go against the humanitarian rules of war founded by the collective consciences of man.

So, even in the case that his actions were political, it was an evil government he was serving which did not respect any humane rules of war. So any way one *honestly looks at it,* Koran, Muhammad, and Allah are morally very corrupt compared to the New Testament Jesus Christ or his Father who sent him! It is honestly impossible to be a Bible-believing Christian and a Koran-believing Muslim, and the issue of loving our enemies is just one of many basic doctrines which conflicts when comparing them!

But what of the Christian crusader wars? As we discuss further in Objection #64, it was only the Roman Catholic popes who started and waged holy wars, not Christ's true Church. The Crusaders who may have claimed to be Christ's Church at the time (carrying out their holy wars) were, in fact, being very poor New Testament Christians if they were even Christians at all, simply because there is no New Testament teaching which would support their militant actions as Christ's Church. Nor did Christ or his disciples ever lead any kind of an example of Crusader holy wars in order to gain land/or anything else.

Additionally, as we have clearly shown (in objection #39) the whole Roman Catholic religion to be an obvious cult with a works-based salvation and not anything set up by Christ, then their crusader actions cannot be fairly linked to the true Church which Christ did set up. The abuse of a religion by others is certainly not the fault of that religion. However, quite to the contrary, Mohammad and his followers were just being good Muslims when they converted men through the sword, simply because their Koran directly commands them to do so. And that's the important difference!

So when we compare the moral fruit produced by the actual

teachings of both because the Koran actually teaches the immoral conduct of Mohammad and his followers, we must honestly conclude that the Muslim religion does, indeed, produce bad moral fruit. And the bombing of our Twin Towers and all the recent Muslim terrorist attacks around the world just bear witness to this same bad moral fruit in our own day!

Additionally, obvious racism is exposed within Islam as it states in 3 Sur, verses 105–106:

> *"In the great and final day of redemption, only white faces will be saved, and all blackened faces will be condemned."*

Even ten-year-old children inherently know that such beliefs which obviously discriminate could never come from a perfect loving God.

Testing Islam against divine power demonstrated

Miracles: There really is no genuine historical record of Allah having demonstrated his divine power through Mohammad in the form of any miracles. And this, too, is a crucial blow to Islam as a whole which claims that Allah himself is both perfect, eternal, all-knowing, and *all-powerful*. Should we just take their word for it in light of the fact that they also claim to prescribe the way of eternal salvation for the entire human race? I don't think so! In fact, the Koran itself explicitly teaches that Mohammad performed *no signs or miracles* apart from the *alleged* inspiration he received in the Koran.

But what inspiration? There is absolutely no evidence that the Koran is even inspired beyond the writings of very imperfect men! In Sura 29:48–51, we read that the Koran itself is *sufficient* as a sign or miracle from God. Well, if the Koran itself is their only miracle, I can assure you they are greatly lacking any real divine power demonstrated! Muslims may claim that the word *al-bayyinat* implies that Mohammad did perform miracles, but such a claim is not substantiated since the term in the Koran is only used in reference to Mohammad receiving or reciting the Koran. In other words, Mohammad's signs or miracles, his *al-bayyinat*, were nothing more than the Koran itself.

Additionally, we have no such reliable historical record of others who witnessed any supposed obvious miracles which came by the hand of Mohammad. Yes, it may be easy for Muslims to claim Allah is the one and only true perfect eternal being, but because the Muslim religion lacks historical record of both miracles and divinely fulfilled prophecy, where's any real proof of it? Again, are we just to take their word for it, even though their religion supposedly prescribes the way of eternal life for all men? Does Allah expect the whole world to just believe in him without taking the responsibility to provide sufficient honest evidence for his supposed divinity? Now that doesn't seem to be very reasonable or loving for a perfect being, does it?

> There really is no genuine historical record of Allah having demonstrated his divine power through Mohammad in the form of miracles. And this, too, is a crucial blow to Islam.

On the other hand, when Christ and his apostles all walked the earth, they fully demonstrated the power of God through major supernatural miracles hundreds of times over in front of many public eye witnesses. Really, what more could they have done to prove Christ was just who he claimed to be? Additionally, the Bible itself is laced with over 2,000 future predicting prophecies which have already been fulfilled, all proving Jesus is just who he claimed to be! And this awesome divine power displayed is something *unique to biblical Christianity alone*. As the saying goes:

> "Jesus did not at all expect the world to follow him blindly. He publicly healed the blind to prove his deity!"

So what then is the big attraction to Islam in today's world anyway?

By far, biblical Christianity is the largest unified religion in the world today as roughly 30 percent of the world believes in the Holy Bible. But since the Muslim religion is believed by about 20 percent of the world's population today, one has to ask why it is believed by such a large following if the character of its founder is deeply flawed. It contradicts itself many times, it has consistently produced warlike fruit throughout history, and the Koran and Islamic traditions lack miracles and are full of false prophecies. Well, it is certainly sad, but like so many false religions in the world, it may just appeal to the sin nature/ emotions of men for a variety of reasons. Please consider the following:

Objection 46
I'm A Muslim

1. *As a religion, Islam compromises more than one of the Bible's teachings on sin.* Ironically enough, one of the first things our sin nature will try to convince us of is that we do not even have a sin nature at all! And as we've already mentioned, Islam basically teaches against mankind being born into sin. To the Muslim, sin is only a personal matter and has not even been passed down genetically from one generation to the other. In a broader sense, Muslims basically believe in the innate goodness of man and that man is basically good and does not need redemption through what Christ did for humanity on the cross, even though all men are obviously morally flawed. And because Islam teaches that man is basically good rather than having a basic inborn sinful nature and needing redemption, this certainly may appeal to many who wish to just live the way they want, even though it may harm others.

However, while many negatives in this life (like man having a sin nature) may not emotionally appeal to any of us, the question still remains: Can we really just make the sin nature of man go away by not believing in it? Does history honestly show that all mankind has been basically good or that he has a definite sin nature, which needs redemption through our perfect creator? And, most importantly, how will such a belief, which basically dodges the plain reality of man's sin nature, affect those who don't believe in the inborn sin nature of man when they stand before their perfect creator some day? Hmm... I guess if I were a Muslim, I'd hate to find out!

As we already covered in Objection #19 in Part 1 of our series, it should be plenty obvious that we all have an inborn sinful nature which we all wrestle with every day if we are honest enough to compare ourselves against the perfect moral standards of God and not just the worst cases of humanity.

2. *Some may be attracted to Islam because of the sexual pleasure it promises.* For example, the Muslim religion teaches and practices polygamy and believes it to be a healthy practice in human society, even though it has been outlawed in many societies because of the bad moral fruit it has produced. For example, in 4 Sur, verse 3, it states:

"Men marry as many women as you like. One, two, three, or four."

Here, again, one can easily see an attraction for the sin nature of man, which, for obvious and very convenient reasons, the Muslim does not believe in. Secondly, while *some* Muslims may not believe in violence (even though their Koran technically does teach conversion through the sword), those Muslims who do believe in violence teach their young men of war that if they should give their lives in any war against the infidels that they will be given great honor by Allah and rewarded with seventy virgin women waiting for them in heaven! This, of course, is a complete lie, but when one is raised a Muslim and trained in their war philosophies, one obviously really believes it as many of their young men have!

> The Muslim religion practices polygamy, and believes it to be healthy, even though it has been outlawed in many societies because of the bad moral fruit it has produced.

3. *Some may be attracted to Islam's doctrine of Pre-destination which essentially relieves man of moral responsibilities.* Islam basically teaches that anything which happens in this life, be it good or evil, is the will of Allah. In other words, again, man is not ultimately responsible for even evil actions. In this sense, everything is predestined by Allah, and man is not morally responsible. However, on the other hand, they believe Islam has the best moral impact on any society because they pride themselves in good morals. But, of course, if they are not good, as in the case of violent Muslims, it was just the predestined will of Allah! So when Muslims are good, they credit themselves, but when evil, it must have been the will of Allah for some mysterious reason we cannot know. However, it, of course, is never the will of Allah that any other nation or religion attack them in self-defense, like Israel has had to do many times if they did not want to let the Muslims just take all their land!

4. *Essentially, the Islam religion in many ways has just cut out*

Objection 46
I'm A Muslim

anything, which may be harder to understand, and that's why Islam may be looked at as simpler and more rational than biblical Christianity, and this, too, may be an attraction to many. However, just because something is made simpler, this in itself does not guarantee that one is believing the truth. Anyone who has lived awhile knows well that life is *not always so simple; even though the more complicated truth may rub us all the wrong way.* For example, it would be much simpler if doctors did not have to receive a lot of complicated education and training before they went into practice. But the truth is that the human body is very complex and all that preparation, while it many times may not appeal to doctors, is quite necessary because it is connected to the truth of reality.

In other words, some things just can't be simplified because in reality; they just are complex and many times even beyond us. But the Muslim mindset seems to be that simplicity must equal truth every time. Additionally, Bible-believing Christians also understand that it has largely been man's sin against God which has made life more complicated than it should be! For example, if it were not for man's disobedience to his creator, we would not need prisons, bigger governments, just wars or probably even hospitals, for that matter. But Muslims simply compromise the truth of man's sin, denying that the two are even connected.

Another obvious example of Muslim simplicity which compromises the truth is their clear rejection of the trinity of God as clearly taught in the Holy Bible. They refuse to believe that a single monotheistic God could ever express himself in three different persons who have the very same will because they are, in fact, one God. Admittedly, many such things to do with God go far beyond our understanding, but does that mean we just throw out those things which may be beyond us, just to simplify?

Quite equally, Muslims cannot any more comprehend the supposed perfection and eternal nature of their Allah, but does that mean they should just simplify and reject him altogether? Simplicity doesn't equal truth any more than complexity does. The truth is that both are actually *irrelevant to truth itself,* which can be either simple or complex.

For example, it is probably much simpler to kill those who may not agree with your spiritual beliefs, rather than try to patiently reason with them in love. But such a solution is not only a wicked solution but also very unloving to say the least! Nevertheless, the *supposed* simplicity of Islam may continue to be an attraction to those who may just value simplicity over truth and morality.

> Simplicity doesn't equal truth any more than complexity does. The truth is that both are actually irrelevant to truth itself, which can be either simple or complex.

5. *The Muslim religion claims to be the final Revelation of God* in the series of three religions, namely Judaism, Christianity, and Islam. Just because it technically came after biblical Christianity, Islam claims to be the new and improved final religion of the world which evolved from Christianity. So, just like they believe simplicity equals truth, they also contend that the latest religion equals truth as well.

However, this flawed logic also makes little sense considering many other religions sprang up in the world after even Islam! And considering both Judaism and biblical Christianity, are so very different from Islam in their basic doctrines (especially as it concerns the very character of God and the salvation of all men), how could Islam have actually come from New Testament Christianity? And how could their perfect Allah have possibly been the source of such contradictions between Islam and the God of Christianity? In a religious evolutionary sense, was Allah just learning from his mistakes when he finally presented Islam to the world? But wait a minute, don't Muslims believe Allah is perfect? On the other hand, if Muslims just believe that Judaism and biblical Christianity were just man-made, then how did Allah expect the entire human race to obtain salvation (and/or believe the truth) prior to the seventh century AD when he finally revealed himself to Mohammad? Either way one looks at it, sound reasoning is abandoned, and Islam itself has no solid ground to stand on.

6. *The Muslim religion claims to be far more compatible with*

Objection 46
I'm A Muslim

science than is biblical Christianity, even though most of our founding scientists were Bible-believing Christians. And, personally, I do not know of one highly influential scientist in the past three to four centuries who was a seriously devout Muslim! If there are any in the last three to four centuries, there can't have been too many, that's for sure. The Muslims constantly parade a book titled *The Bible, The Koran, and Science* by Maurice Bucailles, which supposedly proves that the Koran is far more scientific than the Bible. But, even though it has long been refuted by many prominent scholars, it still can be found in many Muslim bookstores!

Of course, it is quite easy for Muslims to insist that their religion is the *latest revelation of God* which also happens to be *the most scientific*, but that, my friend, does not make it true until it proves to be so with plenty of honest evidence by professionals even outside the Muslim world. The other very reasonable explanation is that both of these assertions are just deceiving lies fueled by the demonic world for the sole purpose of pulling the ignorant away from our one and only true creator and his eternal salvation!

7. In recent decades, it has been quite common for many Black Americans to find refuge in the Muslim religion because, *supposedly, the Muslim religion recognizes how badly Blacks were treated by the whites in slavery days far better than does biblical Christianity*. But we've just cited a passage in the Koran which exposes far worse racism against Blacks than even slavery as it literally condemns all Blacks to eternal hell (3 Sur, verses 105–106, which states: "In the great and final day of redemption, only white faces will be saved, and all blackened faces will be condemned.)!

Muslims today may somehow try to get around this verse, but obviously, Mohammad kept this verse in the Koran because like all other verses in the Koran, he believed it came from Allah, their perfect God. So let us not then even begin to suggest that Islam is not *severely* racist against Blacks as this verse clearly teaches otherwise. Since some skeptics have mistakenly believed that the Bible has actually taught American Black slavery, we've taken some decent time to clear up that whole lie once and for all in Objection #79 of part 4 of our series.

8. Many are attracted to Islam because, *culturally, it may be more structured than biblical Christianity* which does not really tell people just how to live *culturally*. Many people also join the military for that very reason. They want structure imposed on them, to be told what to do so they don't have as much personal responsibility themselves. Even their doctrine of predestination (everything is Allah's will) supports this conclusion as it essentially relieves man of personal responsibility. And perhaps this is what some Muslims mean by "it is simpler than biblical Christianity." However, to the contrary, the New Testament very wisely does not contain as much cultural instruction in order to preserve personal freedoms as much as possible. But with more freedom comes more responsibility and, again, some Muslims may just not prefer that.

9. *Most Muslims are just born into Islam. However, for a minimum penalty, Muslims are typically excommunicated today if they should leave their inborn Muslim religion for any reason.* And more than one reference in the Koran would teach that any who should leave Islam should receive a maximum penalty of death! If this, my friend, is not the true sign of a cult, then what is? In the case of excommunication, from then on, family will not typically associate with those family members who decide to leave the Muslim religion. While this excommunication (or even death threat) practice may certainly not appeal to any Muslim, it nevertheless acts as a strong retaining agent for those who are either born into Islam or became Muslims later on in life.

It is interesting to note that the Catholic religion has always had a similar excommunication practice, and both religions were largely prominent throughout the world from the seventh century to the fifteenth century AD. Hmm... I guess if the historical evidence reveals that Islam was actually started by the Roman Catholic religion accidentally, then their shared excommunication practices would also just make sense!

> If the historical evidence reveals that Islam was actually started by the Roman Catholic religion accidentally, then their shared ex-communication practice would just make sense.

Conclusion

Statistics are always changing, and depending upon the source for one's statistic, presently, there are roughly 1.6 billion people worldwide who attach themselves to Islam or the Muslim religion. Obviously, the Muslim religion may appeal to many in our world today for practical, emotional, or cultural reasons which we've just discussed. However, none of these reasons have anything to do with believing in Islam because it is based on all kinds of honest evidence for the truth…nor should such reasons suffice us for a religion which claims to prescribe our eternal salvation! And, sadly, the more one really looks into Islam and the Koran beyond even what little we've just discussed, the more one can easily see just what a dishonest self-contradicting spiritual mess it really is and that Mohammad himself was an obvious false prophet following a deceiving demonic spirit by the name of Allah.

Unfortunately, because many Muslims are just born into Islam, they may continue to just *blindly* follow family members for their own shallow reasons such as polygamy, cultural structure, the fear of excommunication, etc. However, no matter what the shallow reason is, it is not worth their eternal soul any more than it is honestly without the many unsolvable problems which we've just cited in this objection.

My friend, if you are presently in the religion of Islam, I would simply encourage you to look even deeper into the historical moral character of Mohammad, its founder, the obvious contradictions within the Koran, and Islamic tradition writings as well as their complete lack of divine power displayed in their prophecies. Nevertheless, just the honest evidence which we've already discussed should sufficiently expose Islam as a false man-made religion which should certainly not have our trust for something as important as our eternal salvation. In 19 Sur, verse 66, Mohammad asks:

> *"When I am dead and buried in the ground and go back to dust, is that all? What will happen to me?"*

Obviously, Mohammad himself had no idea where he was going when he died. And he wanted the whole world to follow him? Not cool! Isn't that a true case of the blind leading the blind? But just as Jesus proved his divinity to the honest soul many times over when he walked the earth, so too is his Word completely trustworthy which foretells the awesome eternity which God has for all those who love him. As Revelation 21:3–4 clearly teaches:

> *"[B]ehold, the dwelling place of God is with men, and he will live with them, and they shall be his people, and God himself shall be with them, and be their God. And God shall wipe away all tears from their eyes; and there shall be no more death, neither sorrow, nor crying, neither shall there be any more pain: for the former things are passed away."*

But the Bible teaches us plainly that *only through Christ* can we obtain God's eternal life (John 14:6). If you are one who can easily see through the gross immoralities of the Muslim religion and know that Allah could not possibly be God because of it and would like to give Jesus a fair chance to reveal that he is the one true creator of all things, and would like to be right him and obtain his eternal life, I invite you to just take that first small step of faith by sincerely praying the prayer of salvation located at the end of this book.

Even if you've been a Muslim for years, you can still break away from that obvious false religion today which threatens your true salvation through Christ. And don't be concerned with what your family members may think of you because, simply put, they will not be your judge on judgment day! This decision is between you and God (your creator) alone. No matter what your past is like, God loves you and sincerely wants you to be a part of his awesome eternal kingdom!

> *Jesus said, "I am the resurrection and the life. He who believes in me, will live even though he dies; and whoever lives and believes in me will never die"* (John 11:25-26)

Objection 47

I'm Jewish and Believe in the Old Testament Only

A loving reminder: Before each false belief system we discuss, just so my loving intentions cannot be misunderstood, I will *once again* remind the reader that it's certainly *not the adherents* of any false belief system which the true Church is against but rather just the *false teachings* within them which deceive men away from the one and only true God and his eternal salvation (Ephesians 6:12). Therefore, my dear reader, please know that our discussion of these various different religions or belief systems are very much a *love* issue. (Sidenote: If you happen to be a genetic Jew who devoutly adheres to Judaism, I would encourage you to *first* sincerely read Objections #28 and #37, if you haven't already, before even reading this one.)

Defining Judaism

While Judaism itself is essentially a belief in just the Old Testament scriptures, according to Judaism, even those Gentiles (or non-Jews) who believe in just the Old Testament scriptures can also have salvation through the Old Testament God of Israel, even though they may not be God's covenant people like the genetic Jew (descendants of Abraham and Sarah only; Genesis 17:19–21). Thus, we see within Judaism (as well as even New Testament Christianity) a unique God's covenant people subset which belongs only to the genetic Jew.

The relationship between Judaism and New Testament Christianity

Quite similarly, New Testament Christianity teaches us that ever since Christ died on the cross, all Gentile Christians can *partake* of Israel's *spiritual covenant* through Christ (Romans 11:17), even though Gentile believers in Christ during the church age still cannot partake of Israel's *national* covenants like only the genetic Jew can (Ephesians 2:11–12). But according to Christ in the New Testament, even a genetic Jew has no hope of partaking of even their own national covenants which God made only with the nation of Israel, if he or she should reject what Christ did for them on the cross. Because New Testament Christianity was actually born out of Judaism by way of a spiritual analogy, one could say that the New Testament Christian could view Judaism as their spiritual parent. However, the parent-child relationship between them has always been rather strained indeed simply because New Testament Christianity views their parent as an *unsaved parent* which still needs redemption through Christ who is the Jewish Messiah.

Likewise, Judaism views New Testament Christianity as not really even their own spiritual child, simply because all those who are in Judaism today still believe Christ to either be just a good man who was very deceived or, worse yet, a definite false prophet! However, since true New Testament Christianity believes Israel as a nation will finally recognize Christ as their promised Messiah in the future seven-year tribulation of Revelation, they are at least comforted that their lost parent will finally be unified with them when they find salvation through Christ their own true Messiah (Romans 11:26–27). And because New Testament Christianity actually did start with the genetic Jewish nation of Israel, of course, many Jews have already recognized Christ as their Messiah in the last 2,000 years of the church age and have left Judaism, taking their unique and rightful place of honor in God's New Testament Church. And, of course, continuing to be God's covenant people.

> Many Jews have already recognized Christ as their Messiah in the last 2,000 years of the church age and have left Judaism, taking their unique place of

Objection 47
I'm Jewish and Believe in the Old Testament Only

honor in God's New Testament Church.

The fact is that Jesus was a genetic Jew, and not only was Jesus a Jew, but so were his disciples. In fact, the first 13,000 converts to New Testament Christianity in the first-century Church were also Jewish as New Testament Christianity itself was born right in Israel: the land of the Jews. The New Testament was written by most all Jews and all that was written therein was first addressed to the Jews. And many Gentile Christians today may not even know it, but Jesus himself specifically made a special point of *beginning* the New Testament Church with only genetic Jews. Why? Simply because the New Covenant through Christ was to replace the Mosaic Old Covenant which only belonged to the genetic Jew, even though Gentiles can, of course, *partake* of it spiritually and find eternal salvation through Christ (Matthew 10:5–6; Romans chapters 10–11). So, really, how much more Jewish could the New Testament Church have started when you think about it?

On the other hand, the only comfort which those in Judaism today may have toward their estranged child (which they do not really see as their own) is their very unfulfilled hope that the child will someday grow up when their true Messiah does appear (as they are still looking for him). But so far, after 2,000 years, the Jews still clinging to Judaism still have no Messiah, and their estranged child still isn't growing up; as ever since Christ, the New Testament Church has always grown way past the numbers in Judaism instead! And the fact that world events are continuing to line right up with all Old and New Testament prophecies (especially found in the New Testament book of Revelation) which describe the Antichrist and his short-lived kingdom during the tribulation period is not at all helping to authenticate Judaism as the one true faith which is *still* waiting for their Messiah after about 4,000 years of human history!

> The fact that world events are constantly lining right up with all prophecies in the Old and New Testament which describe the Antichrist and his short-lived kingdom during the tribulation period is not at all helping to authenticate Judaism.

While those Jews within Judaism today may just believe in the Old Testament and totally reject the New Testament as the Word of God, those of us who believe in the New Testament do not, of course, reject the Old Testament as the Word of God. Thus, according to the New Testament, Judaism all by itself must *at least* be described as an *incomplete* faith, which just continues to pass itself off as the complete truth. However, since those Jews still in Judaism today do not yet have salvation through Christ their Messiah, and at the same time consider him to be just a good man or a false prophet, we must say that Judaism as a religion is indeed far more than just incomplete. For, according to the New Testament, because Judaism today totally rejects what Christ did for them on the cross for salvation, and still relies on Old Testament Mosaic laws for their right standing with God, it must certainly be considered a cult, just as much as any other religion in the world today which rejects Christ for their salvation and relies on human works instead for their right standing with God (see Galatians 1:6–9).

The bottom line is that through it (like all other cults), men and women are deceived away from their only way of salvation through Christ. Nevertheless, the child still *respects* their parent as God's future covenant people who are just temporarily blinded by their own sin until they find salvation through Christ in the soon coming tribulation period. But according to God in the New Testament, those adhering to Judaism (the parent or genetic Jew) really should have been a *spiritual example* to their child (the Gentile New Testament Christian) throughout the entire church age so far!

But, again, according to Christ and his apostles in the New Testament, if genetic Jews today fail to find salvation through Christ, they, of course, can never be God's covenant people within the future ages to come.

However, because both Judaism and New Testament Christianity share a common heritage, it is quite common to see that both of these conflicting religions are in spiritual and political support of one another as it concerns their *shared spiritual heritage*. And that's probably one reason why there is strong indication that *most* (meaning over half) New Testament Christians today in America are in support of the nation of Israel, hoping they will find salvation through Christ their Messiah right now, rather than later on in the tribulation period.

Objection 47
I'm Jewish and Believe in the Old Testament Only

However, because *some* professing New Testament Christians (only a minority) have fallen for false doctrines like Replacement Theology which maintains that the physical nation of Israel no longer has its unique place in God's prophetic plans as God's covenant people ever since they helped to crucify Christ their Messiah, they may not support Israel any more than any other nation in the world. In fact, much to their discredit, some such professing Christians tangled in replacement theology may even take a rather anti-Semitic view.

Nevertheless, quite contrary to what replacement theology believers teach, the New Testament clearly teaches that the saved through Christ genetic Jew will continue to hold their unique position as God's covenant people during not only the millennial reign of Christ after his return, but even during the eternal state of mankind which follows. And the saved through Christ genetic Jews will not only be God's covenant people throughout eternity, but also, scripture teaches us that the saved through Christ nation of Israel will actually be the governmental headquarters through which Christ rules and reigns throughout eternity (Matthew 19:28)!

New Jerusalem, as talked about in Revelation chapter 21, is not called New Washington DC for a good reason! Thus, arrogant Gentile Christians today who have already thrown national Israel out of God's prophetic program are indeed in for a major surprise! While replacement theology is a definite heresy which relies heavily on the symbolic method of interpretation, many who believe in it also are tangled in many other heresies born out of the symbolic method of interpretation as well.

> The New Testament clearly teaches that the saved through Christ nation of Israel will continue to be God's covenant people during the millennial reign of Christ and the eternal state of mankind as well.

The origin of Judaism

As we've already mentioned, Judaism, as well as New Testament Christianity, both share the exact same Old Testament history. And quite unlike any other religions in the world, they do not just have a *reliable* historical record which goes all the way back to the beginning of the human race, but also back to the beginning of creation itself. My friend, no other religion in the world even attempts to field such a complete record of human history. And to date, no historian has ever found error in the Bible's genealogical records when cross examining them with other historical records which could confirm or discredit them.

Obviously, no historian doubts human history from our present day back to the time of Christ (when the Roman emperor Tiberius ruled) as there are many genealogical records which would confirm Christ to be roughly 2,000 years ago.

However, you will always have those on the fringe who will even deny obvious historical records which easily validate Christ as a real figure of our history. But because of many nonbiased and even Jewish sources which would confirm otherwise (as we've thoroughly covered in Objection #35), I think we can safely put those who deny Christ as a real historical figure in the same category as those who attempt to deny the Holocaust as a real historical event! The genealogy lists of both the Old and New Testaments combined give us each and every generation from Christ all the way back to Adam and Eve which basically confirms that creation itself is only about 6,000 years old, not 4.5 billion years old as modern evolutionists now claim (see Genesis chapters 5, 10, 11, and Matthew 1:1–17). And even Judaism as a religion does have its list of each and every generation from Abraham back to Adam and Eve in Genesis 5, 10, and 11. However, because Judaism rejects the New Testament and holds only to the Old Testament, only biblical Christianity has the complete inspired chronological list of each and every generation *from Christ* all the way back to Adam and Eve.

Judaism may be able to patch together some of the generations from Christ (who they reject as their Messiah) back to Abraham, but the Old Testament still lacks the inspired consecutive list of each and every generation from Christ back to Abraham which only the New Testament provides. As we've already discussed in Objection #41, our entire genealogy record confirming all of human history back to the beginning of creation is something only unique to biblical Christianity alone!

> Judaism does have its list of each generation from Abraham back to Adam...but only biblical

Objection 47
I'm Jewish and Believe in the Old Testament Only

Christianity has the complete inspired chronological list of each generation from Christ all the way back to Adam and Eve.

Testing Judaism against self-contradictions

Probably one of the biggest self-contradictions within Judaism is its boast of adhering to the Old Testament scriptures, and yet at the same time, those within Judaism completely reject the fact that Christ fulfilled all Old Testament Messianic prophecies with miraculous precision! As we've already mentioned in Objection #36, there are roughly 333 messianic prophecies in the Old Testament, and Christ perfectly fulfilled them all! Thus, any Jew *who really believes the God-breathed Old Testament* must inevitably be *honest* with themselves about who Christ must be according to their own Old Testament prophetic word.

Roughly 2,000 years ago, Christ our creator visited his own creation, died on the cross, and rose again from the dead to prove his deity. By way of a spiritual analogy, Christ could be looked at as a flourishing tree which grew up in the middle of a crop field which represents the nation of Israel. And ever since Christ, it's kind of like the Christ rejecting Jews have been plowing around that flourishing tree in the middle of their crop field, trying their level best to ignore it.

When working in their own field, they have to pass by that flourishing tree in its center all the time, but they just keep denying it's actually there. And just so, when reading their own Old Testament scriptures, those in Judaism have to pass by Christ all the time in their own Messianic prophecies, yet they just keep denying who he really is! Because the Christ-rejecting Jews helped to crucify their own Messiah who was, in fact, the Son of God, it teaches us in Romans 11:1–26 that God then gave them a spiritual *blindness* until the *fullness* of Gentile salvation would be accomplished throughout the church age.

And, sure enough, this is exactly what has happened during the entire church age so far. Just Romans chapter 11 alone (which fully predicts Israel's rejection of Christ throughout the church age) should be powerful evidence to those in Judaism that the New Testament was written by God. There are more than a few biblical realities which actually come to play in all this, but we'll just list a few of the basic ones:

By way of analogy, Christ is like a flourishing tree in the middle of Israel's crop field who Christ-rejecting Jews just keep plowing around and ignore, for when reading the scriptures, those in Judaism have to pass by Christ all the time in their own Messianic prophecies, yet they just keep denying he's there.

1. First of all, God's Word teaches us in passages like 1 Kings 22:1–28 and 2 Thessalonians 2:10–12 that whenever *anyone* continues to reject God or Christ, God will give them just what they want by unleashing the deception of the demonic world upon them so they will actually be spiritually blinded and believe lies instead of the truth! According to God's Word, it doesn't matter whether they be Jews or Gentiles; God ultimately gives men what they persistently want simply because it would not be truly loving for him to do otherwise.
2. Secondly, it teaches in Romans 11:11 that because Israel rejected Christ their Messiah, God not only gave Israel over to a spiritual blindness but also turned toward all Gentile nations with the Gospel to actually make rebellious Israel jealous. And because all the Gentile nations have been partaking of the spiritual covenant through Christ which first of all rightfully belongs only to genetic Israel, many Jews throughout the church age have actually found salvation through Christ and have taken their rightful place of honor in God's New Testament Church.
3. Thirdly, in Matthew 23:34–39, Jesus stated plainly that it wasn't just himself whom Israel rejected, simply because Israel (as a nation) had a long-standing habit of rejecting *almost all the prophets of God* which God sent Israel before Christ (please see 1 Kings 19:10). As Jesus stated, in Matthew 23:34–37:

"[B]ehold, I send unto you prophets, and wise men, and scribes: and some of them ye shall kill and crucify; and some of them shall ye scourge in your synagogues, and persecute them from city to city: that upon you may come all the righteous blood shed upon the earth,

Objection 47
I'm Jewish and Believe in the Old Testament Only

from the blood of the righteous Abel unto the blood of Zacharias son of Barachias, whom you slew between the temple and the alter… O Jerusalem, Jerusalem, thou that kills the prophets, and stones them which are sent unto thee."

Again, in 1 Thessalonians 2:14–16, the Apostle Paul states something similar when he says:

"For ye brethren, became followers of the churches of God which in Judea are in Christ Jesus: for ye also have suffered like things of your own countrymen, even as they have of the Jews: who killed the Lord Jesus, and their own prophets, and have persecuted us; and they please not God, and are contrary to all men: forbidding us to speak to the Gentiles that they might be saved, to fill up their sins always for the wrath of God has come upon them to the uttermost."

Notice that Israel has *not* had a habit of rejecting and killing *false* prophets and *false* men of God but *righteous* men and *prophets of God who were sent by God* unto them throughout the entire Old Testament period. Therefore, historically, it is really God himself which the nation of Israel has constantly rejected and rebelled against because it was even those during Old Testament times whom God sent to represent himself which Israel constantly persecuted and murdered. Thus, since Israel essentially rejected most all the godly prophets throughout their entire history, their rejection of Christ then is just further confirmation that Christ, too, was also from God and the Son of God, just as he claimed and fully demonstrated through many miraculous proofs! So, on one hand, Judaism claims to believe in the Old Testament, but on the other hand, it rebelliously rejected most of the Old Testament godly prophets and Christ whom the Old Testament Messianic scriptures specifically foretell.

Thus, if you are Jewish and holding to Judaism, it is important to understand that it has certainly not just been Jesus whom Judaism has had a problem with: it's most all the men of God and Old Testament prophets which God has sent Israel since it was a nation! This fact is not only thoroughly exposed throughout the Old Testament but other sources which accurately record Jewish history as well. And not only has Israel historically rejected God's prophets, but also, they've worshiped one false heathen god after another while doing so as the two sins went together.

So, if you are Jewish and are still traditionally entrenched in Judaism, why should it be any surprise that Israel as a nation today still largely rejects Jesus as their Messiah when, in fact, they've rejected about every other godly figure in history which God has sent to them? This simple reality should certainly help those in Judaism today to see that their problem has never been Jesus but rather their constant rebellion against God whether we are talking about Old or New Testament times.

> Since Israel also rejected the Godly throughout their entire history, their rejection of Christ then is just further confirmation that Christ too was also from God.

A second contradiction within Judaism today is that it rejects the New Testament, which is their very own New Covenant through Christ. The plain Old Testament history of the nation of Israel clearly reveals that Israel could never begin to even keep all the laws of Moses (and constantly ran after other heathen gods, etc). And that is exactly why according to the New Testament, the Mosaic covenant was largely about proving that no man could actually keep the perfect moral standards of our perfect creator. Thus, the Mosaic law was just intended by God to serve as a *teacher* to bring all mankind to Christ who is, in fact, the only one who could keep all his own moral standards (Galatians 3:24-25).

In fact, collective scripture positively indicates that the covenant which God made through Moses was not an *eternal* covenant because it was clearly a *conditional* agreement between God and the nation of Israel which was essentially dependent upon Israel's human obedience. And because Israel was not obedient within their Mosaic covenant, it must be considered void just on that basis alone. And if the Mosaic covenant is truly void because of Israel's disobedience, then it only makes good sense that God would have to replace it with a new covenant (Christ's sacrifice on the cross) if Israel's very salvation was dependent upon it!

There are actually five major covenants which God made with Israel which we find throughout God's Word. And the first four are all Old Testament covenants, and of those four, only the Mosaic covenant which God made with Israel was not *unconditional* and *eternal* because it was *dependent upon man's performance*. But just to protect against wrong thinking, it should be also mentioned that while all the *eternal*

OBJECTION 47
I'M JEWISH AND BELIEVE IN THE OLD TESTAMENT ONLY

covenants may be *unconditional* themselves (not dependent upon man's performance), we also find in scripture that they may have some blessings attached to them which are indeed *conditional* (and dependent upon man's performance). Nevertheless, please consider the following five major covenants (or agreements) God made with the nation of Israel according to the Old and New Testaments:

1. *The Abrahamic Covenant* (Genesis 17:7, 13, 19; 1 Chron. 16:7; Psalm 105:10): unconditional and eternal. In the unconditional and eternal covenants, God uses the words "I will" in his agreement with Israel.
2. *The Land of Israel Covenant* (Genesis 12:7, 13:15, 17:7–8; Ezekiel 16:60): unconditional and eternal.
3. *The Davidic Covenant* (2 Samuel 23:5; Isaiah 55:3; Ezekiel 37:25): unconditional and eternal.
4. *The Mosaic Covenant* (Exodus 24:3; Deuteronomy 6:25, 7:12, 11:1, 27–28): conditional and meant to be temporary in preparation of the New Covenant. *Unlike the other covenants* which God made with Israel, in the Mosaic covenant, God said, "If you," meaning His agreement with Israel was solely conditioned on the performance of Israel (man and not God).
5. *The New Covenant through Christ* (Isaiah 24:5; Jeremiah 32:40, 50:5; Hebrews 13:20): unconditional and eternal.

The fact that out of all the Old Testament covenants which God made with Israel—only his Mosaic covenant was basically *conditional*—should give us some reasonable credibility to the fact that it was only meant by God to be temporary (just to show man something valuable) and had to be replaced by yet another unconditional covenant which man could not fail through disobedience. And because these *covenants* were just different *agreements* which God had made with Israel for different purposes, it should not be too difficult for Jews today to believe God needed to make one more for all the reasons which even Old Testament scripture gives (please see Isaiah 61:8–9).

Thus, Judaism as a belief system is rather self-contradicting in the sense that it holds to the Mosaic covenant (which the Jews have never been able to keep), while at the same time, it keeps rejecting God's new unconditional covenant through Christ who not only fulfilled all the Mosaic laws of God but also all the Messianic prophecies, just so

Israel could be set free from the impossible! Thus, the New Testament-rejecting Jew today is kind of like someone who is truly drowning but still refuses to grab onto the life-preserver God has thrown them over and over again!

Testing Judaism against the well-known facts of history

As we've already mentioned, Jesus historically fulfilled all the Old Testament Messianic prophecies when he walked the earth. Nevertheless, Judaism today must continue to overlook the most historically reliable ancient document which we possess (the New Testament) in order to continue in their rejection of Christ. In fact, according to historians, the Old Testament technically isn't even as reliable as the New Testament is, even though they are both quite sufficiently reliable. And, yet, Judaism rejects *the more reliable* of the two as a historical record. Thus, Judaism clearly fails this test as well when tested against the well-known facts of history.

Testing Judaism against its prophetic predictions of the future

As we've already mentioned more thoroughly in Objection #36, all 333 Old Testament Messianic prophecies were miraculously fulfilled by Christ. And since Judaism rejects Christ as their Messiah, they must go directly against their own Old Testament prophecies in order to do so. Thus, when tested against their own prophetic predictions of the future, we must conclude that Judaism fails no less than 333 times!

Testing Judaism against the fruit it has produced

While God has blessed Israel ever since 1948, when it became a nation again, there has also been much *trouble* which has surrounded Israel as a nation throughout the entire church age! They were not only scattered all over the world for the better part of the last two millenniums, but God also let them be fiercely persecuted by various Gentile nations throughout the entire church age as well, Hitler's persecution of the Jews just being one more recent example of many which we could cite that cost many Jewish lives.

My point is that according to God's collective Word, all this major persecution and bloodshed of the Jews throughout not only the church age, but also the entire history of Israel, is solely due to the fact that they either went after other false gods or persecuted and killed the

Objection 47
I'm Jewish and Believe in the Old Testament Only

Old Testament *righteous* which God sent them as well as Christ their true Messiah (Matthew 23:37–39)! And the seven-year tribulation is still coming, and according to Scripture, roughly two-thirds of them will actually perish at the hands of the Antichrist (please see Zechariah 13:8–9).

In fact, shortly after Israel rejected Christ as their Messiah, the Roman emperor, Titus, destroyed Jerusalem in AD 70, and over a million Jews perished in the Masada. Even though Christ openly displayed all the divine attributes of God as well as fulfilled all their Messianic prophecies with miraculous precision (Matthew 23:35, 38), the leaders of Israel at the time still persecuted and killed him! And, of course, the honest question for the Jew today is, really, what more could Christ have done to prove he was, in fact, their true Messiah? And when godly men like Stephen stood up and tried to defend Christ as their Messiah, the Jewish leaders murdered him as well as many others like him (please see Acts chapter 7). In Acts 7:52, God inspired Stephen to remind the leaders of Israel of their persecutions and murders with historical accuracy:

> "Which of the (Old Testament) prophets have not your fathers persecuted? And they have slew those who proclaimed beforehand the coming of the Righteous One (Christ), whom you now have betrayed and murdered."

According to God's collective Word, all this major persecution and bloodshed of the Jews is solely due to the fact that they persecuted and killed the Old Testament righteous which God sent them as well as Christ their true Messiah!

And when the Jewish Sanhedrin heard Stephen say this, notice they didn't at all try to deny it because they knew it was the historical truth. Instead, they were so threatened by the truth of it that they just added sin to their past murdering sins and murdered Stephen for speaking the truth. And the New Testament agrees with the Old Testament in that they both prophetically predict that as a consequence, trouble, and persecution of the Jew will continue to be the case right up until Israel as a nation finally recognizes Christ as their true Messiah in the middle of the seven-year tribulation which takes place just before the return of Christ (Zechariah 12:2–3; Jeremiah 30:7; Revelation 12:13).

Thus, according to the collective scriptures of God's Word, it is rather obvious that God has *allowed* Satan and his demonic host to single out and persecute the nation of Israel throughout the entire church age, just because of its rebellious rejection of Christ and his apostles. Wow. You mean if Israel had accepted Christ as their Messiah instead of murdering him, none of their historical bloody persecutions would have happened? Yes, that's exactly what collective scripture teaches us! And not only have millions of Jews lost their lives due to their own rebellion, which brought on this persecution, but historically, the whole world has been negatively impacted and *burdened* by the continued rebellion of Old Testament Judaism, ever since they crucified Christ their own Messiah. And in Zechariah 12:2–3, we read that this negative *burden* on the world will just increase more and more, right up until Christ returns as it says:

> *"Behold I will make Jerusalem a cup of trembling unto all the people round about, when they shall be in the siege both against Judah and against Jerusalem. And in that day will I make Jerusalem a burdensome stone for all people: all that burden themselves with it shall be cut in pieces, though all the people of the earth be gathered together against it."*

And in this great *siege* against Israel in the last days, just before the return of Christ, we once again read in Zechariah 13:8 that roughly *two-thirds* of the nation of Israel will lose their lives in the last days siege, which is considerably worse than even the Masada or Holocaust! However, the good news is that roughly *one-third* of Israel which survives by escaping to their natural fortress Petra will be wise enough to seek the truth in God's word with all their heart and finally recognize Christ as their true Messiah (Revelation chapter 12). God, through the Prophet Daniel, also specifically predicted this when he states in Daniel 12:4, *"[e]ven to the time of the end (of the age): many (of your people Daniel) shall run to and fro, and knowledge (of God's word) shall be increased."*

Nevertheless, despite the good end for one-third of Israel, we must fairly conclude that the overall rebellion of Judaism within its rejection of Christ throughout the entire church age has indeed produced bad fruit and left a wake of destruction behind it. Therefore, the honest question for those Jews today who are still rebelling against Christ (who only proved to be their true Messiah) is: Do you want to continue to be a part of the very violent problem which the last two thousand years of bloody Jewish history bears witness? Or do you want to finally believe in the perfect Christ who very honestly displayed all the divine attributes we'd expect of the Jewish Messiah and take your rightful place of honor within your own God-given eternal covenant?

Conclusion

While Judaism as a belief system does indeed have *some* truth, we must be candid with the fact that according to the New Testament, it cannot represent the *whole truth* and has been *incomplete* and *obsolete* ever since God's new covenant through Christ. If, in fact, believing in Christ is *the only way* of eternal salvation as the New Testament clearly teaches us (Acts 4:12), then it becomes of the utmost importance for all genetic Jews to seek the truth on this matter with all their heart. The truth is that Jews today who dogmatically cling to Judaism must really *want* to know if Christ is their Messiah if they are ever going to see Christ for who he is. And if they really *want* to know if Christ is their true Messiah, then they will *sincerely* seek out the possibility of this critical truth in even their Old Testament with *all their heart*. As the God of Israel has promised in Jeremiah 29:13, *"And ye shall seek me, and find me, when ye shall search for me with all your heart."*

Again, in Deuteronomy 4:29, the God of Israel states, *"[i]f thou shalt seek the Lord thy God, thou shalt find him, if thou seek him with all thy heart and all thy soul."*

> The truth is that Jews today who dogmatically cling to Judaism must really want to know if Christ is their Messiah if they are ever going to see Christ for who he is.

But, obviously, such a promise of God is rather void for those Jews who would only seek God halfheartedly on this issue. And if, in fact, the New Testament's claim is true that the God of Israel in the Old Testament is the very same as the preincarnate Christ (John 1:1–17; 1 Corinthians 10:4, 9; Hebrews 11:24–26), then of course one would simply not find Christ to be God unless they seek him with all their heart, mind, and soul. And this basic reality certainly seems true according to not only many Jews living today who have already come to believe in Christ but also those many Jews who have come to recognize Christ as their Messiah during the entire last 2,000 years! The honest truth is that falsehood and deception has always been so prevalent in our fallen world that unless one seeks out the truth on *any given matter* with all their heart, they will likely be unable to find it!

One of the best ways for Jews to recognize Christ as their true Messiah is of course to study all the Messianic prophecies of the Old Testament. Unfortunately, many Jews just adhere to Judaism today, simply because they've been raised in it and told from an early age that Christ was not their true Messiah. But, as we all know, one is never just grandfathered into the truth through mere blood inheritance. One must always check out what they are taught or raised with to see if it is in fact the actual truth. And for those honest, the honest evidence of the truth must register as such in one's heart, mind, and conscience if one is really going to surrender to it.

But how could any Jew in Judaism today possibly surrender to the honest evidence of Christ being their true Messiah if they never sincerely look at all the Messianic prophecies which confirm it over and over again? Because we have not discussed *all the Old Testament Messianic prophecies*, obviously, a more thorough confirmation that Jesus Christ perfectly fulfilled them cannot be sufficiently accomplished in this short objection or even in our Objections #28 and #36.

Therefore, I would refer you to one of many other good sources called *Evidence* that demands a verdict by Josh McDowell, which provides even more overwhelming evidence that Jesus Christ is, in fact, the son of God and Jewish Messiah. Chapter 9 of Josh McDowell's work specifically shows how Jesus miraculously fulfilled the Messianic prophecies. And, of course, there are many other such books written which also easily confirm Christ as the Jewish Messiah (such as *The Case for Christ* by Lee Strobel).

When honestly examining the Messianic prophecies, it becomes rather difficult for the genetic Jew to *honestly* deny that Christ was, in fact, the true Jewish Messiah when one cannot find even one Messianic prophecy out of the 333 which Christ did not legitimately fulfill! The truth is many Jews have never probably even studied out all the

Objection 47
I'm Jewish and Believe in the Old Testament Only

Messianic prophecies which have proven to be quite powerful in Jewish conversions to Christ throughout the entire church age. If you happen to be a Jew who does not yet know Christ as your Messiah and personal savior, I would encourage you to not only study out the Old Testament Messianic prophecies but also to read a book titled *YESHUA* by Yacov Rambsel which also exposes the fact that Jesus Christ is the Jewish Messiah just through the miraculous Bible codes.

Evidently, over forty names of individuals and places directly associated with the crucifixion of Jesus of Nazareth can be found encoded in the Messianic chapters 52 and 53 of Isaiah, which was written about 700 years before Christ was even born! Another good source which validates Jesus Christ as the Jewish Messiah through the Bible codes is *The Handwriting of God* (chapter 9) by Grant Jeffery. Then, once one has encountered all the overwhelming evidence for Christ being God and the Jewish Messiah in such sources, of course, Matthew, John, Romans, and Hebrews are probably the best books to start reading in the New Testament for those Jews who are sincerely seeking the truth of Jesus Christ being their Messiah.

Since all Jews are not only given a unique place of privilege in God's New Testament Church, but also of course given eternal life through Christ, the neglect of such an awesome salvation would be quite devastating indeed. If you happen to be Jewish without Christ, please know that God loves you very much and has an awesome eternal future for you. And all you really have to do is just give Christ a real chance to prove himself to you! And just as Jesus proved his divinity to the honest soul many times over when he walked the earth, so too is his Word completely trustworthy which foretells the awesome eternity which God has for all those who love him. As Revelation 21:3–4 clearly teaches:

> *"Behold, the dwelling place of God is with men, and he will live with them, and they shall be his people, and God himself shall be with them, and be their God. And God shall wipe away all tears from their eyes; and there shall be no more death, neither sorrow, nor crying, neither shall there be any more pain: for the former things are passed away."*

But the Bible teaches us plainly that *only through Christ* can we obtain God's eternal life (John 14:6). If you are a genetic Jew who knows in your heart that all the Messianic prophecies could not possibly have been fulfilled by any trickery of man and that Jesus must have been just who he always claimed to be and you truly want to be right with God and have his eternal life, I invite you to just take that first small step of faith by sincerely praying the prayer of salvation located at the end of this book. Even if you've been in Judaism for years, you can still break away from that obvious false religion today which threatens your true salvation through Christ. And don't be concerned with what your family members may think of you, because simply put, they will not be you're judge on judgment day! This decision is between you and God (your creator) alone. No matter what your past is like, God loves you and sincerely wants you to be a part of his awesome eternal kingdom!

Jesus said, "I am the resurrection and the life. He who believes in me, will live even though he dies; and whoever lives and believes in me will never die." (John 11:25–26)

OBJECTION 48

I've Been Accused of Being in a Cult, But I'm Not So Convinced Yet

A loving reminder: Before each false belief system we discuss, just so my loving intentions cannot be misunderstood, I will *once again* remind the reader that it's certainly *not the adherents* of any false religion or belief system which the true Church is against, but rather just the *false teachings* within them which deceive men away from the one and only true God and his eternal salvation (Ephesians 6:12). Therefore, my dear reader, please know that our discussion of these various different religions or belief systems is very much a *love* issue.

And as we've already mentioned, when one verifies any false religion simply by way of combing through the honest evidence, it is certainly not to say that there could not be some (or even many in some cases) true believers in Christ within that false religion. However, with that said, if, in fact, there are true believers in Christ within any false religion, it is *despite* their official doctrines, not *because* of them! And to be sure, God would have such a true believer in Christ leave that false religion before they lose their own stability in Christ (Romans 16:17; 1 Corinthians 5:11–13; 2 Corinthians 6:14; Galatians 5:19–21; 1 Timothy 6:3–11; 2 Timothy 3:2–5; Titus 3:9–11).

A Christian cult

A Christian cult is simply a false religious group that claims to be Bible-based (or Christian) but is not because its teachings and doctrines (especially as it concerns the issue of salvation) clearly conflict with the Bible's teachings. However, it is interesting to note that many false religions which reject the main correct teachings and doctrines of the Bible often hypocritically use what scriptures they can from the Bible, just so they can deceive and *appear* more credible. But, reasonably, if their false religion is really the one true faith, why on earth do they even need to *borrow* any scriptures or doctrines from the Holy Bible at all, especially if they have their own books which they deem more *accurate* than the Bible? I can assure you biblical Christianity does not borrow teachings and doctrines from any other religion which contradicts it!

Also, when we consider that all false religions are ultimately hatched by the demonic realm for the sole purpose of deceiving men away from the one true God and his eternal salvation (1 Timothy 4:1), then everything makes sense as we can then see why Satan has to steal *some* truth from God's Word in order to accomplish his devious ends of deception.

Another reality is that *some* cult members often *profess* that they were once a Bible-believing Christian which, if true, may also explain why so many *Christian cults* tend to borrow from the Bible, just to appear more credible. Unfortunately, in such cases, it would seem that those adhering to a cult *after* they fell away from biblical Christianity could have been tested out of the one true faith in some way or another (1 Timothy 4:1–2). However, many who are tangled up in a Christian cult are also often there because they either ignorantly married into it or they are ignorantly born into it.

While it is clearly understood that many within the different conflicting religions of the world are born into it, and thus, emotionally attached to it through family members, we must once again be honest enough to acknowledge the simple fact that no man can really be *just* born into the spiritual truth or grandfathered into heaven. No, we all must take personal responsibility to objectively comb through the honest evidence which confirms the truth of reality and also be honest with ourselves as we do that. Thus, the saying:

Objection 48
I've Been Accused of Being in a Cult, But I'm Not So Convinced Yet

> We are not born winners, we are not born losers, but we are born choosers.

And, yet, as we've also already mentioned in Objection #19, many others are just attracted to cults for things like money, importance, immoral sex, drugs, etc. Nevertheless, the truth remains that none of these reasons are good ones for staying in what we will call a *Christian cult*. And because one's eternal salvation is truly threatened in a cult of any kind, this is what makes them so dangerous, not to mention cults generally spoil man's concept of who God really is. Ironically, while cults will insist you cannot obtain eternal life unless you belong to their particular fellowship, just the opposite is true. For according to the clear teachings of the Holy Bible, one simply cannot obtain the eternal life of God if they truly believe in a Christian cult which traffics in major false doctrines (1 Timothy 4:1–2, 16; 2 Peter 2:1–9)!

> Many false religions which reject the main correct teachings of the Bible often hypocritically use what scriptures they can from the Bible just so they can deceive and appear more credible.

In Objection #19, we've already discussed many selfish reasons for people to stay in a false religion which just exposes man's moral failure. But if you really want the truth in your heart, and you really want to know your one and only true creator and you really love your family members, then you'll *honestly* compare the doctrines you are being taught with the Bible yourself and leave the cult you are in with good reason. Because, let's face it, you won't help (or love) your family members at all by staying in the deception with them and living the lie with them that everything is a-okay, and everyone in the cult is heaven-bound! As the saying goes:

> It is difficult enough to discover the spiritual truth when you really want to know just what it is. But if you really do not want to know the truth, then your ability to find it is greatly decreased.

Of course, not all false religions or belief systems in the world claim to be Christian or Bible-based, so they would not be considered a

Christian cult, but those that do are considered Christian cults and are generally more deceptive than all other false religions simply because they are closer to the truth of the Holy Bible. If you want to know if you are in a cult or even under real cultic influence, it's really not that difficult to determine if you know just what to look for!

Listed below are forty-six different questions which will easily help you determine once and for all whether or not you are being deceived by wolves in sheep's clothing in a cult of some kind (see Matthew 7:15). But, of course, once again, the critical issue is answering the following questions with *sincere honesty*.

> Ironically, while cults will insist you cannot obtain eternal life unless you belong to their particular fellowship, just the opposite is true, for according to the Bible, one simply cannot obtain eternal life if they believe in a cult which traffics in major false doctrines.

Defining a Christian Cult

Want to know if you are in a cult? Does the church, fellowship, or organization you attend:

1. *Teach that your salvation or eternal life is even partially obtained through human performance of any kind?* According to the Bible, good works should, of course, be a natural *result* of genuine saving faith as one has opportunity (James 2:14–18). But never does the New Testament teach us that our good works are a *cause* of genuine saving faith (Ephesians 2:8–9; Romans 3:20–23, 1:17; Mark 10:18)! And, let's be honest, there is a big difference between the *result* of one's salvation and the *cause* of it because one gives glory to God, and the other gives glory to man. When human works are added to the saving Gospel message, we simply cannot obtain eternal life through it, no matter how good we might think our works are (Galatians 1:6–9, 5:4–5; 1 Timothy 4:16)!

When we try to add our good works to what Christ did for us on the cross, we're essentially saying that what Christ did on the cross was

Objection 48
I've Been Accused of Being in a Cult, But I'm Not So Convinced Yet

simply not good enough to save us from our sins and he needed our help! However, Christ clearly stated that the work of man's salvation was completely *finished* on the cross as he said, "*It is finished*" just before he died (John 19:28–30).

2. *Teach that the salvation of man comes through anyone other than Christ?* The Bible clearly teaches us that there is only *one way* to obtain God's eternal life, and that's *his* way by believing his perfect Son, Jesus, took the punishment *for all our sins* on the cross (Acts 4:12; John 14:6; 1 Timothy 2:5; Romans 10:9–10). Any organization which would teach otherwise should definitely be avoided.

3. *Heavily emphasize the teachings of one particular person or group of persons (other than Christ and his apostles)?* Christ proved who he was through the miraculous power of God hundreds of times over, and that's why the Church was built on Christ, and his chosen apostles who also walked in the miraculous power Christ gave them (Matthew 11:2–6). A good pastor or church leader will always teach you to be dependent upon Christ and not themselves or any other mere human being plagued with a sin nature. We should not be dependent upon any fallible man, but only God who is perfect and the teachings of his Word (Colossians 2:3–4; 1 Timothy 6:20–21). There are, of course, Bible teachers in Christ's Church we should learn from (Ephesians 4:11; 1 Timothy 5:17), but no man has any need to be taught by men who are teaching their brand of spirituality which is extrabiblical (1 John 2:27).

4. *Have extra books, pamphlets, etc. other than the Holy Bible which contain extrabiblical teachings that must be believed in order have the full truth, to belong to the true faith, or have eternal life?* The Holy Bible clearly teaches that it is not only the infallible word of the living God (1 Thessalonians 2:13; 2 Peter 1:20–21) but that it is *complete* for all man's spiritual needs, especially salvation (2 Timothy 3:16–17; John 8:31–32). If any organization *adds to* God's Word through other so-called inspired materials or books, according to the Bible itself, they put

themselves in the place of God and endanger their own salvation (Deuteronomy 4:2 12:32; Proverbs 30:5–6; Revelation 22:18–19)!

5. *Teach any other doctrines (or teachings) than those contained within the Holy Bible?* Doctrines are actually mentioned in the New Testament about forty-five times! They are a serious issue because they have everything to do with the *authority of God in our hearts.* Even what some may consider *nonessential* doctrines can affect one's *salvation* because they still change the word of God and are still a rebellion against his authority (1 Timothy 4:1–3; Revelation 22:18–19). If any organization rejects true biblical doctrine, they are really in rebellion against God himself and are basically usurping his authority, putting themselves in the place of God (1 Timothy 4:6,16, 6:3–5; 2 Timothy 4:3–4). False doctrines most often come from the symbolic method of interpretation which attempts to change God's Word through man's private interpretations. But since the Bible itself plainly teaches us that "*no prophecy of scripture is of man's private interpretation*" (2 Peter 1:20), true biblical doctrines will always come from the basic literal method of interpretation which, of course, still recognizes symbolisms within God's Word whenever it is obvious, even though it always rejects man's *private interpretations* of scripture.

6. *Teach that the Tribulation period of Revelation already took place back in Church history?* Since these false teachings essentially get rid of the future tribulation period which Revelation so clearly teaches about, they, too, are *subtracting* from God's Word. Both Preterists and Historicists teach that the Tribulation period, either in its entirety or in part, already happened back in Church history. However, verses like Revelation 22:18 simply make this impossible because according to Gods clear warning in it, those who *add to* God's Word today must still be able to have *all the plagues or judgments* of Revelation's tribulation added to them. But if they already happened back in the history

Objection 48
I've Been Accused of Being in a Cult, But I'm Not So Convinced Yet

of the church age, then, of course, they could not still be added to any violators today.

Thus, Revelation 22:18 only makes sense with a future tribulation and a pre-Tribulation rapture when carefully contemplated. Preterism and Historicism are both heretical doctrines which threaten the salvation of those believing in them because they boldly *subtract* from God's Word and essentially undercut his authority by doing so. According to Revelation 22:18–19, the obvious consequences for adding and subtracting to God's Word is the loss of salvation for those who do not repent from it as it plainly states:

"For I testify unto every man that hears the words of the prophecy of this book, if any man (in the entire church age) shall add unto these things, God shall add unto him the plagues (or judgments) that are written in this book: And if any shall take away from the words of the book of this prophecy, God shall take away his part out of the book of life, and out of the holy city, and from the things which are written in this book."

7. *Teach that the New Testament Church takes over the national covenant promises that God made to the nation of Israel in the Old Testament?* Often, such replacement theology churches will teach that everywhere you see "Israel" in the New Testament, it really means the "Church," and the physical nation of Israel no longer has a place in God's prophetic plans ever since Christ died on the cross. However, this too is subtracting from God's Word as it not only erases the physical nation of Israel from God's future plans, but it causes God to be a liar as he would have to betray all his national covenant promises which he made with the nation of Israel in Old Testament times!

Yes, spiritually, the Gentile Church does *partake* of Israel's spiritual new covenant in Christ. In this sense, the Gentile part of the New Testament Church is spiritual Israel. However, Romans chapters 10–11 (and many other verses) make it clear that the Gentile part of the Church is just grafted into Israel's spiritual new covenant because the New Testament still maintains a clear distinction between the born-again physical nation of Israel part of the Church and the born-again Gentile part of the Church.

8. *Teach that all unbelievers just get annihilated or burned up into nonexistence and do not undergo eternal punishment in the lake of fire?* Since this false doctrine of *annihilation* actually removes eternal punishment hell from God's Word, it too subtracts from God's Word and is an obvious heresy. Many verses like John 3:36, Matthew 25:46, 2 Thessalonians 1:9, Daniel 12:2, Jude 1:7, and Mark 9:43 all make it quite clear that punishment for all unbelievers is *eternal* as it often directly contrasts the *eternal* punishment of unbelievers with the *eternal* life for all believers (Galatians 6:8). And one of the main reasons that all Christ-rejecting unbelievers must undergo eternal punishment is because even after they enter hell, they just keep sinning against God whose perfect justice must continue to be satisfied against their continuing sin.

Even though the Scriptures are clear that God has no pleasure at all in the eternal punishment of the wicked (Ezekiel 18:23, 32), they essentially force his hand as his perfect justice gives him no choice in the matter whatsoever. The doctrine of annihilation is a heretical doctrine which compromises the perfect justice and character of God. It threatens the salvation of those believing it simply because it boldly *subtracts* eternal punishment hell from God's Word and undercuts the very authority of God himself (Revelation 22:18–19).

9. *Teach amillennialism, that the millennial reign of Christ is just symbolic of Christ reigning right now spiritually through the Church and not a literal future time wherein Christ bodily returns to earth to reign for a literal 1,000 years?* Acts 3:19–21 makes this false doctrine (as well as post-millennialism) impossible as it clearly teaches that heaven must bodily receive Christ *until* the millennial reign of Christ on earth and the eternal state of man or the *time(s) of restitution of all things.* Because amillennialism essentially removes the literal millennial reign of Christ from God's Word, it too is heretical and threatens the eternal salvation of those believing and teaching it (Revelation 22:18–19).

Objection 48
I've Been Accused of Being in a Cult, But I'm Not So Convinced Yet

10. *Teach that there is no such thing as a literal rapture resurrection of the Church?* Often, those who hold to the false teachings of amillennialism, historicism, and preterism also reject a literal rapture resurrection for the Church altogether. This, too, is *subtracting* from God's Word and is a heresy which can threaten salvation because of it (Revelation 22:18–19). There are so many scriptures like Matthew 24:36–44, 1 Thessalonians 4:15–18, and 1 Corinthians 15:50–52, which plainly describe a literal rapture event for the Church that one has to over symbolize many scriptures of God's Word in order to get rid of it. Additionally, many verses like Luke 21:34–36, Revelation 3:10, and Revelation 22:18 even teach us plainly that the Church will be raptured out of this world before the seven-year Tribulation of Revelation hits, which is called a *pre-*Tribulation rapture.
11. *Teach that their specific church or organization title (or name) is the only true church?* According to the Bible, there is only one true faith because there is only one true God, which only makes sense (Ephesians 4:5–6). And there is only one true Church, which was pardoned by Christ's sacrifice on the cross. However, God's spiritual true Church is defined by all those who believe Christ fully paid for their sins on the cross (which is the largest unified faith in the world, making up about 30 percent of the world's population). But it may attend many different church buildings which all have different titles (or names) on their church building. Their doctrines just must check out with the clear teachings of the Holy Bible itself, but they may have different names.

Nowhere in the Bible will you find that the true Church has to have a single specific name because the true Church is not defined by a specific name; it is defined by biblical doctrine. Therefore, any church which truly believes in biblical doctrine, no matter which specific title hangs above its door is, in fact, part of the true Church according to the Bible.

12. *Teach that their particular denomination is the only true church?* Technically, according to the Bible, there are no *denominations* in the true Church or body of Christ. You will never see denominations taught anywhere within the New Testament, and thus, they are all man-made concepts. Most denominations are simply named after men who did not even intend to start them. Examples would be the Lutheran church which was named after Martin Luther and the Baptist church which was named after John the Baptist. But no matter what the denomination was named or how it got started, because their particular denomination name cannot even be found in the Bible as the only title of the true church, they certainly do not have the authority to teach that their particular denomination is the only true Church and salvation cannot be found outside it (1 Corinthians 1:11–17).

Ironically, insisting that one must belong to their particular denomination in order to secure salvation is exactly what would make that denomination a cult which endangers one's salvation! Of course, not all denominations are cults, but the Roman Catholic religion would be a good example of a so-called denomination which actually insists that one must belong only to it for true salvation to be secured. However, most other true denominations do not insist that one must belong to them in order for salvation to be secured.

Examples of these true Church denominations, which are not *typically* cults, are Baptist, Lutheran, Methodist, Episcopal, Church of the Nazarene, etc. But, again, one must specifically look at their salvation doctrines to finally determine which particular churches of even a given denomination are a cult and which are not. For example, some Lutheran churches still believe that water baptism and communion are actually essential for salvation, showing that they never really made a clean enough break from the Roman Catholic religion. Thus, according to the Bible itself, they would still technically be a cult which traffics in salvation threatening heresies (Ephesians 2:8–9, Titus 3:5, Romans 11:6; Galatians 1:6–8; John 10:1).

All this having been said, denominations which are cults (like the Roman Catholic religion) generally do not only insist that you belong

Objection 48
I've Been Accused of Being in a Cult, But I'm Not So Convinced Yet

to their particular denomination to secure your salvation, but they also typically insist that salvation must be earned in part through many good works of man. They may also contain many other false doctrines which the Holy Bible simply does not teach in any way. For example, you will not even find the word or the concept of a pope taught in the entire New Testament! In fact, the Roman Catholic religion itself didn't even believe in popes (or many of its other strange doctrines) until centuries after it started!

13. *Have a chain of churches with a certain person (or group of persons) at its head which claim to be God's only true apostles or prophets?* Just because someone claims to be an apostle or prophet doesn't mean they are one. Don't be fooled! The Apostle Paul actually said that his apostleship was proved to the Corinthian church because the "*signs of an apostle were wrought among*" the Corinthians "*in all patience, in signs, and wonders, and mighty deeds.*" Often in *Christian cults,* deceiving demonic spirits work through false prophets and apostles, but those false prophets and apostles do not even display any real supernatural power to prove who they say they are (Matthew 7:15–23; 2 Corinthians 11:13–15). In fact, if there is a *heavy constant emphasis* on apostles and prophets (which display no real supernatural power to back them up), this too may be a sign that you are in a cult.

14. *Have leadership which openly claims that no other church has the special revelation of God which they have?* Pride goes before destruction (Proverbs 16:18), and according to the Bible, spiritual pride is the worst in the sight of God.

15. *Have leadership which operate in a secret or semi-secret manner and act above all else who attend because only they have an "in" with God?* Anyone can claim or act like they are close to God by saying, "The Spirit showed me" because there is no way to argue with what God supposedly told them. However, since it was the Holy Spirit who wrote God's Word, you can check out everything they are saying and teaching with God's Word, and if the Spirit of God really is working through them, then their teachings certainly

should check out with God's Spirit-inspired Word! We are to test the spirits (1 John 4:1). If what you are being taught does not check out with God's Word, then such leaders are just walking in pride and self-deception (Proverbs 16:18), and you need to leave that false fellowship!

16. *"Teach that you should not use your mind to understand the deep spiritual truths of God which they impart to you but that you should just learn to accept and experience the reality of God in the way they teach you?"* Verses like Matthew 22:37, 2 Timothy 2:15, John 8:31–32, and Acts 17:11 make it clear that all Christians should use their own mind and check out all things they are being taught with the Holy Bible.

17. *Heavily emphasize the Spirit of God over the Word of God and good doctrine?* Many cults seek experience instead of truth. But the truth of God's Word is the best experience because only it sets us free (John 8:31–32)! Again, since the Holy Spirit wrote God's Word, any so-called revelation of the Spirit should never conflict with the clear teachings of God's Word. Knowing the Word of God ensures we will not be deceived by other seducing spirits (Psalm 119:105; 1 Timothy 4:1–2; 2 Timothy 3:16–17; 2 Corinthians 11:13–15). Anyone can claim God is with them using the Holy Spirit (in an isolated way without the Word of God). But if God is with them, they should often cite God's Word to back up what they are saying or teaching (Psalm 119:105; 2 Timothy 3:16–17)! And remember always that if church leaders are not teaching from a *literal method of interpretation*, then their teachings should not be trusted!

18. *Tell you that you should earnestly pray about the things they teach you (rather than pray and seek the truth from the Bible), and if they are true, you will receive an inner witness or an assurance within yourself?* It is true that an inner witness can come from the Spirit of God within the true believer (Colossians 3:15). However, once again, the Spirit and the Word of God will always be in harmony with each other.

Objection 48
I've Been Accused of Being in a Cult, But I'm Not So Convinced Yet

For if they are not, it is always the spirit which is wrong, not only because there can be deceiving demonic spirits but because the Word of God (which is to be interpreted literally unless symbolism is obvious) is God's primary revelation to us so we won't be deceived (Psalm 119:105)!

19. *Teach that you need to regularly attend special meetings where certain God-appointed prophets and apostles tell the Church just what God is doing in the Church and what his will is for the Church?* There should be no big mystery as to just what God wants his Church to do. The great commission was the Church's last commission, and that is quite enough to keep us all busy (Matthew 28:18–20). Just how the Church chooses to share the Gospel, the New Testament never prescribes a set way to do it, other than accurately and in love using the gifts God has given you. If Church leaders insist on a certain way, saying others are not in God's will using other ways, then they walk in pride and go against scripture (Mark 9:38-40).

20. *Put constant pressure on you to attend their organization several times a week and to give finances and service in order to be considered a member in good standing?* First of all, technically, church membership itself is not even biblical! The Bible teaches us plainly that when we are *born again* (with a spiritual birth; John 3:3), we automatically become *members* of Christ's Church (1 Corinthians 12:12–27). Secondly, when church leaders constantly push you to give money to be a member in good standing, that is the sin of extortion (1 Corinthians 6:10; *extortioners* will not inherit the kingdom of God). Thirdly, we must always remember that Christ's *yoke is easy and his burden is light* (Matthew 11:28)! The religious Pharisees heaped heavy burdens on people, but they were not even true believers as they played a major role in crucifying Christ.

21. *Have a pastor or prophet with an angry spirit who constantly displays anger in their sermons to influence you to do what they want* (Proverbs 22:24; James 1:20)? In order to keep letting yourself be abused in this manner, you have to be a

willing participant. The Bible calls men to *"speak the truth in love, gentleness, kindness,* and in *joy"* (Ephesians 4:15; Galatians 5:22; 2 Timothy 2:24). If your pastor is always angry when preaching, leave. You don't deserve that kind of spiritual abuse. Such preaching can give people the false impression that God is that way, but please know that he is not! Christ was gentle, meek, kind, and never raised his voice in any loud angry manner (Isaiah 42:2–3).

22. *Have leaders who require that all members be discipled or shepherded to the degree that they are constantly guiding you in your personal life (who you should marry, what car you should buy, what job to get, etc.)?* Nowhere in the New Testament do we see even one example of the apostles or pastors having say over the personal lives of those in their spiritual care, telling them who to marry or what donkey to buy, etc.! New Testament Church leaders never tried to use God's Word to manipulate the personal lives of others; they were only concerned about spiritual matters!

23. *Tell you that if you should you leave their fellowship that you will backslide, fall into Satan's hands, become ill, get divorced, or have some other evil befall you?* If this is the case, then I would certainly test their theory and leave! Nowhere in Scripture do church leaders teach such threatening and controlling things. The Church is commanded to fellowship in a Bible-believing Church, but as soon as leadership would say anything like that, they prove they are not Bible-believing right there. Just the opposite is true: if you were to stay in such a threatening Church, then you just might fall into Satan's hands!

24. *Teach that you must love each other (within their organization) but must hate God's enemies (outside their fellowship), implying that only you, as part of their particular group, are on God's side?* Those who do not love man whom they do see cannot love God whom they do not see (1 John 4:20). Those who do not love do not know God, for God is love (1 John 4:8).

Objection 48
I've Been Accused of Being in a Cult, But I'm Not So Convinced Yet

25. *Teach that there may be other true believers in the world, but since they are not part of your particular group that they are in darkness, confusion, Babylon, sin, etc.?* Do such cult leaders want everyone in the professing church to crowd into their church building so they won't be in darkness? How very narrow and completely unrealistic! I'm afraid just the opposite is true; these cult leaders are actually in the spiritual darkness, which they have pronounced for others. As Jesus said: *"Judge not, that you be not judged. For with what judgment you judge, you shall be judged: and with what measure you mete, it shall be measured to you"* (Matthew 7:1–2).

26. *Teach that if you are faithful to their true church, you will find special favor with God which will in turn spare you from the Great Tribulation or from any other harm?* Scripture does clearly teach a pre-Tribulation rapture, but that is the case no matter which particular Bible-believing church you attend (Revelation 22:18; Luke 21:34–36). No particular Bible-believing church has dibs on the pre-Tribulation rapture! However, any such threats are not of God and should make the door of their church look better and better! Just walk out of it and find a healthy Bible-believing church.

27. *Teach that if you are faithful or keep the laws of God's Word, you will one day come to possess his nature in the sense that you will become a god?* Such a teaching not only puts one under the law in order to please God but also goes directly against God's first commandment: *"Thou shall have no other gods before me"* (Exodus 22:3). Only faith in Christ (not our own abilities) pleases God (Hebrews 11:6). As a general rule, most all false religions tend to lower God down to man's level and/or raise man up to God's level. However, the reality is that both God's thoughts and ways are higher than ours as high as the heavens are above the earth (Isaiah 55:8–9)!

28. *Teach that you should disregard your own opinions and assume the opinions of your leaders because they are more learned in*

spiritual matters or because their opinions are given in your best interest? Never just take someone's word for their own spirituality. They must demonstrate it by displaying the fruits of the spirit and have a deep understanding of God's Word, which first and foremost includes not teaching false doctrines (Galatians 5:22–23; 1 Timothy 4:6, 5:17; 2 Timothy 2:15). See also the biblical qualifications for leadership (1 Timothy 3:1–13).

29. *Require that you tithe or give money in order to be a member in good standing? First of all,* as we've already mentioned, Church membership is not even in the New Testament because as soon as we are born again, we become members of Christ's Church through spiritual adoption. *Secondly*, if a church has to have something like membership, it is certainly not connected with financial giving anywhere in the New Testament! *Thirdly*, the whole concept of *tithing* was actually only an Old Testament custom, specifically observed by the nation of Israel. In fact, nowhere in the New Testament is the Church specifically commanded to *tithe*, which means to give exactly a tenth of your income to the Church! To the contrary of such a law, the New Testament Church is called to only give from their heart (2 Corinthians 9:7).

Hebrews briefly talks about *tithing* in one place, but Paul there is referring to what saints (like Abraham) did in the Old Testament; he's not commanding the New Testament Church to tithe! If the New Testament Church was to give precisely 10 percent (tithe), then undoubtedly, we would see more than one obvious command of God to that affect within the New Testament! And if the Church is called to tithe, then why shouldn't we be called to perform all of Israel's other ordinances as well, like keeping the Sabbath, etc.?

But Paul also makes it clear that keeping the Sabbath has changed from Old Testament to New Testament times (Romans 14:5–6), and the Church is not to be under the law *in any area* because the Mosaic covenant that God had with the nation of Israel is replaced by God's new covenant of grace! The truth is God wants Church leaders to be dependent upon the Holy Spirit to put the amount of giving on the

Objection 48
I've Been Accused of Being in a Cult, But I'm Not So Convinced Yet

hearts of each person in his Church. If a Church leader cannot trust God enough to let those in his fellowship hear from God themselves on this issue of giving and has to always push the 10 percent giving, then there is a definite weakness of faith there!

Since the doctrine of tithing uses the Old Testament law to guilt people into giving, this practice can definitely be considered extortion for those Church leaders who secretly just want more money for themselves by constantly pushing 10 percent giving (1 Corinthians 6:10). We can be sure God knows the secrets of a man's heart, but regardless, when Church leaders push 10 percent, giving which is unbiblical in the New Testament, it's not a good sign. If your pastor does that, challenge him to give you one obvious *New Testament* verse which clearly teaches God's Church to do that! Please know that quite often, cults use Old Testament verses (which were intended only for the nation of Israel in Old Testament) to put their members under the law and control them.

30. *Teach that you should stop thinking as an individual and start thinking corporately, following the will of the leaders or the will of God as defined by your church leaders?* According to the New Testament, the Church is the spiritual family of God, or the *body of Christ*, but it's never a business! Unfortunately, the American Church tends to struggle more with treating the Church as a business, just because our American culture has been all about big business. But the Church must avoid this big business mentality completely, just like it needs to avoid greed and extortion because that's what it leads to.

31. *Teach that you should be willing to sacrifice everything in order to please God as defined by your leadership?* Make sure your leadership is leading by example. All too often, abusive cult church leadership calls its members to sacrifice while they do not make the same sacrifices because they directly benefit from your sacrifice. For example, more than one house has been built in the name of God by cult members for cult leadership! But rarely do cult leaders actually help build houses for all of its members!

32. *Teach you that you should shun those who leave the group and give them certain labels?* As we've already mentioned, those who do not love man whom they do see cannot claim to love God whom they do not see (1 John 4:20). And nowhere in the New Testament are we constrained to any certain church or fellowship. We have freedom in Christ; the main thing is that you attend a Bible-believing church. What if you had to move out of state for some reason? Did any of the apostles always attend the exact same fellowship? Certainly not. In fact, many times, they were in prison for their faith and could not even attend church at all! God is not so narrow or unwise as to command you to attend a certain fellowship group the rest of your life, my friend; it's just not biblical.

33. *Encourage you to cover up or ignore the sins of your church leaders, but tattle-tale to the leaders on the sins of the members?* "Do unto others as you'd have them do unto you" (Matthew 7:12). God shows no partiality in the Church (Romans 2:11). All those in the body of Christ should have the same care, one for another (1 Corinthians 12:25). Such partiality is definitely the mark of cultic leadership.

34. *Teach that the true Church has not functioned rightly since the first century and, therefore, must be restored through your leader's new truths?* According to the Bible, the *times of restoration* are not *until* Christ returns bodily to earth to set up his millennial reign (Acts 3:19–21). Anyone teaching that the *times of restoration* are right now are not only going against God's Word but must also be pretty disappointed! If your leadership teaches this, please leave that group you are in, and trust me, you won't be disappointed.

35. *Have leadership which claims that only their particular teachings will usher in the kingdom of God?* Christ alone already ushered in the *spiritual* kingdom of God when he came the first time (Matthew 4:17). And he will usher in the kingdom of God *politically* when he comes the second time (Revelation 11:15). He just wants his Church

Objection 48
I've Been Accused of Being in a Cult, But I'm Not So Convinced Yet

to preach the Gospel in some way, love others into the kingdom, and *occupy* till he comes again (Luke 19:13).

36. *Stress the idea of covenants, teaching that if you do not remain in covenant with the leadership, then you are out of covenant with God?* According to the Bible, all of God's covenants are with the nation of Israel only (Romans 10–11). The Gentile part of the Church may be grafted into Israel's new covenant *in the spiritual sense*, but there is no New Testament teaching which even remotely indicates that the members of God's Church should be in some kind of a covenant with its leaders. Please find it. I'll give you a million dollars if you can!

37. *Use the concept of sowing your seed, teaching that the more you give financially to their church, the more you are going to reap a harvest?* True, as it concerns our giving to God, there is a New Testament verse which teaches us that *"He which sows sparingly, shall reap also sparingly; and he which sows bountifully shall reap also bountifully"* (2 Corinthians 9:6). But the very next verse 7 says, *"Let every man give according as he purposes in his heart not grudgingly or of necessity: for God loves a cheerful giver."*

In other words, we are not under the law; we are to operate from love in our hearts when we give! We shouldn't give because we are constantly guilted into it or poked and prodded to do so by prosperity teachers who are just lining their own pockets. Additionally, there is nothing in the New Testament telling us that our financial giving to God has to be to a certain fellowship which preaches more on financial giving than it does about Jesus! *Extortioners* will not inherit the kingdom of God (1 Corinthians 6:10). If any organization or teacher talks more about financial giving than it does Jesus, please leave that organization so you don't find out ten years later and many dollars later that you've been had.

38. *Teach that the Church is literally some sort of ongoing embodiment of God himself?* No, the Church is not God nor is God the Church. Yes, by way of analogy only, Paul says the Church is the *body of Christ*, simply because Christ is the spiritual *head* of it (1 Corinthians 12:12–27;

Ephesians 4:15–16). But all throughout the Bible, God maintains a clear distinction between the creator and us the created (Romans 1:25). All men are *made in God's image*, but that's all. Nor does that imply the created was somehow blended into becoming the creator (Isaiah 43:10, 45:6–8). If the group you are attending blurs these lines of distinction between man and his creator, I would strongly encourage you to leave. Trust me, no matter how many good works you do, you will never be divine!

39. *Concentrate their teachings on just one or a few subjects and ignore the rest of the Bible?* Balance of the whole Word is important. God gave us his whole Word for a reason (2 Timothy 3:16–17; Matthew. 4:4) because it is actually needed! Any fellowship which simply does not teach the whole Word of God (which even includes end-time Bible prophecy) is out of balance or *may* be a cult or have cultic tendencies.

If a pastor refuses to teach on end-time Bible prophecy, then it is probably because they themselves cannot figure out the biblical truth in that area. And if they cannot discern truth from error concerning end-times, then that, too, is a red flag. It may not automatically mean that you are in a cult, but it may mean that in time, that pastor will eventually fall prey to false doctrines in that area. If that happens, the salvation of those they are teaching will be endangered.

40. *Have a clergy-laity mentality that keeps the congregation to the status of mere pew warmers with the leaders effectively operating as a priesthood through whom God speaks?* According to the New Testament, all those in the body of Christ are equally considered a *royal priesthood* (1 Peter 2:9; Revelation 20:6). Other than that, there is nothing in the New Testament which indicates that Church leadership have their own *priesthood*. The term *laity* cannot even be found in the Bible. All these ideas are Roman Catholic inventions which just served to control people during the Middle Ages so they could abuse the biblically ignorant common people through extortion. All should be on the same level in God's Church because we are all saved by

Objection 48
I've Been Accused of Being in a Cult, But I'm Not So Convinced Yet

grace alone, and truly, no one is any better than others (1 Corinthians 12:25)!

41. *Have a board of elders who operate as mere puppets for the head pastor?* Again, what good is a board of elders if they can't hold the pastor(s) accountable to God's Word? Clearly, even the apostles of the New Testament held each other accountable (Galatians 2:11–13). If elders are just pushovers which follow the pastor blindly, then they are simply loving *man* or *money* more than God!

42. *Have its visions always coming from a single person (pastor, apostle, or prophet) who sets the direction for the whole fellowship?* Again, it is essential for any church (if it is large enough) to have a board of elders which can hold the head pastor accountable to God's Word. Whenever the word *vision* is used in the New Testament, it referred to the apostles (or some godly man) receiving a real supernatural *vision* from God.

For example, when the Apostle Peter received a vision from God in Acts 10:9–33, he literally *fell into a trance* to receive it from God (v. 10). He didn't just have a personal thought which he believed was from God; it was a completely supernatural event wherein God literally communicated with Peter." All too often, cult groups just throw around biblical terms like "vision," saying, "God gave me a vision." Or if they are always saying, "*God spoke to me*," you probably should suspect the leadership of cultic tendencies, especially if their *vision* or *God speaking to them* concerns specific instructions for you and what you should do in your personal life.

43. *Have leadership whose beliefs or teachings cannot be challenged with the Holy Bible?* As we've already mentioned, even Christ's apostles all challenged each other if they needed to (2 Timothy 3:16–17; Galatians 2:11–14). If you can't question the teachings of your leadership with plain scripture without them getting upset, you are definitely in a cult. Or if they just don't heed the plain teachings of the Bible when you do challenge them, then you are also probably in a cult.

44. *Teach that Jesus was or is an angel or anything else other than the one and only true creator God of all things within the trinity Godhead?* As we've already mentioned, it's helpful to know that, generally speaking, all false religions bring God down lower than what he is and raise man up higher than what he is. For example, the Jehovah's Witnesses teach that Jesus was just Michael, the Archangel, and a god while the Mormons teach that we can actually become a god (Philippians 2:6–8; 1 Peter 5:6). However, Jesus was just who he said he was. He was fully God in human form, nothing less. It is true that when Jesus came to earth in the form of a man that he was fully human (Galatians 4:4; Hebrews 4:15). However, when he humbly became a man for our sake, he also retained 100 percent of his divinity and remained sinless the whole time (John 1:14; Colossians 2:9). If the organization you attend teaches that Jesus is anyone else other than God Almighty in the New Testament and God incarnate in the Old Testament, please leave that group because you are not in a real church!

45. *Teach that water baptism, baptism in the Spirit, or Communion is essential for salvation?* Jesus said to the thief on the cross that believed in him, "*Today, you will be with me in paradise*" (Luke 23:43). Yet, that thief did not even get a chance to be baptized in water, observe communion, or even become a member of a certain church. Thus, we can be quite sure that *only trust in what Christ did for us on the cross is essential for salvation!* According to scripture, water baptism is a symbol of our saving faith, but it does not save us as then we would be justified by *works of the law* and that would go directly against the rest of God's Word, such as Romans 3:20 and Ephesians 2:8–9. Other clear examples of salvation without water baptism would include Zacchaeus (Luke 19:9) and the Apostle Paul who clearly believed in Christ and was saved three days *before* his water baptism (Acts 9:3–18). Notice also that the eunuch from Ethiopia was saved by *first* believing in Christ *before* he was even baptized (Acts 8:36–37).

Objection 48
I've Been Accused of Being in a Cult, But I'm Not So Convinced Yet

Conclusion

No false *Christian cult* out there in the world is going to have a sign hanging over their door which says, "This is a cult. Stay away because we already have enough money!" You must take the personal responsibility to check out all their teachings and practices with the Word of God yourself if you are going to avoid deception!

As we've already mentioned, most all false religions tend to lower God down to man's level and/or raise man up to God's level. However, the reality is that both God's thoughts and ways are higher than ours, as high as the heavens are above the earth (Isaiah 55:8–9). If you answered yes *to any of the above questions*, then you are most likely either in a cult or there is certainly a cult mentality at work where you fellowship.

Those who stay in cults are typically constantly battling *confusion, fear, a negative concept of God,* and *guilt,* not to mention *their very salvation may be in danger,* depending upon what they believe really saves them or gives them eternal life. Additionally, those who attend cults may also struggle financially because they are giving a lot of their hard-earned money to their cult leaders! If you are constantly struggling with these things, it may be another indicator of cultic activity in your fellowship, and you should sincerely seek counsel at another healthy Bible-believing church that adheres to the literal method of interpretation.

In order for us to get constantly abused by others, most of the time (unless you are in a German concentration camp), we must be a *willing participant!* If you are in a cult, you should get out as soon as possible because simply put, no fellowship is better than attending a cult that pretends to be the true Church!

After you get out of a cult, please don't continue to just keep believing in all the false doctrines they taught you! If you do, then in the spiritual sense, you really haven't even left, and Satan wins either way. If you leave a cult, you want to start correcting all the wrong things you've been taught by taking personal responsibility to read only the Holy Bible daily. Sincerely ask the Holy Spirit to expose and correct the wrong things you were taught so your trust is in God and his word and not in any man.

If you know you have been wrongly taught the scriptures of God's Word, please know that it is almost always because that cult has convinced you to adopt the *symbolic or allegorical method of interpretation* which truly allows false teachers to make the Scriptures say whatever they want it to say! However, much to the contrary, the literal method of interpretation—while it does honestly acknowledge all obvious symbolism given to us in God's Word—safely protects the intended meaning of God's Word, just as it does with any other piece of literature we read.

In 2 Peter 1:20, God's Word teaches us plainly that *"no prophecy of the scripture is of any private interpretation."* And if none of scripture should be given the personal or *private* interpretations of man, then obviously, it has an easy to see meaning of its own which can be understood by all. In other words, it says just what it means and means just what it says unless symbolism is obviously indicated. As Jesus promised in John 8:31–32, *"If you continue in my word, then you are my disciples indeed; and you shall know the truth, and the truth shall set you free."*

Obviously, Jesus could not have made this basic promise if one could not really understand his word with certainty! But since there is simply no way to unify all symbolic or allegorical interpreters, then we know the symbolic method of interpretation makes very little sense with many such verses like John 8:31–32! Other verses which easily teach us we can all be *absolutely sure* of the true meaning of God's word are:

"Study to shew thyself approved unto God, a workman that needeth not to be ashamed, rightly dividing the word of truth." (2 Timothy 2:15)

"If any man do his will, he shall know of the doctrine, whether it be of God." (John 7:17)

"All scripture is given by inspiration of God, and is profitable for doctrine, for reproof, for correction, for instruction in righteousness." (2 Timothy 3:16)

"For we write you nothing but what you can read and understand; I hope you will understand fully, as you have understood in part, that you can be proud of us as we can be proud of you on the day of the Lord Jesus." (2 Corinthians 1:13–14)

Objection 48
I've Been Accused of Being in a Cult, but I'm Not So Convinced Yet

If you are one who has been tangled in a cult (even for years) and sincerely desire to meet the real biblical Jesus and get the healing, life, and love you need, I invite you to begin a new and right relationship with God today on the authority of his Word alone, which is accurately interpreted. If you have never understood the true biblical Gospel, the prayer of salvation located at the end of this book with its discipleship guidance will get you started right. For unless one genuinely obtains God's salvation first through the true biblical Gospel which is not based on the *good works* of man in any way, they will simply not have the Spirit of God living in them to guide them into all doctrinal truth (1 Corinthians 2:14; John 16:13).

Even if you've been tangled up in an obvious cult for years, which threatens your true salvation in Christ, you can still break away from it today if you just choose to with the powerful free will which God gave you. And don't be concerned with what your family members may think of you because, simply put, they will not be your judge on judgment day! This decision is between you and God (your creator) alone. No matter what your past is like, God loves you, my friend, and sincerely wants you to be a part of his awesome eternal kingdom!

OBJECTION 49
I'm a Catholic

Catholicism

A loving reminder: Before each false belief system we discuss, just so my loving intentions cannot be misunderstood, I will *once again* remind the reader that it's certainly *not the adherents* of any false religion or belief system which the true Church is against but rather just the *false teachings* within them which deceive men away from the one and only true God and his eternal salvation (Ephesians 6:12). You see, God loves everyone, and everyone *has the right to know* if a religion or belief system is truly steering people away from him and his eternal salvation. In fact, if the true Church did not expose false belief systems which do not pass the reasonable tests which we can apply to them, then it most certainly would be a reflection of its love!

Therefore, my dear reader, please know that our discussion of these various different religions or belief systems is very much a *love* issue. However, with that said, even though one confirms that a given religion is false by way of combing through the honest evidence, that is certainly not to say that there could not be some (or even many in some cases) true believers in Christ within that false religion. This is especially true with those false religions which are *closest* to the biblical truth.

In such cases, the Bible teaches us that "*The lord knows them that are his*" (2 Timothy 2:19). However, if, in fact, there are true believers

Objection 49
I'm a Catholic

in Christ within any false religion, it is certainly *despite* their official doctrines, not *because* of them! And to be sure, God would have such a true believer in Christ leave that false religion before they lose their own stability in Christ (Romans 16:17; 1 Corinthians 5:11–13; 2 Corinthians 6:14; Galatians 5:19–21; 1 Timothy 6:3–11; 2 Timothy 3:2–5; Titus 3:9–11).

The origin of the Roman Catholic religion

Catholics often claim that their *"church"* goes all the way back to Christ and his apostles. But since the *entire* New Testament (even in the Catholic Bible) does not really contain *any* of the unique teachings of the Roman Catholic religion (including its Catholic name), is that belief even very reasonable? The truth is most all the unique teachings of the Roman Catholic religion (I can't call it the church) come from either their own Catechism, the leaders of their own religion, or the fallible writings of *some* early Church fathers of the second, third, and fourth centuries, long after the New Testament was written. And so, if indeed the Roman Catholic religion does go all the way back to Christ and his apostles, then why didn't Christ or his apostles even mention the Catholic church by name or any of its unique teachings even once in the entire New Testament?

My friend, this is just a very fair question to ponder. Of all the following unique Catholic religion teachings (without which today's Catholic religion would not even exist), really, none of them can be specifically found in the entire New Testament (of even the Catholic Bible)! Please observe the historical dates of just when the Catholic religion officially adopted them long after the New Testament was written:

1. AD 300: Prayers for the dead first instituted.
2. AD 300: Making sign of the cross first instituted.
3. AD 375: Worship of saints and angels first instituted.
4. A.D 394: Mass first instituted.
5. AD 431: Worship of Mary first instituted.
6. AD 500: The different dress code between priests and laypeople first instituted.
7. AD 526: Extreme unction first instituted.
8. AD 593: Doctrine of purgatory first instituted.

9. AD 600: Latin worship services first instituted.
10. AD 600: Prayers directed to Mary first instituted.
11. AD 607: The concept and position of a pope first instituted (Boniface III).
12. AD 709: Kissing the Pope's foot first instituted.
13. AD 786: Worshiping of images and relics first instituted.
14. AD 850: Use of holy water first instituted.
15. AD 995: Canonization of dead saints first instituted.
16. AD 998: Fasting on Fridays during lent first instituted.
17. AD 1079: Celibacy of priesthood first instituted.
18. AD 1090: Prayer beads first instituted.
19. AD 1184: The Inquisition first instituted.
20. AD 1190: The sale of indulgences first instituted.
21. AD 1215: Transubstantiation first instituted.
22. AD 1220: Adoration of the wafer (host) first instituted.
23. AD 1229: Bible forbidden to laypeople first instituted.
24. AD 1414: Cup forbidden to people at communion first instituted.
25. AD 1439: Doctrine of seven sacraments first instituted.
26. AD 1508: The Ave Maria first instituted.
27. AD 1534: The Jesuit order first instituted.
28. AD 1545: Tradition granted equal authority with the Bible first instituted.
29. AD 1546: Apocryphal books first instituted.
30. AD 1551: Confessing sins to a priest and being absolved by him first instituted.
31. AD 1854: Immaculate conception of Mary first instituted.
32. AD 1864: Syllabus of Errors first instituted.
33. AD 1870: Infallibility of the pope first instituted.
34. AD 1930: Condemnation of public schools first instituted.
35. AD 1950: Assumption of the Virgin Mary first instituted.
36. AD 1965: When Mary was first proclaimed Mother of the Catholic church.

After learning of these late adoption dates within the Catholic religion for these many nonbiblical teachings, of course, the first honest question which arises in one's heart is, if all of the above are so critical and needed for the one and only true Church, then how on earth could the Roman Catholic religion even claim to be the one and only true Church prior to their quite late adoption dates? Clearly, we can see that the early adherents of the Roman Catholic religion did not even believe in half of what the later adherents believed in. This in itself is quite self-contradicting as is the case with any false religion which has evolving doctrines over many years time. And even more importantly, if all these strange teachings are indeed so critical to the one true church, again, why can't we obviously find any of them within the entire New Testament of God's inspired Word?

> If all the unique teachings of the Catholic religion are indeed so critical to the one true Church, then why can't we obviously find any of them within the entire New Testament of God's inspired Word?

The truth is that one has a very difficult time trying to affirm the historical roots of the Roman Catholic religion any further back than about AD 300 when the Roman emperor, Constantine, ascended to his throne. In the second century, just before Constantine became the emperor of Rome, Satan tried (through Roman emperors like Diocletian) to annihilate Christ's Church just through the fierce physical persecution of all Christians. But it largely failed and backfired because Christianity just spread all the more across Asia when he did so; kind of like when you pour water on an oil fire! As a result, both Roman history and Church tradition indicate that the Roman emperor, Constantine (after Diocletian), was firmly convinced that Christianity was the political answer to Rome's problems. In other words, "If you can't beat 'em, join 'em!"

> If all of the unique teachings of the Catholic religion are so critical to the one true Church, then how could the Roman Catholic religion even claim to be the one true Church prior to their late adoption dates?

Allegedly, Constantine even saw a vision of a fiery cross in the sky and heard a voice saying, "In this sign, conquer." And Constantine believed this was a message from God indicating that if he would embrace the Christian religion, he would be able to conquer his enemies; thus, the Roman Catholic religion was largely born through him. Constantine not only legalized Christianity but also set up churches for it and produced about fifty copies of the Holy Scriptures for use in the churches. Because Constantine even declared himself to be the defender and protector of the Christian religion, some believe his conversion to biblical Christianity was genuine.

However, a historical examination of Constantine's life and actions indicate that he had a very *skewed* concept of New Testament Christianity and that he had never been truly born again by the Spirit of God (as the Bible teaches is necessary) while in his political office (John 3:3). In fact, from AD 312 on, the Catholic religion in Rome became more and more *Roman* and less *biblical* in its practices as our previous list clearly indicates.

> A historical examination of Constantine's life and actions indicate that he had a very skewed concept of New Testament Christianity and that he had never been truly born again by the Spirit of God as the Bible teaches is necessary.

Up until the time of Constantine, the biblical Church of Christ was an independent collection of local churches which worked together and were not dominated by a single governmental authority, which is only biblical. But when Constantine tried to marry the Church of Christ to the Roman government, the strange mutated hybrid of the Roman Catholic religion was the result which eventually taught an unbiblical works-based salvation. However, while this was once again Satan's strategy to destroy Christ's Church, it too failed as the Protestant believers of Christ's Church (which adhered to the scriptures of God's word without compromise) officially and finally broke away from the Catholic religion during the reformation period in about AD 1500. But, unfortunately, it took about 1,000 years for the true Church to see through Satan's deception of the Roman Catholic religion and break away by employing the literal method of interpretation to the Scriptures!

However, obviously, not everyone in the world managed to escape the deception, for even today, the Roman Catholic religion remains one of the largest cults in the world.

Objection 49
I'm a Catholic

Interestingly enough, when you ask a Roman Catholic if they are a born-again Christian, they will often respond by just saying, "I'm a Catholic." They typically do not even say, "Yes, I'm a Christian." They just say, "I'm a Catholic." This in itself is rather disturbing and should be a red flag. Once again, this does not necessarily mean that there are no true Bible-believing Christians trapped within the Roman Catholic religion. There may be many. But, again, if there are, it is certainly *despite* Roman Catholic doctrine and not *because* of it as we will sufficiently demonstrate.

Though our following examination of the Roman Catholic doctrines are based on their 1994 Catechism, their stance today has largely stayed much the same on the subjects we'll be discussing. Nevertheless, just considering that the Roman Catholic religion has kept adding their *new and approved* basic doctrines over the centuries as our previous list testifies, this too is a major red flag of a cult as any religion representing the reliable spiritual truth for all mankind (which prescribes the way of eternal salvation) should certainly not be ever-changing in its beliefs! The bottom line is reliable eternal truth should not evolve any more than our eternal perfect God should be always changing in his character!

Testing Roman Catholicism against the true moral condition of man

According to the catechism doctrines of the Roman Catholic religion, the pope is actually infallible in matters of doctrine, faith, and morals. Of course, the Roman Catholic religion is always changing its traditional teachings and catechism doctrines; nevertheless, the 1994 Catechism of the Roman Catholic religion states:

> *"In order to preserve the church in the purity of the faith handed on by the apostles, Christ who is truth, willed to confer on her (the church) a share in his own infallibility. By a supernatural sense of faith, the people of God, under the guidance of the church's living magisterium, unfailingly adheres to this faith."* (P. 235, #889)

> *"The Roman Pontiff…enjoys this infallibility in virtue of his office, when, as supreme pastor and teacher of all the faithful:who confirms his brethren in the faith:he proclaims by a definitive act a doctrine pertaining to faith or morals… This infallibility extends as far as the deposit of divine revelation itself."* (P. 235 #891)

These clear statements not only teach that the pope is infallible (or perfect) in matters of morality but also in matters of doctrine which extends as far as the deposit of divine revelation itself. This essentially means that the authority of the pope himself is equal to the authority of God's Word. But because the Roman Catholic religion actually follows their popes in the case when their proclamations may conflict with the Holy Bible, we must conclude that the authority of the pope himself within the Catholic religion is actually *greater than* the authority of God and his Word!

However, when we honestly consider that, historically, all popes within the Roman Catholic religion have certainly disagreed with each other in matters of doctrine (along with the constant change we see in the doctrinal beliefs within the Catholic religion), such a belief of the pope's infallibility puts the Catholic in a very difficult place! Because how can any of the popes be without doctrinal error if they have all disagreed with each other in doctrine ever since they were established in the Catholic religion in AD 607 (Boniface III was the first Pope)?

For example, some more recent popes have believed that God used Darwin's Theory of Evolution in the creation week of Genesis. And, of course, many past popes have not. So just who are the Catholics to believe anyway if all Popes are infallible? Is our perfect God actually double-minded, even though Hebrews 13:8 and James 1:8 (even in the Catholic Bible) clearly teach us that he isn't? And whatever did the Catholic religion rely on for infallibility of doctrine before the first pope if the pope himself is so necessary for such a thing? My friend, these are some fair and honest questions which really cannot have any sensible answer to the honest soul!

> Some popes have believed that God used Darwin's Theory of Evolution in the creation week of Genesis. And, of course, many have not. So just who are the Catholics to believe anyway if all Popes are supposedly infallible?

On the other hand, the Holy Bible (which includes the lion share of the Catholic Bible) teaches us plainly that all people (which must include all the popes) are sinners and that *no one* is morally perfect or infallible! Please consider what even the Catholic Bible clearly teaches:

Objection 49
I'm a Catholic

"As it is written, There is none righteous, no, not one: There is none that understandeth, there is none that seeketh after God. They are all gone out of the way, they are together become unprofitable; there is none that doeth good, no, not one." (Romans 3:10–12)

"Therefore by the deeds of the law, there shall no flesh be justified in his sight: for by the law is the knowledge of sin." (Romans 3:20)

"For all have sinned, and come short of the glory of God." (Romans 3:23)

According to Scripture, Jesus himself is the only infallible person who ever walked the earth, and that was simply because he was God in the flesh who didn't even have a sin nature and was visiting his own creation in human form (2 Corinthians 5:21; 1 Peter 2:22). But to make matters worse for the Roman Catholic religion, its Catechism has also plainly taught that even other Catholic religion leaders can somehow reach this same state of infallibility when it states:

"The pastoral duty of the magisterium is aimed at seeing to it that the people of God abides in truth that liberates. To fulfill this service, Christ endowed the church's shepherds with the charism of infallibility in matters of faith and morals." (p. 235, #890)

"The infallibility of the magisterium of the pastors extends to all the elements of doctrine, including moral doctrine, without which the saving truths of the faith cannot be preserved, expounded, or observed." (p. 495, #2051)

Thus, according to even the Catholic Bible, it is important to understand that it certainly could not have been God who declared these leaders in the Roman Catholic religion to be infallible or perfect as they were only declared so by other very fallible men within the traditional writings of the Catholic religion. Why, even the Apostle Peter himself denied Christ three times (Luke 22:54–62). And, obviously, the Apostle Paul thought himself worse than Peter, for he referred to himself as *"less than the least of all saints"* (Ephesians 3:8; 1 Corinthians 15:9). And finally, the Apostle John said even in his later years that if any man said he was without sin, they were not even saved (1 John 1:8–10)!

So if God's inspired Word teaches us this basic truth, what does that really say about the true spiritual condition of any Roman Catholic religious leader (including the popes) who claims to be infallible or sinless? Just the opposite is not only confirmed, but according to the Apostle John, they are not even right with God when they claim such things!

My friend, just this issue alone should not only expose to the honest soul that *all such* Roman Catholic religious leaders are not even right with God but that there is something seriously wrong with the whole Roman Catholic religion which is standing on such teachings! So, if then, according to their own Bible, the leader of the Catholic religion cannot even be saved if he claims infallibility, then we truly do have the blind leading the blind. Truly, the Roman Catholic religion completely fails this first very reasonable test as we test it against the true moral condition of man.

> The Apostle John said that "if any man claimed he was without sin, they were not even saved" (1 John 1:8–10). So where does that leave all the Catholic popes and Catholic leaders who have claimed to be morally infallible?

Testing Roman Catholicism against self-contradictions

As we have already pointed out, the Roman Catholic teachings within their Catechism clearly disagree with even their own Bible on the issue of man's fallibility or sinfulness. The Roman Catholic Catechism has plainly taught that Catholic religious leaders are infallible in all matters of doctrine and morality while the Catholic Holy Bible clearly teaches that no man living on earth has been infallible other than Christ himself. So if you claim to be a Catholic, my friend, which source do you believe when they both clearly contradict each other? Do the leaders of the Roman Catholic religion truly have authority over God our creator and his Holy Word to us? The Catholic Bible clearly teaches that God's Word is the only final authority on all matters which pertain to this life and the next as it states:

> *"All scripture is given by inspiration of God, and is profitable for doctrine, for reproof, for correction, for instruction in righteousness, that the man of God may be perfect, thoroughly furnished unto all*

Objection 49
I'm a Catholic

good works." (2 Timothy 3:16–17; see also Psalm 19:7; 1 Peter 1:23; Proverbs 30:5–6; 2 Peter 1:21)

The word *perfect* here in the original Greek just means mature. It doesn't mean morally perfect like only God is. But as you can see from this passage, whenever any other source would disagree with God's Word, God's Word is good for *doctrine, correction*, and *reproof*. Thus, according to the Bible itself, the Bible is *the only* final authority on all matters of doctrine and morality, not any pope or church leader. So if Roman Catholic religious leaders are infallible and do claim to have authority over God and his inspired Word, then why on earth do they even need the Holy Bible? If they truly do not have authority over God and his inspired Word, but nevertheless still claim to, then if you presently belong to the Roman Catholic religion, are you not in the largest Christian cult in the world?

Please think for yourself, my Catholic friend, because as we will continue to show you it is truly your eternal salvation which is hanging in the balances of these spiritual battles for the souls of men. If leaders of a religion claim to have authority over God and his infallible Word, and that is not a cult in the truest sense, then we might as well say there is no such thing as a cult anywhere in the world! The following are many more obvious major self-contradictions within Roman Catholic church doctrine:

> If leaders of a religion claim to have authority over God and his infallible word, and that is not a cult in the truest sense, then we might as well say there is no such thing as a cult!

Salvation through the Church

The Roman Catholic religion Catechism teaches that the eternal salvation of man can only be obtained through the Roman Catholic religion as it states:

"*The second Vatican council's decree on Ecumenism explains: For it is through Christ's Catholic church alone, which is the universal help towards salvation, that the fullness of the means of salvation can be obtained.*" (p. 215, #816)

"*[A]ll salvation comes from Christ the head through the Church which is his body: Basing itself on scripture and tradition, the counsel teaches that the Church, a pilgrim now on earth, is necessary for salvation:... Hence they could not be saved who, knowing that the Catholic church was founded as necessary by God through Christ, would refuse either to enter it or to remain in it."* (p. 224, #846)

"It is in the Church that the fullness of the means of salvation has been deposited. It is in her that by the grace of God we acquire holiness." (p.218, #824)

"In her (the Church) subsists the fullness of Christ's body united with its head (who is Christ)"—this implies that she (the Church) receives from him. The fullness of the means of salvation." (p.220, #830)

However, when one searches for the truth on this matter, even within the holy Catholic Bible, we find a very different reality presented which manifests in two different facts:

1. The Bible never even begins to indicate (much less teach) that one must be a member of any certain church organization (by a specific title) in order to obtain salvation.
2. But many other scriptures of God's inspired Word do clearly teach that salvation is a free gift of God readily available to anyone, but only by believing in what Jesus did for them on the cross.

And both of these biblical realities clearly contradict what we've just read in the Roman Catholic Catechism. Let's just take a look at a few verses within God's Word which just represent these many more verses in God's Word which clearly teach us that salvation can only be obtained through believing what Christ did for us on the cross:

"For the wages of sin is death; but the gift of God is eternal life through Jesus Christ our Lord." (Romans 6:23)

"Neither is there salvation in any other (except Jesus): for there is none other name under heaven given among men, whereby we must be saved." (Acts 4:10, 12)

"Whoever believes in the Son has eternal life, but whoever rejects the Son will not see life, for God's wrath remains on him." (John 3:36)

Objection 49
I'm a Catholic

> *"To him (Jesus) give all the prophets witness, that through his name whosoever believeth in him shall receive remission of sins."* (Acts 10:43)

Never do we see that both believing in Christ and being a member of a certain church organization are necessary for salvation in the scriptures of God's inspired Word. Once one is saved by truly believing in what Christ did for them on the cross, they automatically become part of Christ's true spiritual Church and have his eternal salvation! But the Church itself cannot and does not give anyone salvation according to any scripture within the Holy Bible. So, in all this, the Roman Catholic Catechism directly contradicts even the Catholic Bible. So, if you claim to be Catholic, which do you believe?

If you choose God's Word, you have chosen wisely. And if you do, you must admit that the Roman Catholic religion (which tries to pass itself off as the one true Church) is once again failing this simple test of self-contradictions and once again proves to be a false man-made religion.

> Never do we see that both believing in Christ and being a member of a church organization are necessary for salvation in the scriptures of God's inspired Word.

Salvation through good works

To obtain the eternal salvation of God, the Roman Catholic religion also teaches that one must not only belong to the Roman Catholic religion but also continually perform *good works*. Please consider the following references within the 1994 Catechism which teach that certain human performances must be accomplished in order to obtain salvation:

1. First of all, as we just discussed, one must be a member of the Roman Catholic religion in order to even have eternal salvation (p. 216, #816; p. 224, #846), and even this is a type of a *good work* for their salvation.
2. One must be water-baptized in the Roman Catholic religion in order to have eternal salvation (p. 320, #1257).

3. One must perform various sacraments in order to have eternal salvation (p. 292, #1129).
4. Additionally, one must also perform many other good works in the Roman Catholic religion in order to have eternal salvation. Time and written pages just do not permit us to expose them all.

Once again, the Catechism teachings of the Roman Catholic religion on this very important issue directly contradicts the plain scriptures of God's Word. And once again, this makes the Roman Catholic church an obvious cult which also contradicts itself because it claims to also believe in the (Catholic) Bible. If the Roman Catholic religion insists that there is no salvation outside the Roman Catholic religion, where does that leave all those millions of *Bible-believing saints* who do not belong to the Roman Catholic religion?

According to the Roman Catholic, it must mean we don't have salvation! If the Roman Catholic religion insists that one must be infant-baptized in the Roman Catholic religion in order to be saved, where does that leave the millions of people who sincerely believe in Christ but just never got baptized as an infant in the Roman Catholic religion? And where does that leave all aborted or miscarried babies who never even got a chance to be baptized in the Roman Catholic religion? Similarly, if any religion insists that those who did not get infant-baptized must be water-baptized as an adult in order to be saved, then where does that leave the millions of people who have believed in Christ on their death beds and had no opportunity to even get water-baptized as an adult at all (kind of like the thief on the cross)?

Thus, if any religion in their theology does not fairly accommodate all such situations of man's experience, it cannot be fairly representative of our just and loving creator and, therefore, should not be worthy of our trust!

The Word of God clearly teaches many times over that no man is saved through human performance *of any kind* but only through *faith* in what Christ did for us on the cross. It is true that after one is genuinely saved by believing in what Jesus did for them on the cross, good works and a morally clean life will be the *results*, but never the *cause* of one's salvation; and that, my friend, is the big difference! If anyone professes to believe in what Christ did for them but is living

Objection 49
I'm a Catholic

in some lifestyle of unrepentant sin or believing in basic false doctrines which directly contradict God's Word, then they really could not have believed in what Christ did for them on the cross. Why? Because true belief will always be accompanied by a righteous life! Not a perfect life but a basically righteous life. Think of it like a train engine pulling box cars behind it. The engine represents our salvation through Christ, which pulls behind it the boxcars which represent our good works.

> If any religion in their theology does not fairly accommodate all situations of man's experience, it cannot be fairly representative of our just and loving creator and, therefore, should not be worthy of our trust.

Those who believe we are saved by performing any religious good works believe the boxcars are in front of the engine, pulling it. Thus, their misguided faith is backward and ultimately gives glory to men and not God. But we all know that only the engine of a train can pull boxcars. Thus, the true simple faith Gospel message of salvation does, in fact, accommodate all men who didn't even have a chance to get (infant or adult) water-baptized (or never belonged to the Roman Catholic religion). In fact, the true Bible Gospel is so simple that even a child can understand it and find salvation through it, and that's exactly why Jesus said that, *"Verily I say unto you, except ye be converted, and become as little children, ye shall not enter into the kingdom of heaven"* (Matthew 18:3). You see, the Gospel message of salvation is all a heart issue, not a religious good works or human performance issue!

The true Gospel is so simple, then, that it actually trips and stumbles all those who are unwilling to let their own creator have his perfectly deserving glory. It is so simple it even accommodates those millions of men who have died in battle as Romans 10:13 has always clearly taught that *"whosoever shall call upon the name of the Lord shall be saved!"* If a soldier, mortally wounded, calls out for Christ to save him in his last moments, he will be saved by God's promise, just like the thief on the cross got saved (Luke 23:39–43)!

But according to all the ordinances which the Roman Catholic religion attaches to salvation, no soldier could even find salvation in their last moments on the battlefield! Notice it doesn't say "whosoever shall call on the name of the Lord within the Catholic religion shall be saved." Nor does it say "whosoever shall call upon the name of the Lord in addition to being water baptized shall be saved."

The sad truth is that the Roman Catholic religion has added *many* religious good works to the "true faith in Christ alone" gospel and has not only made it much more complicated than it really is but also actually damns all those who really do trust in good works for their salvation! And not only has the false Roman Catholic religion done this, but pretty much every other cult or false religion out there has done this to the true Gospel as well. *Only biblical Christianity stands alone,* declaring that salvation is obtained through *faith in Christ alone.* My friend, if you belong to the Catholic religion, please carefully consider the following verses of God's Word on this very critical issue of our eternal salvation:

"For by grace ye are saved through faith; and that not of yourselves: it is the gift of God: Not of works, lest any man should boast. (Ephesians 2:8–9)

"Therefore by the deeds of the law there shall no flesh be justified in his sight: for by the law is the knowledge of sin." (Romans 3:20)

"Therefore we conclude that a man is justified by faith without the deeds of the law." (Romans 3:28)

Thus, what we only see throughout *the entire New Testament* is that the true salvation Gospel message is simply *faith in Christ (believing in what he did for us on the cross) and nothing else—period!* And so it is important to understand that whenever man tries to add any good works whatsoever (whether they be religious in nature or not) to the pure salvation Gospel message of God's Holy Word, he immediately nullifies it and makes it of no effect.

According to the Holy Bible, one simply cannot even begin to *earn* the eternal salvation of Almighty God through their own very imperfect merits (Galatians 5:2–4)! *By way of analogy,* one could think of the "pure faith in Christ alone" gospel as a pure unpolluted glass of crystal clean water from God for mankind to drink in order to obtain his eternal life. But when deceived men attempt to even add one small good work to the pure Gospel, it is essentially like adding a small drop

Objection 49
I'm a Catholic

of poison to that clean glass of water! That glass of water may look just as good as pure water, but Satan knows it will kill you just as surely as a full glass of pure poison! And since the Catholic religion has made many good religious works a requirement for their true salvation, they've added many drops of poison to their glass of pure water.

To further emphasize the true catastrophe involved when man changes or perverts the true salvation Gospel message, let's just read the Apostle Paul's solemn warning to all who do so. Here he is talking to the Church in Galatia who drifted from the true Gospel in the same way the Roman Catholic religion clearly has:

> *"I marvel that ye are so soon removed from him who called you into the grace of Christ unto another gospel: which is not another; but there be some that trouble you, and would pervert the gospel of Christ. But though we, or an angel from heaven, preach any other gospel unto you than that which we have preached unto you, let him be accursed. As we have said before, so say I now again, if any man preach any other gospel unto you than that ye have received, let him be accursed."*

Only biblical Christianity stands alone, declaring that salvation is obtained through faith in Christ alone.

The true consequences laid out here for adding any legalistic good works to the Gospel could not be any more clear or severe as the Greek word for *accursed* here in the original manuscripts basically means "damned or the loss of one's salvation!" And that's exactly why the entire New Testament has made it abundantly crystal clear that the eternal salvation of our creator cannot be obtained, *even in part* through the imperfect religious good works of men in any way shape or form.

When Christ died on the cross, he clearly said that the work of man's salvation was *completely finished on the cross* (John 19:30). So, for any man to add even small religious good works to what Christ did for us is simply very ugly pride in the sight of God (Ephesians 2:8–9) because it is not only saying that what our perfect creator did on the cross for our salvation was not good enough but that sinful mankind must actually help God out in this critical matter! Again, we read in Titus 3:5, *"Not by works of righteousness which we have done, but according to his mercy he saved us, by the washing of regeneration, and renewing of the Holy Ghost."*

The *washing of regeneration* here mentioned in Titus 3:5 is not actual water baptism as some cults may try to teach but only the spiritually cleansing symbol of salvation which is a gift of the Holy Spirit when one gets saved through faith alone (Romans 1:17). If it was an actual reference to water baptism, then this verse would clash with many other verses which directly teach against a works-based salvation. And then God would, of course, be double-minded, which we know he simply cannot be. Yes, after we get saved, water baptism is a beautiful symbol of the spiritual cleansing *which already took place* when one gets saved *through faith alone*. And all true believers should follow Christ's command to get water-baptized, just for a symbol of their salvation (Matthew 28:19). But nowhere in scripture does it teach that water baptism itself is necessary *for salvation*.

Without saving faith occurring first, the act of water baptism in obedience to Christ's command is absolutely meaningless. Verses like Acts 8:36–38 just confirm the basic truth within God's Word that the true Church is saved first by faith alone, then it is to be water baptized just as a symbol of their conversion:

> *"[S]ee, here is water, what doth hinder me (the Ethiopian eunuch speaking) to be baptized? And Philip (the apostle of Christ) said, if thou believest with all thine heart, thou mayest. And he answered and said, I believe that Jesus Christ is the Son of God. And he (Philip) commanded the chariot to stand still: and they went down both into the water, both Philip and the eunuch; and he baptized him."*

As we can clearly see, Philip made sure the Ethiopian eunuch fully believed in Christ as his Savior with all his heart *first* before he would let him be water-baptized. In the conversion of Zacchaeus, it is also apparent by Christ's own words that he was completely saved before he even had the chance to be water-baptized (Luke 19:1–10). Other obvious examples of salvation occurring before or apart from water baptism would be the Apostle Paul's conversion (see Acts 9:17–18; Ananias clearly refers to Paul as a *brother* before he was water baptized). And, of course, the thief on the cross (Luke 23:39–43).

And so, because the New Testament scriptures collectively teach us that one must be saved through faith in Christ *before* one is water-

Objection 49
I'm a Catholic

baptized, this of course makes even infant water baptism completely meaningless since infants cannot yet understand the Gospel and what Christ did for them on the cross. Not to mention there is not one single clear *example* of infant baptism given to us by Christ or the apostles.

Perhaps one reason the Roman Catholic religion (and other false religions) have held to infant sprinkle baptism is because during the Middle Ages, they simply failed to understand that the Bible has already taught that all infants and little children (below the age when they can understand the Gospel) are automatically graced into eternal life should they die before the age when they can understand the Gospel. Since infants are, of course, ignorant and incapable of understanding the Gospel, God graces them with the gift of eternal life, even though they are, of course, born with a sin nature. We must remember God is perfectly just and would never hold anyone accountable for something they simply cannot yet understand!

Another reason why the Roman Catholic religion (as well as even some Lutheran churches) may have held to infant sprinkle baptism is because they simply fail to understand that biblical water baptism truly symbolizes death to self for the Christian (Romans 6:3–6). And because it actually symbolizes death to self, this is exactly why we can know that infant sprinkle baptism is not the biblical model. Let's face it: no one ever died by just getting *sprinkled* with water!

But many have died due to being submerged in water as adult water baptism accurately symbolizes. At the same time, this pretty much rules out any biblical infant submersion baptisms because it is obviously unsafe for infants to get completely submerged under water as we see with our biblical example of adult submersion water baptism. And, of course, the reason infant sprinkle baptism for salvation is so spiritually dangerous is because once those who are sprinkle-baptized as an infant grow up, if they really do trust in both their sprinkle baptism, plus in what Christ did for them on the cross for their salvation, then they are not really saved when they may think they are!

Satan has been working on earth for a reason, and it is deceptions like these which have kept him occupied for past millennia (1 Peter 5:8)! Because, once again, they are at least in part trusting in their own good works to save them, and this is simply unacceptable to our perfect creator who had to die for our sins! You can have the best boat to sail in, but if it even has one single hole in the bottom, you're in trouble! As the Apostle Paul well said, *"I do not frustrate the grace of God: for if righteousness came by the law, then Christ is dead in vain"* (Galatians 2:21).

But perhaps the apostle Paul said it best in Romans 11:6, when he said, *"And if (salvation is) by grace, then it is no more of works: otherwise grace is no more grace. But if it be of works, then it is no more grace: otherwise work is no more work."*

When we add any good human works to what Christ did for us on the cross, we really haven't understood the "true faith alone" saving gospel, and we are still in our sins eternally separated from God. Let's be *honest*: if our salvation is at all about doing religious good works, then why did our *perfect* creator even have to die on the cross for our salvation? If our imperfect good works can save us, then why couldn't we as imperfect humans just die for our own sins? If our imperfect good works are truly what saves us, then just who actually determines just what good works are required for salvation and which ones are not, since the Bible itself actually condemns good works for salvation?

> Let's be honest: if our salvation is all about who, as imperfect human beings, can do the most religious good works, then why did our perfect creator even have to die on the cross for our salvation?

More than one scripture teaches us that little children automatically belong to the kingdom of heaven (with absolutely no mention of sprinkle or water baptism), even though they, too, were born into sin (see the death of King David's child; 2 Samuel 12:23; Matthew 18:3; Luke 18:16). And this is also why God's Word clearly teaches us that *"unto whomsoever much is given, of him shall be much required"* (Luke 12:48). And respectively, if that is true, then we must also assume the very opposite is true as well: to him who is given little, less is required.

The bottom line is God is perfectly just in all his ways, especially when it comes to the gift of eternal salvation of all men (Psalm 19:9). And only this biblical truth that all small children and babies are automatically saved by God's grace has an answer for the reasonable question: If infant sprinkle water baptism is actually *necessary* for salvation, then reasonably and logically, all those many millions who have been either aborted or miscarried (who never had the chance

Objection 49
I'm a Catholic

of sprinkle water baptism) could not have been saved. One simply cannot have it both ways. And even if the Roman Catholic religion has yet another man-made exception built into their doctrines for those many millions of babies who have been aborted and miscarried, their exception still makes no sense with their insistence that all born babies must be sprinkle baptized in the Catholic church since neither live infants in or out of the womb can begin to understand the gospel message. And what about those Catholic infants who did not even get sprinkle-baptized in the Catholic religion before it *officially adopted* its practice of infant sprinkle baptism? Can you hear a pin drop like I can?

But, of course, we know that our *morally perfect* God would never be so cruel as to send babies to hell if they died somehow in or out of the womb before they had the chance to get sprinkle-baptized in the Roman Catholic religion. Just as we also know from Scripture that all aborted or miscarried children are saved *through God's grace*, just like all adults who respond to the Gospel message! Once again, the bottom line is if any theology (especially those salvation-related) does not fairly accommodate all situations of man's experience, it cannot be fairly representative of our just and loving creator and is therefore not worthy of our belief or trust. Additional scriptures (among many) which absolutely confirm that the eternal salvation of God cannot be won through *any* human effort like some stuffed animal at the fair (which would certainly include sprinkle or water baptism) are Galatians 2:16, Romans 5:1, 3:20, Matthew 7:21–23, Galatians 2:21, John 3:16, 6:40, and 6:29.

So, in light of all this, we cannot only see that once again, the Roman Catholic religion doctrines in their Catechism directly contradict what is plainly taught in the Catholic Bible but that also the Roman Catholic religion proves to be a cult in the truest sense because it *insistently maintains that many human works are absolutely essential for salvation!* Some may try to use Philippians 2:12 to justify trying to obtain God's eternal salvation through religious good works. It simply states: *"Wherefore, my beloved, as you have always obeyed, not in my presence only, but now much more in my absence, work out your own salvation with fear and trembling."*

However, Paul here is obviously talking to the *already saved* Philippians Church and is only encouraging them to *work out the salvation which they already have*, not work *for* their salvation! As we've already mentioned, while the biblical truth is that good works are certainly a *result* of genuine saving faith (James 2:14–18), they are never the *cause* of it (Ephesians 2:8–9). And there is, my friend, a big difference between the two because one glorifies God, and the other glorifies man!

That Jesus was against any tradition of man which nullified the Word of God is quite evident throughout the gospels when he often confronted the religious Pharisees of his day who were also ignorantly trying to work their way to heaven. Mark 7:9 is just one of many confrontations Jesus had with them, saying, *"Knowing full well, ye reject the commandment of God, that ye may keep your own tradition."*

If you belong to the Roman Catholic religion, again, you must choose what you are ultimately going to put your trust in: the traditions of very fallible men inside the Roman Catholic religion (which are always changing) or the Word of the living God (which never changes). What say you?

> While the biblical truth is that good works are certainly a result of genuine saving faith, they are never the cause of it. And there is a big difference between the two because one glorifies God, and the other glorifies man.

Catholic penance

Penance in the Roman Catholic religion is simply confessing one's sins to a priest and being forgiven by God *through him*. And according to the Roman Catholic doctrine of penance, one cannot be forgiven their sins without it, and this is precisely where the Catholic religion once again contradicts even its own Bible. As it clearly states in the 1994 Catechism:

"One who desires to obtain reconciliation with God and with the Church, must confess to a priest all the unconfessed grave sins he remembers after having carefully examined his conscience." (p. 374, #1493)

While the Catholic religion makes the eternal salvation of God contingent upon confession to a Catholic priest (who was also born into sin), the Word of God itself has never taught that such a thing is necessary for salvation. Again, if it did, the salvation of the thief on

Objection 49
I'm a Catholic

the cross would make no sense! Please consider the following verses of God's Word, which clearly teach that all men can pray to God directly for the forgiveness of all sins with no other men necessary:

"I acknowledged my sin unto thee, and my iniquity have I not hid. I said, I will confess my transgressions (sins) unto the Lord; and thou forgavest the iniquity of my sin." (Psalm 32:5)

"If we confess our sins, he (Jesus:vs. 7) is faithful and just to forgive us our sins, and to cleanse us from all unrighteousness." (1 John 1:9)

"Peter answered (Simon)… Repent of this wickedness and pray to the Lord. Perhaps he will forgive you for having such a thought in your heart." (Acts 8:20–22)

During penance, the Catholic religion teaches that the priest being confessed to can even *absolve (or forgive) sins himself*. As it states in their Catechism:

"Only priests who have received the faculty of absolving from the authority of the church can forgive sins in the name of Christ." (p. 374, #1495; see also p. 364, #1448)

But, clearly, this strange teaching goes directly against God's word. Please consider the following:

"Why does this man speak blasphemies? Who can forgive sins but God only?" (Mark 2:7)

"For there is one God, and one mediator between God and men, the man Christ Jesus." (1 Timothy 2:5)

Catholics will typically try to justify their practice of penance with New Testament scriptures, such as James 5:13–16 which states:

"Is any among you afflicted? Let him pray… Is any sick among you? Let him call for the elders of the Church; and let them pray over him, anointing him with oil in the name of the Lord: And the prayer of faith shall save the sick, and the Lord shall raise him up; and if he have committed sins, they shall be forgiven him. Confess your faults one to another, and pray for one another, that you may be healed. The effectual fervent prayer of a righteous man availeth much."

However, to make this passage fit with the Roman Catholic practice of penance is a rather *awkward* affair to say the least.

1. First of all, the main context of James 5:13–16 is *healing*, not even forgiveness of sins. *If* one has committed sins, God can forgive them through the prayer of the elders, but the main context is still physical healing for the sick.
2. Secondly, the passage says elders (plural), not a single Catholic priest in some private confessional booth. In fact, verse 16 even teaches that *anyone* in the Church can be confessed to, and God will hear.
3. Thirdly, the sick person and the elders are all praying directly to the Lord in this passage. It doesn't teach that the elders are the ones absolving others of their sins. It clearly teaches that *the Lord* is the one forgiving of sin, not the elders.
4. And, fourthly, even if you dishonestly force this whole passage to mean the unbiblical practice of Roman Catholic penance, it still isn't even teaching that one *has to* be prayed for by a group of elders in order to be forgiven for sins, like Catholic penance insists. Obviously, according to many other scriptures in the New Testament (some of which we've cited), anyone can go directly to God in prayer for the forgiveness of their own sins!

Some Catholics even try to back up Catholic penance with Acts 2:38. But when you just read Acts 2:38 in its proper context, such an interpretation proves to be rather ridiculous, not to mention impossible! Acts 2:38 simply says, *"Then Peter said unto them, Repent, and be baptized everyone of you in the name of Jesus Christ for the remission of sins and you will receive the gift Holy Ghost."*

1. First of all, this verse *in proper context* is clearly referring to Peter's evangelistic gospel message toward *only those who have never known Christ*. He's not addressing those already saved in the Church who have just fallen into sin. These people he's addressing are clearly not saved yet because they don't even have the *gift of the Holy Ghost* yet. Since the rest of the New Testament makes it clear that if we do not have the Holy Spirit living inside us, we're not saved, then we can be sure Peter here can only be evangelizing

non-Christians (Romans 8:9–11).
2. Secondly, it is clear that Peter is addressing *non-Christians*, simply because he calls them to water baptism. Therefore the *repent* here in Acts 2:38 can only refer to one repenting unto salvation, not repenting of various sins after one is saved and already has the Holy Spirit. I'm quite sure most Catholics who go to confession have already been water-baptized (which should only be a one-time occurrence for the Christian according to the Bible). So, if Catholics are typically already water-baptized when going to confession, how does that honestly fit with Acts 2:38 if Peter calls them to be water-baptized within it? The honest truth is that it doesn't and simply should not be used by anyone to back up the practice of Roman Catholic penance.
3. Thirdly, Peter here does not specifically call those he is addressing to go to him for their repentance or any man, for that matter. Where does it say that? Again, the *honest* truth is that it doesn't; especially as it concerns salvation (which is the clear context with Acts 2:38), scripture always directs unsaved man to God for salvation repentance, not any man. And this is simply because our unsaved condition is only the result of our broken relationship with God, not a result of our broken relationship with any man.

The Bible always directs unsaved man to God, not any man. And this is because our unsaved condition is only the result of our broken relationship with God, not a broken relationship with any man.

Testing Roman Catholicism against the fruit it has produced

Truly, there are many abominations that the Roman Catholic religion has committed against God throughout its awful history, which the confines of time and written page do not permit us to expose. But just to begin with, the history of the Catholic religion is indeed quite bloody. Back in the Middle Ages, many—even godly men, such as Jon Hus, William Tyndale, and many others—were persecuted, tortured, and even put to death in the name of Christ by the Roman Catholic religion. Even its practice of burning supposed witches (like Joan of Arc) at the stake was a serious moral wrong which was also burned into the bloody history of the Catholic religion.

My friend, no matter what the Catholic religion thought some guilty of at the time, nowhere in the entire New Testament is the Church taught by Christ or his apostles to kill or hurt anyone through any means for any reason whatsoever—period! Such evil practices could never have been done by God's true Church any more than Christ himself could have lit men on fire! Even the Roman Catholic religion's bloody Crusader wars in the name of Christ were just more bad historical fruit which the Roman Catholic religion produced. More on this is covered in our Objection #64 of part 4 of our series. Other bad fruit was just the fact that through the constant extortion of its laypeople, it grew to be one of the wealthiest cults in the world and likely owns more land today than any other organization.

> No matter what the Catholic religion thought some guilty of at the time, nowhere in the entire New Testament is the Church taught by Christ or his apostles to kill or hurt anyone through any means for any reason!

Additionally, their doctrines stipulating the celibacy of their nuns and priests not only goes directly against the teachings of their own Catholic Bible (1 Corinthians 7:9, 28, 9:5; 1 Timothy 3:2, 12, 4:1–3) but has long tempted them into fornication and other sexual sins with children. Additionally, many of the leaders of the Roman Catholic religion proved to be corrupt along the way in its history. For example, St. Augustine, who was a religious leader in the Roman Catholic religion about AD 400, declared that prostitution was a necessary evil and soon thereafter had 100,000 prostitutes employed!

My friend, this is not just some small character defect for someone who claimed to be a teacher of God's Word in the Roman Catholic church. Nor could this immoral statement which encouraged fornication just be considered an abuse of the one true Roman Catholic church because even to this day, Catholics herald St. Augustine as one of their great historical Church fathers.

Objection 49
I'm a Catholic

But, again, probably the worst bad fruit which the Roman Catholic religion has displayed is its boldness to not only add to God's Word but also subtract from it. Revelation 22:18–19 clearly forbids it, teaching us that all those who do so lose their salvation if they ever had it. And the reason it is such a serious sin in the sight of God is not only because it undercuts the very authority of God himself but also because it can endanger the very salvation of men, if, for example, works are *added* to the Gospel message of salvation.

And this, my friend, the Roman Catholic religion has done many times over! As we've already mentioned verses like Galatians 1:6–9 also forbids anyone to *add* anything to God's message of salvation and warns of damnation if anyone does. Unfortunately, probably millions have been deceived away from the true Gospel message within the Roman Catholic religion because it has added so many different religious good works of men to what Christ did for us on the cross!

Adding to God's Word the extra apocrypha books within the Catholic Bible

All their extra apocrypha books (added to the Catholic Bible) are another real example of the Catholic religion *adding* to God's Word. The word *apocrypha* just means hidden, and is simply used to describe the extra books added to the Catholic Bible which were written by Jews between 300 and 100 BC. Despite the fact that these certain historical writings *lacked Old Testament prophet authorship* and contained things which clearly *conflict with the teachings within the rest of the Bible (even the Catholic Bible),* the Roman Catholic religion still added them to their canon of scripture anyway and taught that they were inspired of God. But if the rest of the Bible obviously conflicts with some of the teachings within their extra books, which Catholic Holy Spirit is right and which is wrong? They both can't be right if they conflict with each other, any more than a perfect God could contradict himself!

While the Catholic religion added the apocrypha books to their Bible, at that very same time, *most* of the Protestant Church refused to accept them as divinely inspired Scripture for the following very good reasons:

    1. The Jews themselves never considered the apocrypha to be a part of the divinely inspired Scriptures because they firmly believed that there was no voice of God given to Israel after their Prophet Malachi in about 430 BC.

2. Jesus and the apostles never considered the apocrypha as part of the Scriptures and never quoted from them *once* as though they were inspired of God.
3. Unlike the Old Testament Scriptures, the apocrypha itself never claimed divine inspiration.
4. Some parts of the apocrypha contain historical mistakes as well.
5. The community who copied the Dead Sea Scrolls never gave inspired authority to the apocrypha like they did the Old Testament books.

Despite the fact that the apocrypha books lacked Old Testament prophet authorship and clearly conflicted with the teachings of the rest of the Bible, the Roman Catholic religion still taught that they were inspired of God.

My friend, none of these are small reasons for rejecting the apocrypha books which the Catholic religion has added to their Bible! The following are just some of those apocrypha books which the Catholic religion has added to their Bible because they chose to accept them as the inspired Word of God: Tobit, Judith, Maccabees 1, Maccabees 2, Wisdom of Solomon, Sirach (or Ecclesiasticus), and Baruch. Other books of the Catholic apocrypha are Esdras 1 and 2, the rest of Esther, The Letter of Jeremiah, Song of the Three Young Men, Susanna, Bel and the Dragon, The Additions to Daniel, and The Prayer of Manasseh. Again, this is not to say that all these apocrypha writings don't contain *any truth* or *historical value at all*; they just cannot be considered inspired by God for the true Church for all the obvious reasons we've cited.

Subtracting from God's Word—the removal of God's Second Commandment

Just how has the Roman Catholic religion subtracted from God's Word? If you just look into the official list of the Ten Commandments, which the Vatican of the Roman Catholic religion holds to be true, you'll find that the Roman Catholic religion has taken upon itself to remove the Second Commandment of God completely from the original Ten Commandments, and then it has split the Tenth Commandment into two separate Commandments just to hide it!

Even the Catholic Bible (NRSV) contains the Second Commandment of God, but when looking for it in the official Vatican doctrines of the Roman Catholic religion, it is completely gone from the list, and the tenth commandment is mysteriously split into two, so the total number of commandments remains ten in number.

So, if you are a Roman Catholic, which are you to believe? And just why did the Roman Catholic religion remove the Second Commandment of God from God's inspired Word anyway? Once you read it, it becomes rather obvious as to just why it was such a threat which could not be ignored by the Roman Catholic religion as it states, *"Thou shalt not make unto thee any graven image, or any likeness of anything that is in heaven above, or that is in the earth beneath, or that is in the water under the earth"* (Exodus 20:4).

Historically, the Roman Catholic religion has always been full of graven images, which, of course, would have been quite difficult to explain in light of this Second Commandment of God. Therefore, they boldly just took it out of God's Word! Unfortunately for those responsible, according to Revelation 22:19, to remove anything from God's Word is a serious salvation threatening sin in the sight of God!

> The Catholic religion has removed the Second Commandment of God completely from the original Ten Commandments and then split the tenth commandment into two separate commandments just to hide it.

Conclusion

Statistics are always changing, and depending upon the source for one's statistic, presently, there are roughly 1.3 billion people trapped in the false Roman Catholic religion and may not even realize that it truly is a cult which threatens their eternal salvation, depending upon how seriously that individual may hold to extrabiblical Catholic doctrine. If you happen to belong to the Roman Catholic religion, I would sincerely encourage you to reevaluate just what you have been taught and compare it carefully with the plain teachings of God's Word in even the Catholic Bible. One day soon, we will all stand before our perfect creator to give account of our lives and our beliefs. And I can assure you when it is your time to do so, the Roman Catholic religion leadership will be of no aid to you whatsoever! What you did with the true biblical Gospel message of salvation and the rest of his inspired Word will ultimately be your own responsibility before God on that day.

And I sincerely do not wish that you will have any major regrets because you chose to put your trust in fallible men within the Roman Catholic religion instead of the infallible Christ and his eternal Word. I would seriously encourage you to look up the Bible verses which we've cited in this objection (in even the Catholic Bible, if you wish) and prayerfully ask God to reveal the real truth of his salvation message to you. If you search out the matter at all, Jesus and his apostles never taught that man had to earn his eternal salvation through religious good works of any kind (John 3:16, 3:36). It was only a *free gift* to be humbly received through faith (Romans 1:17, 11:6). As Jesus himself said in John 8:31–32, *"If ye continue in my word, then ye are my disciples indeed; And ye shall know the truth, and the truth shall set you free."*

Someone once asked Jesus how many will be saved. And Jesus replied, *"Make every effort to enter through the narrow door (which is just faith in Himself), because many, I tell you, will try to enter and will not be able"* (Luke 13:24).

If anyone truly believes that even *one small good work* of their own (added to the true Gospel of faith alone) will save them, according to Scripture, they will simply *not be saved* (Galatians 1:6–9)! If you are one who is simply unwilling to let the mere traditions of men within the Roman Catholic religion destroy your opportunity to enter God's awesome eternal kingdom, I invite you to just take that first small step of faith by sincerely praying the true biblical prayer of salvation (which doesn't include the religious works of men) located at the end of this book.

To be sure, even praying a certain prayer doesn't even save us because salvation is truly a heart issue. But if we sincerely mean the true biblical prayer of salvation (with no works added to it) in our hearts when we do pray it, then God can give us his eternal life through it because it is his own Word to us which we are praying. However, with that said, if we truly believe in what Christ did for us on the cross, which we could not have done for ourselves, then we won't just pray the prayer of salvation and then just live for ourselves afterward either. We will just be inspired from the inside out to live for Christ because we truly want to return some of the love he showed us on the cross!

Objection 49
I'm a Catholic

If you were born into the Roman Catholic religion, it doesn't matter. If you married into it, it doesn't matter. If you've been tangled up in the Roman Catholic religion for many years, it doesn't matter because right now, you can choose with your very own free will which God gave you to break free from that major cult today which threatens your true salvation. And don't be concerned with what your family members may think of you because, simply put, they will not be your judge on judgment day! This decision is between you and God (your creator) alone. No matter what your past is like, God loves you, my Catholic friend, and sincerely wants you to be a part of his true Church, which is even more "universal" than the Roman Catholic religion realizes!

Jesus said, "I am the resurrection and the life. He who believes in me, will live even though he dies; and whoever lives and believes in me will never die." (John 11:25–26)

Note: Another good resource which may help you do this is titled *Understanding Roman Catholicism* by Rick Jones.

OBJECTION 50
I'm a Mormon

A loving reminder: Before each false religion and/or belief system we discuss, just so my loving intentions cannot be misunderstood, I will *once again* remind the reader that it's certainly *not the adherents* of any false religion or belief system which the true Church is against but rather just the *false teachings* within them which deceive men away from the one and only true God and his eternal salvation (Ephesians 6:12). Therefore, my dear reader, please know that our discussion of these various different religions or belief systems is very much a *love* issue.

The origin of Mormonism

Unlike biblical Christianity, which goes all the way back to the first man Adam (Genesis 1:26–27; Matthew 19:4; 1 Corinthians 15:45), the Mormon religion (again, I can't call it a church) was basically founded by Joseph Smith from AD 1820–1830. And all Mormon scripture apart from the Holy Bible (*The Book of Mormon*, *Doctrines and Covenants*, and the *Pearl of Great Price*) was manufactured sometime after 1830. In light of this, then, one must certainly ask the reasonable question: If Mormonism is really the one true faith for all humanity, how did all mankind have access to the vital truth which pertains to their eternal salvation during the many centuries prior to the very *late* birth of

Objection 50
I'm a Mormon

Mormonism? Would a perfect God really be so neglectful of his own creation? And, again, Mormonism can't at all claim that Christ and his apostles actually spearheaded their particular religion with all its unique doctrines because they never once even mention their religion by name or taught *any* of their unique doctrines in the entire New Testament! As we will demonstrate, the late origin of Mormonism is just one *among many* real problems for those claiming that Mormonism is the one true faith.

> If Mormonism is really the truth, how did all mankind have access to the vital truth which pertains to their eternal salvation during the many centuries prior to the late birth of Mormonism?

Mormons claim that after the death of Jesus's apostles, the whole Christian Church fell away from the faith, which they refer to as the Great Apostasy. During this apostasy, Mormons claim that there was a complete and universal abandonment of Christian principles. However, while of course the true Church has never been perfect throughout the entire church age so far, there are still no historical records whatsoever which would back up their claim that the true Church completely abandoned all Christian principles after the apostles died! In fact, there are enough historical records which would easily confirm that there has always been a large body of true believers, which have not compromised the teachings of Christ and his apostles, even during the worst times of church age history.

Yes, there were the dark ages wherein the Roman Catholic religion did dominate and abuse the common people simply because they did not have access to the Bible in their own language. But that didn't even stop the true church as the reformers did pull the church out of the dark ages when the printing press was invented and they once again applied the literal method of interpretation to the Bible in the language of the people. But for some reason, the Mormon religion cannot see those abundant historical records. Thus, they claim that a *complete restoration* of the Church was necessary, and that is why God the Father and Jesus Christ appeared to Joseph Smith in 1820, giving him *visions* of how the existing Christian Church was an abomination to God and that their doctrines and creeds were *all wrong*. However, while such a rash and sweeping belief about the true Christian Church would be a fast justification of the Mormon religion which Joseph Smith set up, it is, at the same time, plagued with some real basic obvious problems which certainly expose the Mormon religion as false:

1. First of all, if, in fact, the whole true Church fell into complete apostasy starting right after the apostles died, then why did God wait 1,700 years before he set up the supposed Mormon church? Especially if it only took about thirty years for Joseph Smith to get it going?
2. And if the Mormon religion, which Joseph Smith started, is really the true Church restored by the hand of God, then why is there only about 16 million Mormons in the world today against over seven billion? This would mean the true church only consists of 16 million people after 2,000 years! Even if there were 70 million Mormons on planet earth right now (which there isn't close to that number), that would only be about 1 percent of the world's population! Thus, 16 million is only about one-fourth of 1 percent of the world's population. One must then ask the reasonable question about this tiny fraction of a single percent: what on earth is God doing, if anything?

On the other hand, the Christian faith today based solely on the New Testament is the largest united faith on earth and makes up roughly 30 percent of the world's population, which of course has a much better reflection upon God and despite man's free will that he has not been too incompetent to have any impact upon his own creation.

3. And most obvious of all, if the Mormon religion today is truly the restored Church which Jesus Christ and his apostles had originally set up, then it is common sense that all their unique Mormon teachings would line right up with all that Jesus and his apostles taught in the New Testament. For if the Mormon religion is truly the restoration of the Church that Christ and his apostles originally set up, then the Mormons would at least retain all that Christ and the apostles taught! However, when it comes to all the doctrines which are unique only to

Objection 50
I'm a Mormon

Mormonism (without which the Mormon religion would completely crumble), you cannot find a single one within the entire New Testament! Therefore, we only have so many conclusions we can draw given these realities. Either the process of true Church restoration is a lot longer than we thought (like a billion years, even though the supposed apostasy started within only decades of Christ and his apostles) or Joseph Smith and the following founders of Mormonism all had a very difficult time reading and understanding the New Testament, even though the King James version is at a tenth- to twelfth-grade reading level.

However, at this point, the Mormon religion would say that *much* of the New Testament has been corrupted in the supposed Great Apostasy and cannot be relied upon as it has been mistranslated over the centuries since Christ and his apostles. And, of course, everywhere where the Bible does not agree with Joseph Smith's three other books is right where the Bible has been conveniently corrupted or mistranslated. However, as we already covered in our Objection #29, there is *absolutely no historical evidence* for today's New Testament having lost its original meaning or content as it has proven to be 99.5 percent textually pure and accurate when thoroughly examined by professional historians.

But, quite hypocritically, the same simply cannot be said of the three extra books of Mormonism when tested by professional historians. Again, for some reason, Mormons are either ignorant of this well tested fact or they simply deny it despite all the honest and sure methods of our professional historians.

It is interesting to note that many false religions (like Mormonism) which reject the main correct teachings and doctrines of the Bible often hypocritically use what scriptures they can from the Holy Bible, just so they can deceive and appear more credible. As we've already mentioned earlier, according to the New Testament (which has not lost its accuracy), all the contradicting false doctrines and religions in the world are ultimately hatched from the demonic realm for the purpose of deceiving mankind away from the one true God and his eternal salvation. And because the devil and his demonic host do need some truth mixed in with their lies in order to effectively deceive the ignorant, this then gives us some real insight as to why some false religions constantly *borrow only parts* of the Bible. Let's explore just *some* of the main unsolvable problems within Mormon teachings:

> Many false religions (like Mormonism) which reject the main correct teachings of the Bible often hypocritically use what scriptures they can from the Bible just so they can deceive and appear more credible.

Testing Mormonism against the true moral condition of man

Like many man-made cults, the Mormon religion rejects the Bible's clear teaching that all men have a sin nature, which is inherited from the first man, Adam, and the first woman, Eve. While they may believe all men can presently choose good or evil, like the Muslims, they basically reject the reality of *inherited sin from Adam and Eve*. Thus, because according to the Bible all men have inherited a sin nature from Adam and Eve, the Bible has always taught that *only Christ's shed blood on the cross* paid the separating penalty for all our sins (Colossians 1:20). But the Mormon religion obscurely teaches that man's own blood must pay for certain sins (such as fornication and murder)! But how can any sinful man pay for his own sins if he doesn't even have the sinless authority to do it? That, my friend, is like a thief trying to be his own civil court judge so he doesn't have to go to jail? He would simply not have the authority to do so because it was he who broke the law in the first place.

But I guess the Mormon religion wants the world to believe lawbreakers can be their own judge! However, it should be quite obvious to the honest soul that only a perfect God could keep his own perfect laws, so only he has the authority to pay for and forgive our sins when we break his own perfect moral standards.

Salvation

The Bible has always taught that God's eternal life is a free gift to be humbly received because it was paid for by Christ's death on the cross (in our place). However, Mormonism teaches that we (who wrestle with a sin nature every day) must partially earn our eternal life by keeping the Ten Commandments and other laws of God. However,

Objection 50
I'm a Mormon

isn't that a bit like a woman trying to win a beauty contest with dirty drain oil poured over her head? I guess the Mormon religion wants us to believe it can be done and base our very salvation on it!

On June 23, 1843, Joseph Smith said:

> *"I see no faults in the Church, and therefore let me be resurrected with the saints, whether I ascend to heaven or descend to hell, or go to any other place. And if we go to hell, we will turn the devil out of doors and make a heaven of it. Where this people are, there is good society. What do we care where we are, if the society be good."*

Obviously, Joseph Smith, the founder of the Mormon religion, didn't even know if he was going to heaven or hell. And is it not safe to say that he was being quite presumptuous to tell the world he was just going to turn the devil out of hell should he go there? So how could he possibly expect the rest of sane humanity to follow him? Not me!

Additionally, according to all related scripture in the Bible, the devil himself (including most of his demons) have never even set foot in hell yet nor will he until during and after the Millennial reign of Christ when an angel of God puts him there (Revelation 20:1–3). In many such instances, when Joseph Smith touches upon the realities of the Bible in his writings, he plainly shows how little he actually knew about the Bible!

According to the Bible, Satan and most of his demonic hosts are not at all in hell right now (nor have they ever been throughout the entire history of man) but rather they are on earth, looking for men to deceive, like Joseph Smith (1 Peter 5:8)! And when the devil finally does go to the hell as Scripture teaches, he will not be in charge of anything as he himself will be helplessly confined in torment just like anyone else there. In fact, the whole idea that the devil is in hell right now, tormenting the wicked is completely contrary to the plain teaching of God's Word.

> Many times, when Joseph Smith touches upon the realities of the Bible in his writings, he plainly shows how little he actually knew about the Bible.

Testing Mormonism against self-contradictions

There are actually many unsolvable contradictions within the Mormon religion. However, because we could easily write a whole book on just the contradictions, we will only cite a few obvious unsolvable contradictions which should be sufficient to show it simply cannot be the one true faith.

Self-contradiction #1

The Mormon religion teaches that there are many gods, not just one. In contradiction to both the Holy Bible and the *Book of Mormon*, today's Mormon doctrine teaches that the Father, the Son, and the Holy Spirit are actually three completely different gods instead of one god just manifested or expressed in three persons, which the Bible has always taught. As Deuteronomy 6:4 states, *"Hear, O Israel: The Lord our God is one Lord."*

As Isaiah 43:10 states, *"[b]efore me there was no God (not gods plural) formed, and neither shall there be after me."*

Isaiah 44:6, 8 states, *"Thus saith the Lord the King of Israel… I am the first, and I am the last; beside me there is no God… Is there a God beside me? Yea, there is no God; I know not any."*

Isaiah 45:6 states, *"[I] am the Lord, and there is none else."*

In John 10:30, *Jesus stated to the pharisees: "I and the Father are one."*

In John 14:9, *Jesus told his disciple, Philip, "He who has seen me has seen the Father: how can you say show us the Father?"*

Additionally, Ephesians 4:5 affirms there is only *"one Lord, one faith,"* not to mention the Mormon teachings about *many gods* flies in the face of the First Commandment: *"Thou shalt have no other gods."*

And the *Book of Mormon* actually agrees with the Holy Bible as it clearly states, *"I say unto you, that the Father and the Son, and the Holy Ghost are one"* (*Book of Mormon*, 3 Nephi 11:27).

In addition, 2 Nephi 31:21, 1 Nephi 13:41, Mormon 7:7, and Alma 11:44 in the *Book of Mormon* teach the same thing: the Father, Son, and the Holy Spirit are one God which just manifest in three different persons, not three different Gods. And, actually, the earlier part of the Mormon book, *Doctrine and Covenants*, also agrees with the Bible and the *Book of Mormon* as it also states: *"Which Father, Son, and Holy Ghost are one God, infinite and eternal, without end. Amen"* (Doctrine and Covenants 20:28).

Objection 50
I'm a Mormon

However, all this contradicts modern Mormon teaching which holds that the Father, Son, and Holy Ghost are actually three different Gods (which would all have to have different wills).

> In contradiction to both the Holy Bible and the book of Mormon, today's Mormon doctrine teaches that the Father, the Son, and the Holy Spirit are actually three different Gods.

Self-contradiction #2

Modern Mormon doctrine also recognizes a Mother God, not to mention the Mormon religion also teaches that its members can reach a state of exaltation and become gods themselves, having all power. But very reasonably, how can all exalted Mormons have *all power?* To have all power is to be all sovereign over everyone else. Logically, only one single being could have all power and be all sovereign over everyone else. Nevertheless, as we've just previously cited, both the *Book of Mormon* as well as their book, *Doctrine and Covenants,* both teach that there is only one God.

Self-contradiction #3

Strangely, Mormons actually study their genealogies, looking for dead relatives who have not been water-baptized. When they find one, they believe they can actually be baptized for them by proxy (in their place), hoping that they will have accepted the Gospel in the spirit world. However, Mormon proxy baptism directly contradicts both the Bible as well as the *Book of Mormon*, which teach such a practice is useless because once one finally dies in their sins, they simply cannot have any other chances for eternal life after that. Even the *Book of Mormon* states, "For behold, this life is the time for men to meet God" (*Book of Mormon*, Alma 34:32).

> "For behold, if ye have procrastinated the day of your repentance even until death, behold ye have become subjected to the spirit of the devil, and he doth seal you his; therefore the Spirit of the Lord hath withdrawn from you and hath no place in you, and the devil hath all power over you; and this is the final state of the wicked." (Book of Mormon, Alma 34:35)

While this last passage in the *Book of Mormon* has an unbiblical teaching about the devil having all power over the damned, it nonetheless does clearly agree with the Bible that after one dies in their sins, any repentance after that is simply impossible. This, too, then is another obvious unsolvable contradiction with the modern Mormon teaching of proxy baptism for dead relatives that they might be saved. Not to mention the Holy Bible (which Mormons claim to believe in) teaches against any works of man (like water baptism) being added to the Gospel for salvation! Additionally, not only is it impossible for anyone to be water baptized for salvation, but it is also impossible for any other imperfect human being to do any good works to get another into heaven. It doesn't matter if you are related to them or not! So, either way, the doctrine of proxy baptism is false on at least three accounts within God's Holy Word.

> Mormon proxy baptism directly contradicts both the Bible as well as the Book of Mormon.

Self-contradiction #4

After Joseph Smith had finished the *Book of Mormon* and almost all of *Doctrine and Covenants*, he had the new idea of men having more than one wife and wrote new Mormon scripture to accommodate that belief, namely *Doctrine and Covenants 132*, which actually commands men to marry more than one wife:

> "[I] the Lord justified my servants Abraham, Isaac...as touching the principle and doctrine of their having many wives and concubines...prepare thy heart to receive and obey the instructions which I am about to give unto you... For behold, I reveal unto you a new and everlasting covenant; and if ye abide not in that covenant, then ye are damned; for no one can reject this covenant and be permitted to enter into my glory."

According to this passage of Mormon scripture, anyone who rejects this new and everlasting covenant of plural wives is actually *damned* forever. However, in the *Book of Mormon* (Jacob 2:24–27), Joseph Smith himself clearly taught that polygamy is wrong and an abomination to God as he wrote:

Objection 50
I'm a Mormon

> "Behold, David and Solomon truly had many wives and concubines, which thing was abominable before me, saith the Lord. Wherefore, thus says the Lord, I have led this people forth out of the land of Jerusalem, by the power of mine arm, that I might raise up unto me a righteous branch from the fruit of the loins of Joseph. Wherefore, I the Lord God will not suffer that the people shall do like unto them of old. Wherefore, my brethren, hear me, and hearken to the word of the Lord: For there shall not any man among you have save it be one wife; and concubines he shall have none."

Clearly, the *Book of Mormon* here directly contradicts *Doctrine and Covenants*, which was also written by Joseph Smith. Notice how clearly *Doctrine and Covenants 132:9* contradicts the passage we just quoted out of the *Book of Mormon*:

> "David's wives and concubines were given unto him of me, by the hand of Nathan, my servant, and others of the prophets who had the keys of this power; and in none of these things did he sin against me save in the case of Uriah and his wife."

However, you cannot find one scripture in the Bible which teaches us that God or his prophets ever gave David (or anyone else) the permission to even take many wives! And there certainly is no scripture that says that Nathan (God's prophet at the time of David) gave David permission to take many wives. The New Testament certainly forbids polygamy (1 Corinthians 7:2) and calls it the sin of *fornication*. And we are also taught that God himself (from Old Testament times to New Testament times) is the very same yesterday and today and forever (Hebrews 13:8).

When Abraham doubted and had a child with Hagar his servant, it is quite apparent God was not pleased, and constant warfare between Hagar's descendants (the Arabs) and Sarah's descendants (the Israelites) reveals the bad fruit which came of Abraham's doubt. Solomon fell away from his faith due to his many wives, and David's many wives ensued many family problems on him. Thus, we can conclude that the many wives of these Old Testament patriarchs were simply not even God's will.

Self-contradiction #5

Mormons teach that all Mormons can reach the state of exaltation and become an all-powerful god by keeping the laws of God. And because of this teaching, Mormons also actually teach that the first man, Adam, actually became God the Father (which, again, is blasphemy). So when Mormons pray to the Father, they are actually praying to Adam! But then you have to ask the very reasonable question: Who created the first man, Adam, if Adam became God the Father? And if it was the Holy Spirit that created Adam, then why didn't the Holy Spirit come from a man also? And if the Holy Spirit came from a man, who created that man? What a mucked up spiritual mess, huh?

Self-contradiction #6

Why did Joseph Smith try to join the Methodist church in 1828 when in his 1820 *vision,* the Lord supposedly commanded him to join none of them (Baptist, Methodist, and Presbyterian churches) as they were all an abomination in his sight (*The Amboy Journal*, April 30, 1879, p. 1, and June 11, 1879)? Obviously, Joseph was disobeying his god (which really only could have been a demon deceiving him). But more than that, if Mormonism was truly the one true faith in his eyes, then in his mind, Joseph was actually trying to join a cult by trying to join the Methodist church. But, in truth, the Methodist church back then was a very legitimate church of Christ and quite biblical. But according to Joseph who had taught it was an abomination in the sight of God from a supposed vision he got from God, Joseph had to be literally falling away from his counterfeit faith in order to even attempt joining the Methodist church. Hmm…he seems rather unstable indeed, does he not?

> Why did Joseph Smith try to join the Methodist church in 1828 when in his 1820 vision, the Lord supposedly commanded him to join none of them (Baptist, Methodist, and Presbyterian churches) as they were all an abomination in his sight?

OBJECTION 50
I'M A MORMON

Self-contradiction #7

Joseph Smith admonished his people not to drink wine or strong drink (*Doctrine and Covenants* Sec. 86). But then he attempted to construct a bar in the mansion house he lived in and only removed it when his wife, Emma, scolded him by saying: "Either that bar goes or I go" (*Saints Herald*, Feb. 1999, p. 18; and *Doctrine and Covenants,* Sec. 86). Are you getting the impression that Joseph Smith was a very mixed-up hypocrite who also probably had a drinking problem? I sure am.

More self-contradictions

Other whole doctrines of the Church of Jesus Christ of the Latter-Day saints which cannot even be found in the *Book of Mormon* (and some of them directly contradicting the *Book of Mormon*) are:
1. God as an exalted man.
2. A heavenly mother.
3. The degrees of glory.
4. The word of wisdom (hot drinks forbidden, such as coffee, etc.).
5. The preexistence of people's spirits.
6. Eternal progression (the belief that men may become gods). The *Book of Mormon* also teaches that God does not change (*Book of Mormon*, Mormon 9:9–11 and Moroni 8:18).

Testing Mormonism against the well-known facts of history

The *Book of Mormon* claims that the languages spoken by the first people to live in America were Hebrew and Egyptian. However, if this were true, at least some of the Native American languages would contain words which clearly show this to be true. If the *Book of Mormon* is correct, then many Indian words would contain Hebrew and Egyptian roots: but, in fact, *none* of them do. According to the *Book of Mormon*, the Hebrew immigrants knew how to read and write. If Hebrew really was an original language in America, it would seem with all the archaeological finds in the Americas that Hebrew writings or inscriptions would have been found, but they have not. But against all *professional* archaeological evidence, I guess the Mormon religion just wants us to take their word for it blindly. Hmm…not good.

> If the Book of Mormon is correct, then many Indian words would contain Hebrew and Egyptian roots, but none of them do.

Testing Mormonism against the well-known facts of science

As we've already covered in our previous Objection #41, any religion which touches upon *science* can be objectively tested against the well-known facts of science to see if its source of truth is really the eternal God who must be perfect by definition. For example, Joseph Smith, the founder of the Mormon religion, seriously taught back in the 1800s (before modern science) that the moon was actually inhabited by 1,000-year-old men who dressed like Quakers (see *The Young Woman's Journal*, Vol. 3, p. 263–264; and reprint of a book called *Mormonism: Shadow or Reality?*)!

Today, modern science has easily disproved such an absurd notion just through our modern space exploration and technologies. But if Joseph Smith seriously taught that (before our modern technologies could prove otherwise) and at the same time claimed to be God's true prophet for the whole world, just what does that do for his credibility? My friend, it should destroy it on the spot! Men not only have the perfect right to judge his credibility against the obvious scientific discoveries of modern man but also the perfect right to judge the credibility of Mormonism in general against the credibility of Joseph Smith! Thus, Mormonism as the one true religion fails this reasonable test of modern scientific discovery and can be ruled out as the one true faith, just on this fantastic claim alone. Would you trust such a misguided mess of a man to show you the way of eternal salvation? I hope not!

> Joseph Smith, the founder of the Mormon religion, seriously taught back in the 1800s (before our modern science) that the moon was actually inhabited by 1,000-year-old men who dressed like Quakers!

Testing Mormonism against archaeological discovery

According to the Mormon religion, the *Book of Mormon* is presented as true history. It gives us many details which can easily be checked

Objection 50
I'm a Mormon

out. Mormons themselves often claim that the *Book of Mormon* can be authenticated as divine through archaeological discoveries. However, while many cities mentioned in the Bible have been uncovered right where the Bible says, no real archaeological evidence has been found in America that directly verifies the claims within the *Book of Mormon*.

One such claim is that the *Book of Mormon* tells of the final battle between the Nephites and the Lamanites. This battle supposedly took place on Hill Cumorah in New York where the gold plates were hidden. If hundreds and thousands of people fought in this great war as the *Book of Mormon* claims (p. 702–703), why are there no artifacts as evidence to be found by archaeologists? Oh, and by the way, no one has, of course, ever found the supposed golden plates of Mormonism either.

While no one has found the original Ten Commandments within the biblical Ark of the Covenant either, it is hardly a fair comparison, considering the supposed golden tablets of Mormonism are not even 200 years old! Going by all the other deceptions we've plainly exposed in this objection, do you honestly think that they ever really existed?

Even though the golden plates supposedly weighed about 230 pounds (Joseph gave their exact dimensions), in Lucy Mack Smith's book, titled *Joseph Smith and His Progenitors*, p. 120, she tells of an incident where her son (Joseph) fought off three attackers while running at the top of his speed through the woods for three miles with the golden plates tucked under his arm! But the problem is, according to the dimensions of these gold tablets which Joseph Smith himself gave us, they would have weighed no less than 230 pounds! Obviously, he was divinely inspired to run with supernatural strength, right?

Going by his moral character, I highly doubt myself that the golden plates ever even existed. I personally believe Joseph was a natural born liar, and it doesn't look like his own mother was much different, unless you really believe Joseph Smith ran at top speed for three miles fighting off attackers with 230 pounds tucked under one arm!

My friend, no bodybuilder or football player today could probably pull off such a run! Since Joseph Smith was probably not even a runner, he'd probably even have a difficult time running three miles without carrying anything! Additionally, it doesn't make much sense for his wife, Emma, to even move them *"from place to place as it was necessary in doing my work,"* if indeed they weighed 230 pounds going by their dimensions (*Saint Herald*, Oct. 1, 1879)? In my opinion, there are some real unsolvable problems here which directly defy basic science as well as the common sense of a ten-year-old. What do you think?

> Even though the golden plates supposedly weighed about 230 pounds, Lucy Mack Smith (Joseph's mother) testifies in her writings that Joseph Smith ran at top speed for three miles with the golden plates tucked under one arm!

Testing Mormonism against the character of its founder

In the *Teachings of the Prophet Joseph Smith*, p. 363, Joseph Smith declared, *"God made Aaron to be the mouth piece for the children of Israel, and he will make me be God to you in his stead, and if you don't like it, you must lump it.'"*

Anyone who would follow such a self-absorbed blasphemous creep would have to be completely ignorant of this statement which he sincerely made, especially considering all Mormons today are supposed to have a reputation in the community of politeness and courtesy! First of all, according to the Bible, once again, Joseph Smith is not even accurate when he says that Aaron was the mouthpiece for the children of Israel. According to the Bible, Aaron was, in fact, the mouthpiece for the Prophet Moses, not the whole nation of Israel. Moses was the prophet for Israel, but Aaron was not.

Secondly, notice Joseph doesn't just say here that he'd speak for God (as in the case of a prophet, which he claimed to be) but that he'd actually be God (through force) to the Mormons in God's place! Since this is *obvious blasphemy*, this statement alone should completely disqualify Mormonism altogether as the one true faith in the eyes of anyone being honest with themselves. And considering Mormonism claims to be the restored church of Christ and the apostles who would definitely consider Joseph's statement to be quite blasphemous, that too should be a real problem!

> Joseph Smith doesn't just say that he'd speak for God (as in the case of a prophet, which he claimed to be) but that he'd actually be God (through

Objection 50
I'm a Mormon

force) to the Mormons in God's place!

Testing Mormonism against its prophetic predictions of the future

The Bible has always taught men to test anyone claiming to be a prophet of God, simply by seeing if what they said came to pass. Because if it was from the eternal God, who must be perfect, the prediction would surely come to pass, including its details if it has any. 1 John 4:1 states, *"Beloved, believe not every spirit, but try the spirits whether they are of God: because many false prophets are gone out into the world."*

In Deuteronomy 18:20–22, God not only commanded the Old Testament nation of Israel to test prophets but to also put them to death if they should prove false as it states:

> *"But the prophet which shall presume to speak a word in my name, which I have not commanded him to speak, or that shall speak in the name of other gods, even that prophet shall die. And if thou say in thine heart, How shall we know the word which the Lord hath not spoken? When a prophet speaketh in the name of the Lord, if the thing follow not, nor come to pass, that is the thing which the Lord hath not spoken, but the prophet hath spoken it presumptuously: Thou shalt not be afraid of him."*

Joseph Smith not only claimed to be God to his deceived followers, but clearly, he also claimed to be God's prophet. But, of course, the obvious problem for anyone honest is that he made many prophecies of the future which were proven false with time! This obviously makes him a false prophet who obviously then founded a false religion. The following are just a few of many:

1. Smith wrote out several of his prophecies in *Doctrine and Covenants*, which had time limits put on them. One such prophecy Smith gave in 1832 (*Doctrine and Covenants* 84:3–4):

> *"Which city shall be built, beginning at the temple lot, which is appointed by the finger of the Lord, in the western boundaries of the state of Missouri, and dedicated by the hand of Joseph Smith... Verily this is the word of the Lord, that the city New Jerusalem shall be built by the gathering of the saints, beginning at this place, even the place of the temple, which temple shall be reared in this generation. For verily this generation shall not all pass away until an house shall be built unto the Lord."*

This prophecy of Joseph Smith's which predicts that Mormons would build a whole city (called New Jerusalem) and a temple in western Missouri before Joseph Smith's generation died simply did not come to pass at all. My friend, this is not just some little error where most of the prophecy came to pass, except a few minor details. His whole prophecy did not come to pass at all! Joseph Smith is clearly not hearing from the Lord in this prophecy which clearly makes him a false prophet of a false religion, probably hearing from the demonic realm instead.

> The prophecy of Joseph Smith's which predicted that Mormons would build a whole city (called New Jerusalem) and a temple in western Missouri before Joseph Smith's generation died simply did not come to pass at all.

2. In 1832, in Doctrine and Covenants (87), Smith made another prophecy about the Civil War which was only accurate on two minor points and false on many other accounts. Though it accurately predicted that the southern states shall be divided against the northern states, by 1932, this kind of division rumor was already in the air because South Carolina opposed a new tax law. In other words, it was not a difficult guess on Joseph's part!

Joseph also accurately predicted where the Civil War would start. But again, in 1832, it was also rumored to start right where it started in 1861. So it could have easily been just another educated guess on Joseph's part. However, the false prophet is really exposed when he also predicted that Great Britain would step in to help the South, thus starting a world war. He further states: *"And then war shall be poured out upon all nations"* (87:3). And, of course, his biggest blunder in the prophecy was when he also predicted the Civil War would bring a full end of all nations (87:6)!

This prophecy is even a much bigger failure than the last which we discussed. And Mormons cannot try to say that the full end of all nations just meant that the Civil War would just lead into the book of Revelation because even in the book of Revelation, all nations never come to an end. And you still have to explain why Great Britain did not help the South in the Civil War as predicted. Any which way, the prophecy is false along with the prophet and his very man-made demonic religion.

3. In another of Smith's prophecies given in 1932, the bishop Newel K. Whitney was to warn the cities of New York, Albany, and Boston of impending judgment if they rejected his gospel. It stated:

> "Nevertheless, let the bishop go unto the city of New York, also the city of Albany, and also to the city of Boston, and warn the people of those cities with the sound of the gospel, with a loud voice, of the desolation and utter abolishment which await them if they do reject these things. For if they do reject these things, the hour of their judgment is nigh, and their house shall be left unto them desolate."

Like many of his other prophecies, many years have passed, and the thing which he spoke did not at all come to pass. Utter abolishment are big words to predict for those major cities, and nothing of the kind ever happened. My friend, how much more of a false prophet could Joseph Smith have been? If anyone cannot acknowledge Joseph Smith's obvious false prophecies, they must indeed have some real *honesty* issues! There are many more false prophecies given by Joseph Smith in *Doctrine and Covenants*. Some of them are found in Doctrine and Covenants 97:19, 111:2–4, 124:56–60.

Testing Mormonism against the moral fruit it has produced

In a book called *Secret History (An Eyewitness Account of the Rise of Mormonism)*, the fact is fully exposed that many were even murdered when they tried to leave the Mormon church in their day when it was first being established. Since Christ and his apostles always taught men to love one another (1 John 3:10–11), how much more polar opposite could the murderous history of the Mormon church be from biblical Christianity? If Christ or his apostles had done any such thing, I can assure you that the New Testament Church would never have been born!

> In a book called, Secret History (An Eyewitness Account of the Rise of Mormonism), the fact is fully exposed that many were murdered when they tried to leave the Mormon church in their day when it was first being established.

Testing Mormonism against its divine power demonstrated

The Mormon religion basically teaches that Christ is just one of many gods and is actually just the spirit brother of Lucifer, the devil, who is also a created being. But, when looking at all historical documents of the New Testament which quote Christ and his apostles, since none of them ever taught such a thing about Christ, then where's any proof for such a fantastic claim? And if the New Testament nowhere teaches that Jesus is the spirit brother of Lucifer, then how can Mormons claim their religion is the actual restoration of the true Church which Christ and his apostles set up?

Once again, I guess we are just to blindly take the Mormon's word for it, even though no Mormon leader has ever done the divinely empowered miracles which Christ and his apostles did hundreds of times over in front of many historical witnesses. Ultimately, the Mormon religion must solely rely on their extra man-made books (*The Pearl of Great Price, Doctrine and Covenants,* and *The Book of Mormon*) for such a teaching about Christ. But Mormonism still lacks any real divine power demonstrated through public miracles or accurately fulfilled prophecy.

The Bible

The Mormon religion also teaches that their three other books (*The Book of Mormon, Doctrine and Covenants,* and *Pearl of Great Price*) are at least equal to the Holy Bible. However, if there is a discrepancy between the Holy Bible and their extra books, Mormons will typically insist that the Holy Bible was mistranslated and their other books are correct. Therefore, let's be quite honest: Mormons actually place their extra books *above the Holy Bible, not equal to it.* And if you think about it, they almost have to, simply because many of their unique teachings cannot be found within the Holy Bible. But when looking for any amazing fulfilled predictions of the future in their three other books, which would prove divine authorship (such as we see hundreds of times within the Holy Bible), there are none.

Again, I guess we're just supposed to take their word for it that their three other books are more correct or more inspired than the Holy Bible, even though the lack of evidence for divine authorship through fulfilled prophecy completely indicates that their three extra books are not divinely inspired at all.

Objection 50
I'm a Mormon

Considering these three extra books actually claim to prescribe the vital way to eternal life for the entire human race (after 1830, of course), maybe we should expect some honest evidence for divine authorship before we should ever believe that such books ever came from God. After all, many different contradicting religions within history have written many so-called holy books and claimed they came from God; and when you think about it, really, anyone could do that! However, the Holy Bible stands alone as nearly 2,000 prophecies within it have already miraculously come true, just as it foretold hundreds of years in advance! Only a perfect and all-knowing God could have predicted the future so many times with 100 percent accuracy! And that's the kind of evidence we need before we would trust a source as divinely prescribing the way of eternal life for all mankind.

Our faith should never be blind faith or faith just in man's word which does not have such proof; it should be in the power of the living God which should be self-evident to any honest soul.

The birth of Christ

Within the Holy Bible, all the apostles were in agreement on all the basic doctrines of the Christian faith with no indications that they were in disagreement. And one of those basic doctrines was that Jesus was born of a virgin and conceived by the Holy Spirit (Luke 1:35). And when Christ and his apostles lived on earth, they all performed many great miracles of God which demonstrated that God was with them and that they taught the truth of God (Matthew 9:35; Acts 2:22, 2:42–43; 1 Timothy 4:6, 16). Therefore, if both Jesus and his disciples taught that Jesus himself was conceived by the Holy Spirit, we can be sure that their doctrine on this issue was correct! However, strangely enough, the Mormon religion teaches that Jesus Christ was conceived by the Father, not the Holy Spirit.

But if it is the Mormon religion's word against Christ and his apostles as to who conceived Christ, who within the Mormon religion has displayed all the divine attributes of Christ that we should believe them over Christ and his apostles? Did Joseph Smith raise the dead and control the weather to show God was with him? Did Brigham Young heal many sick and crippled people to show God was with him? I guess, once again, we are expected to just blindly take their word for it!

The Holy Bible (backed by original Greek manuscripts which date close to the time of Christ) teaches us plainly that Christ was conceived by the Holy Spirit. How far back do the three extra books in Mormonism date? Not any further back than the 1800s, I can assure you! So, honestly, why should we trust them (on a teaching about Christ) over the Bible which dates right back to Christ himself?

Who Is God?

As we've already mentioned, the Mormon religion basically teaches that if Mormons keep the whole law of God in this life, they'll reach a state they call exaltation and become a god which possesses immortality and actually rules over other whole worlds for all eternity. They teach that even the angels and all things will be subject to those who reach exaltation and that they will have *all power* (Doctrine and Covenants 132:19–22; *Doctrine of Salvation, Vol. 2,* p. 39,48). But, again, if Mormons can reach a state of godhood where they can have *all power,* then how can God our creator have *all power* at the same time (Matthew 28:18)? You can't have two all-powerful beings, much less many more than two!

Obviously, such a teaching, while it may appeal to the sin nature of some, defies all logic and common sense. This whole Mormon teaching on becoming a god by reaching the state of exaltation cannot be found within the Bible at all. Additionally, the Holy Bible has always taught that there is only one God who is separate and distinct from his own creation (which includes all deceived Mormons). Yes, man is created in God's image, but the reality remains we were created, and there is only one God who is defined as the creator who was himself never created. As God clearly teaches us through his Prophet Isaiah in Isaiah 43:10, *"Before me there was no God formed, and neither shall there be after me."*

In Isaiah 44:6, God says, *"I am the first and I am the last; besides me there is no God."*

> If Mormons can reach a state of godhood where they can have all power, then how can God our creator have all power at the same time? You can't have two all-powerful beings, much less many more than two!

Objection 50
I'm a Mormon

Clearly, Isaiah 44:6 teaches that there is no God besides the one true God, so how can Mormons teach that all mankind can become a god by reaching exaltation and eternally produce spirit children who all in turn can also reach exaltation and become a god as well? If that process continues forever, which is what the Mormon religion ultimately teaches, then the number of gods produced is eternally unlimited! You in fact can't get more polar opposite of what the Bible actually teaches, that there is only *"one God and Father of us all, who is above all, and through all"* (Ephesians 4:6). In fact, there is only one single verse that I know of in the entire Bible which could possibly be *misunderstood* to mean that man can be a god, and that is Psalm 82:1,6.

John 10:34–36 is just a reference to Psalm 82:1, 6, and according to both Psalm 82:1, 6, and John 10:34–36, they collectively refer to the human judges of Israel as *gods,* simply because they were appointed by God *to act in the name of the true God* while judging civil and spiritual matters within their nation. In this sense, they were the *children of the Most High* as evidenced in Psalm 82:6.

But, obviously, God (or Jesus) did not mean to suggest that the created could become the creator who himself was never created. And even this verse could not teach that men could become gods through such a Mormon idea like exaltation by trying to keep the whole law of God. Whatever was meant by those human judges of Israel being gods, they already were gods; they did not have to earn it and become a god through keeping the whole law of God and eventually reach a state the Mormon religion calls exaltation. So, either way, Psalm 82:1, 6 does not at all fit with the Mormon religion teaching that man can become a god through a process of good works. And considering those in Psalm 82:1, 6 who were called gods surely failed to keep the whole law of God themselves, it is rather impossible to use Psalm 82:1, 6 to teach that men can become gods by keeping the whole law of God. In fact, it was because all Israel did fail to keep the whole law of God that God had to send his perfect Son, Jesus, to die for the sins of the whole world, even the sins of all Mormons. And that's why the Apostle Paul stated in Galatians 2:21, *"I do not frustrate (or violate) the grace of God: for if righteousness came by the law, then Christ died in vain."*

Is it just a coincidence that Satan told Eve that she and Adam could become *as gods* just before they disobeyed God in the garden of Eden and plunged the whole world into sin for at least 6,000 years (Genesis 3:5)? I think not. For it was also Satan's main sin to think he could become like the Most High (Isaiah 14:12–15). So, while the Mormons claim that man can become a god by keeping God's laws, the Bible actually teaches us that man trying to become a god (by just doing our own thing) is the very definition of sin! Passages like Isaiah 30:1, 53:6, 65:2, Jeremiah 18:12, and Ezekiel 13:3 all discuss this. Even some powerful political dictator types throughout history have claimed to be a god. However, the consistent evil fruit of those men throughout history also showed us that when men foolishly try to be equal with God, it just leads to pride and destruction every time and shows us that Satan (who first wanted to be God) has influenced them to do so.

Conclusion

The Mormon Tabernacle Choir may be well known. But it is simply not enough for the one true faith to have a talented choir. It also must have the truth backed by solid honest evidence, which Mormonism obviously lacks. After all, they want to worship God in heaven, don't they? Statistics are always changing, and depending upon the source for one's statistic, presently, there are *roughly* 16 million people worldwide who have been deceived into Mormonism. While that may seem to be a lot to a Mormon, as we've already mentioned, it is *less than* a fourth of 1 percent of the world's population! It should be truly difficult for anyone to believe that more than 99.75 percent of today's world population is deceived and unable to make it into the Mormon religion concept of heaven or exaltation (not to mention all those who lived prior to 1830)!

Jesus proved his divinity to the honest soul many times over when he lived a sinless life, fulfilled all the Messianic prophecies, and did hundreds of miracles so powerful that they could only come from God. But, honestly, what are Joseph Smith's spiritual credentials beyond that of just another weak human being deceived by demonic spirits? Or Brigham Young's, for that matter? God's Word foretells the awesome eternity for all those who put their trust in Christ. As Revelation 21:3–4 clearly teaches:

Objection 50
I'm a Mormon

"[B]ehold, the dwelling place of God is with men, and he will live with them, and they shall be his people, and God himself shall be with them, and be their God. And God shall wipe away all tears from their eyes; and there shall be no more death, neither sorrow, nor crying, neither shall there be any more pain: for the former things are passed away."

But the Bible teaches us plainly that *only through Christ* can we obtain God's eternal life.

Jesus said, "I am the way and the truth and the life. No one comes to the Father except through me." (John 14:6)

Someone once asked Jesus how many will be saved. And Jesus replied:

"Make every effort to enter through the narrow door, because many, I tell you, will try to enter and will not be able." (Luke 13:24)

If anyone believes that even *one small good work* of their own (added to the "true faith alone" gospel) will save them, according to scripture, they will simply *not be saved* (Galatians 1:6–9)! If you are one who is unwilling to let the false doctrines in the Mormon religion destroy your chance for eternal life in God's awesome eternal kingdom to come, then I would encourage you to give Christ your creator a chance by embracing the true biblical Gospel of salvation. If you are one who can easily see that the Mormon religion is clearly man-made because it fails the very reasonable basic tests we've applied to it, and you'd like to know for certain that you too are right with God and have his eternal life, I invite you to just take that first small step of faith by sincerely praying the prayer of salvation located at the end of this book. It doesn't matter if you've been a Mormon for many years; you can still break away from that obvious cult today which threatens your true salvation through Christ.

And don't be concerned with what your family members may think of you because they will not be your judge on judgment day! This decision is between you and God (your creator) alone. No matter what your past is like, God loves you and sincerely wants you to be a part of his awesome eternal kingdom!

Jesus said, "I am the resurrection and the life. He who believes in me, will live even though he dies; and whoever lives and believes in me will never die." (John 11:25–26)

Note: Other good resources which clearly expose the Mormon religion as false are *Mormonism: A Way that Seemeth Right* and *Mormonism: Shadow or Reality?*

OBJECTION 51
I'm a Jehovah's Witness

A loving reminder: Before each false belief system we discuss, just so my loving intentions cannot be misunderstood, I will *once again* remind the reader that it's certainly *not the adherents* of any false belief system which the true Church is against but rather just the *false teachings* within them which deceive men away from the one and only true God and his eternal salvation (Ephesians 6:12). Therefore, my dear reader, please know that our discussion of these various different religions or belief systems is very much a *love* issue.

The origin of the Jehovah's Witnesses religion

Unlike biblical Christianity which goes all the way back to the first man, Adam (Genesis 1:26–27; Matthew 19:4; 1 Corinthians 15:45), the Jehovah's Witnesses religion which exists today came out of the Bible Student movement which was largely founded in the 1870s by a man named Charles T. Russell. After Russell's death in 1916, the Bible Student movement split into several rival organizations, one of which was headed by Joseph Judge Rutherford who made significant changes to the doctrines of Russell which resulted in many long-term members leaving the organization. Nevertheless, the group quickly grew, and in 1931, it adopted the name of Jehovah's Witnesses. Further changes to its doctrines led to the forbidding of blood transfusions, the symbol of the cross of Christ, birthday celebrations, and the Christmas holiday.

The religion was actually banned in Canada during WWII and in Germany, Soviet Union, Canada, and Australia and has even suffered mob violence in those countries as well as the United States.

Once again, in light of the fact that the Jehovah's Witnesses religion basically started in the 1870s, one must certainly ask the very reasonable question: If the Jehovah's Witnesses religion is the truth for all mankind, how indeed did all mankind have access to the vital truth which pertains to their eternal salvation during the many centuries prior to its very late starting date? Would a perfect God really be so neglectful of his own creation? And, again, the JW religion can't at all claim that Christ and his apostles actually spearheaded their particular religion with all its unique doctrines because neither Christ nor his apostles never once even mention their religion by name or taught any of their unique JW doctrines in the entire New Testament. Nor can the Jehovah's Witnesses claim that Christ's Church went into complete apostasy and needed to be restored or that the New Testament lost its accuracy through mistranslations because there is simply no *professional* historical evidence for such claims. These are just some among many unsolvable problems within the Jehovah's Witnesses religion as we will reasonably show.

> If the Jehovah's Witnesses religion is the truth for all mankind, how indeed did all mankind have access to the vital truth which pertains to their eternal salvation during the many centuries prior to its very late starting date?

Again, it is interesting to note that many false religions (like the Jehovah's Witnesses) which reject the main correct teachings and doctrines of the Bible often hypocritically use what scriptures they can from the Holy Bible, just so they can deceive and appear more credible. But, reasonably, if their false religion is really the one true faith, why on earth do they even need to borrow any scriptures or doctrines from the Holy Bible in the first place? If Jehovah's Witnesses rely on their New World Translation whenever there's a disagreement between the Holy Bible and their New World Translation, then why do they even need the Holy Bible at all? I can assure you that biblical Christianity certainly does not borrow any of the unique teachings of the Jehovah's Witnesses just to appear more credible!

Objection 51
I'm a Jehovah's Witness

Testing Jehovah's Witnesses against self-contradictions

As we already mentioned, any religion can be tested against self-contradictions. According to their religion, the King James Bible has many mistakes, so they created their own version. It's called the New World Translation. However, the problem is that it is not only the Bible but even their New World Translation which contradicts their beliefs and other written material. For example, like a lot of other small false cults out there, they teach that Jesus Christ is not God the creator but rather just a created being. However, according to the Bible itself, all these religious groups which teach this must be considered non-Christian cults trafficking in basic heresy which threatens their salvation. And most all such cults must heavily rely upon their own books and literature other than the Bible or they have corrupted versions of the Bible which support their false teachings. Or like the Jehovah's Witnesses, they have both.

For one example, the Jehovah's Witnesses do not just teach that Jesus is not God but rather he is actually Michael the Archangel, who was just a god, the first being God ever created. But this basic teaching of theirs not only goes directly against the Holy Bible but also their own New World Translation as well.

While their New World Translation does greatly obscure the basic biblical truth that Jesus Christ is God the creator, even it still teaches that Jesus Christ is, in fact, God who created everything and not just some created being. And obviously, common sense does not allow one to have it both ways! First, we'll further confirm that the Jehovah's Witnesses belief that Jesus Christ is just a created being does go directly against the authorized version of the Holy Bible as the Bible has always plainly taught that Jesus Christ is God and not just some created being like an angel (John 1:1–17, 20:28; 1 Timothy 3:16; Isaiah 9:6-7; John 10:30-33; Matthew 16:16–17; 1 John 5:5; 1 Peter 2:21–22). And as we've already mentioned, in Colossians 1:16–17, the Apostle Paul plainly confirms Christ's unique claim to deity when he writes:

"For by Him (referring to Christ; see v. 13) were all things created, that are in heaven, and that are in the earth, visible and invisible, whether they be thrones, or dominions, or principalities, or powers: all things were created by Him and for Him: and he is before all

things, and by him all things are held together."

> If, in fact, according to even their New World Translation (John 1:1–17; Hebrews 1:8, 10; Colossians 1:16), Christ created everything that was ever created, then how could he himself possibly be God's first created being?

So, of course, the honest question is: If, in fact, according to their New World Translation, Christ created everything that was ever created, then how could he himself possibly be God's first created being? The amazing thing is that Jehovah's Witnesses will still claim to believe in the Bible. But how can they make such a claim when even their own corrupted version of the Bible goes directly against their own basic beliefs? Nevertheless, with all that said, one can easily prove through even their corrupted New World Translation that Jesus Christ is still unmistakably our one true God and creator of all things. For example, if one compares all the divine attributes of *Jehovah*, the *Lord*, or *God* with those of *Jesus Christ* within even their corrupt version of the Bible, they will find that they are consistently describing one and the same person, just like the Holy Bible does. For example, please consider the following from the New World Translation used by the Jehovah's Witnesses:

1. *Who will judge us?*

Isaiah 33:22: Jehovah is our judge.

Psalm 50:6: For God himself is judge.

2 Timothy 4:1: I solemnly charge you before God and Jesus Christ who is destined to judge the living and the dead.

2. *Who is the shepherd?*

Psalm 23:1: Jehovah is my shepherd.

John 10:11: I (Jesus) am the fine shepherd.

3. *Who is the light of the world?*

Psalm 27:1: Jehovah is my light.

Micah 7:8: Although I dwell in darkness, Jehovah will be a light to me.

John 8:12: Therefore Jesus spoke again to them, saying: I am the light of the world.

Objection 51
I'm a Jehovah's Witness

4. Whose judgment seat will we appear before?

Romans 14:10: For we shall all stand before the judgment seat of God.

2 Corinthians 5:10: For we must all be made manifest before the judgment seat of Christ.

5. Whose name do we use in baptism?

Matthew 28:18: Baptizing them in the name of the Father, and of the Son, and of the Holy Spirit.

Acts 19:5: They got baptized in the name of the Lord Jesus Christ.

6. Who is the King of the Jews?

Isaiah 44:6: This is what Jehovah said, the King of Israel.

Isaiah 33:22: Jehovah is our King.

John 19:21: But that he (Jesus) said, I am the King of the Jews.

7. Who raised Jesus from the dead?

Acts 3:15: But God raised him from the dead.

John 2:19, 21: Jesus said to them: break down this temple, and in three days I will raise it up… But he was talking about the temple of his body.

8. God and Jesus Christ are the creator.

Genesis 1:1: In the beginning, God created the heavens and the earth.

Hebrews 3:4: But he that constructed all things is God.

John 1:1–17: In the beginning was the word…all things came into existence through him, and apart from him; not even one thing came into existence…grace and truth came by Jesus Christ.

Hebrews 1:8, 10: But unto the Son he said, thy throne oh God is forever and ever…thou Lord, in the beginning has laid the foundation of the earth; and the heavens are the works of thy hands.

Colossians 1:16: For by Him *(referring to Christ: see v. 13)* were all things created, that are in heaven, and that are in the earth, visible and invisible, whether they be thrones, or dominions, or principalities, or powers: all things were created by Him and for Him.

9. Jehovah and Jesus are Lord of Lords

Deuteronomy 10:17: For Jehovah your God is the God of gods and the Lord of lords, the great, mighty awe inspiring God.

Revelations 17:14: These will do battle with the Lamb, but, because He is the Lord of lords and the King of kings, the Lamb will conquer them.

1 Corinthians 8:6: And there is one Lord, Jesus Christ, through whom all things are.

10. Jehovah and Jesus are the first and the last.

Isaiah 44:6: This is what Jehovah has said, "I am the first and the last, and besides me there is no God."

Revelations 22:13, 16: I am the Alpha and the Omega, the beginning and the end, the first and the last… I Jesus have sent my angel.

Since it is quite obvious that their New World Translation teaches us that Jesus Christ is both God and creator of all, then it is just as obvious that it directly contradicts their belief that Jesus Christ was also the first being God created. And since this is just one of many other contradictions within the Jehovah's Witness religion, it should be equally obvious that it easily fails when tested for self-contradictions.

> If one compares all the divine attributes of Jehovah, the Lord, or God with those of Jesus Christ within even the New World Translation, they will find that they are consistently describing one and the same person.

Testing Jehovah's Witnesses against their prophetic predictions of the future

As we've already mentioned in Objection #41, one of the ways we can reasonably test any religion to see if the one true God is behind it is to test it against its own prophetic predictions of the future. It is common knowledge among religious scholars that the Jehovah's Witnesses religion has set exact dates and falsely predicted the return of Christ on many different occasions. The following are just some examples from their own writings:

1899: The battle of the great day of God Almighty (Revelation 16:14), which will end in AD 1914 with the complete overthrow of earth's present rulership, is already commenced. (*The Time Is at Hand*, p. 101; 1908 edition)

1916: The Bible chronology herein presented show that the six great thousand-year days beginning with Adam are ended and that on the great seventh day, the 1,000 years of Christ's reign began in 1873. (*The Time Is at Hand*, p. ii forward)

1918: Therefore, we may confidently expect that 1925 will mark the return of Abraham, Isaac, Jacob, and the faithful prophets of old (particularly those named by the apostle Paul in Hebrews

Objection 51
I'm a Jehovah's Witness

11) to the condition of human perfection. (*Millions Now Living Will Never Die*, p. 89)

1922: The date, 1925, is even more distinctly indicated by the scriptures than 1914. (*The Watchtower*, 9/1/1922, p. 262)

1923: Our thought is that 1925 is definitely settled by the scriptures. As to Noah, the Christian now has much more to base his faith than Noah had upon which to base his faith in a coming deluge. (*The Watchtower*, 4/1/1923, p. 106)

1925: The year 1925 is here. With great expectations, Christians have looked forward to this year. Many have confidently expected that all members of the body of Christ will be changed to heavenly glory during this year. This may be accomplished. It may not be. In his own due time, God will accomplish his purposes concerning his people. Christians should not be so deeply concerned about what may transpire this year. (*The Watchtower*, 1/1/1925)

1925 (September): It is to be expected that Satan will try to inject into the minds of the consecrated, the thought that 1925 should see an end to the work. (*The Watchtower*, p. 262)

1926: Some anticipated that the work would end in 1925, but the Lord did not state so. The difficulty was that the friends inflated their imaginations beyond reason and that when their imaginations burst asunder, they were inclined to throw away everything. (*The Watchtower*, p. 232)

1931: There was a measure of disappointment on the part of Jehovah's faithful ones on earth concerning the years 1914, 1918, and 1925, which disappointment lasted for a time, and they also learned to quit fixing dates. (*Vindication*, p. 338)

1968: True, there have been those in times past who predicted an end to the world, even announcing a specific date. Yet nothing happened. The end did not come. They were guilty of false prophesying. Why? What was missing? Missing from such people were God's truths and the evidence that He was using and guiding them. (*Awake*, 10/8/1968[(see Luke 21:8])

1968: Why are you looking forward to 1975? (*The Watchtower*, 8/15/1968, p. 494).

Going by these quotes, it would seem that 1914, 1918, and 1925 were some of the main dates which Jehovah's Witnesses set for Christ's return. Nevertheless, not only the fact that Christ did not return on those years, but also the fact that the Bible does not teach Christ's return on those years, makes them quite false indeed. Again, we must remember how seriously God takes false prophecies which really did not come from him.

Let's read, again, Deuteronomy 18:20-22, where God not only commanded the Old Testament nation of Israel to test prophets but also to put them to death if they should prove false as it states:

> *"But the prophet which shall presume to speak a word in my name, which I have not commanded him to speak, or that shall speak in the name of other gods, even that prophet shall die. And if thou say in thine heart, How shall we know the word which the Lord hath not spoken? When a prophet speaketh in the name of the Lord, if the thing follow not, nor come to pass, that is the thing which the Lord hath not spoken, but the prophet hath spoken it presumptuously: Thou shalt not be afraid of him."*

While we are not commanded to put to death such false prophets in the New Testament era, we can be assured that such men are not right with God and heavenbound whenever they misuse the authority of God himself, just to imagine their own spiritual realities. Even if it only happened once, this would be ample evidence against the Jehovah's Witnesses religion and would immediately disqualify it from being the one true faith. Why? Simply because a God claiming to be perfect cannot make even one such false prophecy through his true prophets. If he could, then he certainly couldn't be a perfect eternal being and we might as well all just make up our own religion and sign ourselves in to the nearest insane asylum!

The truth is that whenever any false religion in the world gives prophecies, not many of their prophecies *can really be correct* because the only source they are influenced from for their prophecies is the demonic realm as God himself would have no part of any such thing. And since the demonic realm is, of course, not all-knowing like God is, the stage is just set for the failure of such prophecies. That's why in Isaiah 41:22–23, God himself also teaches us that it is rather impossible for false religions to be accurate in their prophecies of the future:

Objection 51
I'm a Jehovah's Witness

"Let them bring forth, and show us what shall happen: let them show the former things, what they be, that we may consider them, and know the latter end of them; or declare us things to come. Show us the things that are to come hereafter, that we may know that you are gods: Yea, do good, or do evil, that we may be dismayed, and behold it together."

However, we must contrast that passage with what God says of himself in Isaiah 46:9–10:

"Remember the former things of old: for I am God, and there is none else; I am God and there is none like me, declaring the end from the beginning, and from ancient times the things that are not yet done, saying, my counsel shall stand, and I will do all my pleasure."

Obviously, just based on all their false prophecies, any *honest* judge in a civil court of law would also disqualify the Jehovah's Witnesses religion as truly representative of the one true *perfect* and eternal God. And it would appear that *most everyone* else in the world who has a conscience would also agree. And the fact that it is a very small percentage of the world's population that even claims to be a Jehovah's Witness does not exactly give their prophecies credibility either. For what did the world do for prophetic truth prior to their very late starting date in 1870 by Charles T. Russell?

> God claiming to be perfect cannot make even one false prophecy through his true prophets. If he could, then he certainly couldn't be an eternal being!

Biblical Christianity

On the other hand, unlike many cults which touch upon the subject, biblical Christianity based upon the Holy Bible does not give us any specific dates for the return of Christ. One will never find such a verse in God's Word because it is simply does not exist. In fact, Christ specifically says that *no man* can know the *day or hour* of his return (Matthew 24:36) nor does the Bible ever give us even a *year or month date* for Christ's return. And the simple reason for this is because God wants mankind to be in a state of readiness for Christ's return. God knows human nature, and if he gave us a specific date for Christ's return, much of the world would likely take advantage of that and probably not even think as much about God until just before Christ's return.

Since this would undoubtedly destroy men spiritually, in his wisdom, God has determined that Christ's rapture return for his Church should be a surprise event, like a *thief in the night* (Matthew 24:43; Luke 12:39; 1 Thessalonians 5:2-4; 2 Peter 3:10; Revelation 3:3, 16:15). While most Bible scholars would agree that the table is now basically set for Christ's return, any man setting specific dates for it simply could not be speaking for God according to what the Bible has always taught on the *surprise nature* of Christ's return for his Church. Obviously, all the year date setting by Jehovah's Witnesses for Christ's return which did not come to pass backs up the fact that the surprise *thief in the night* nature of Christ's return does not even allow us to know the *year* it will happen, even though Christ just says we cannot know the *day or hour*.

What about some who have set dates claiming to believe in the Holy Bible?

As we've already mentioned, since nowhere in the Bible will we find exact dates of any kind set for Christ's return, those who do so cannot be speaking for the true Church which is founded upon the New Testament Bible. Unlike cults who have put their stamp of approval on their false prophets, the true Church never does approve of anyone trying to set a date for Christ's return simply because there is no backing for it in the entire New Testament. Even if they have claimed to be a Bible-believing Christian while setting their dates, they simply cannot be speaking for the true Church! Quite reasonably, the abuse of the one true faith should, of course, never discredit the one true faith.

However, cults usually have plenty of written material outside the Bible which would back up their false prophecies, and that's the clear difference! Just prior to 1988, there came out a small booklet titled *88 Reasons Why Jesus Will Return in 1988*. However, this man acted independently from the true Church, simply because the New Testament does not teach even year date setting for Christ's return. Thus, most all true Church leaders rejected the prophecy before it was even proven wrong.

This is a perfect example of a false prophet within the professing Church who obviously exposed his own sin when Christ did not return in 1988. While it is possible for a false prophet to repent and get right

Objection 51
I'm a Jehovah's Witness

with God, most probably do not change, simply because there can be many more underlying spiritual problems which they also struggle with as well. On the other hand, obvious false cult groups like the Jehovah's Witnesses often have set many different dates for Christ's return within their own written materials given from their own prophets who they have put their stamp of approval on. So not only have their many different specific dates for Christ's return all proven to be wrong with time, but all their false date setters have also all contradicted each other, which really proves that *all* their date setting prophets and their entire religion is false and completely unworthy of our trust!

Testing Jehovah's Witnesses against the fruit it has produced

Many cults grossly misinterpret passages of the Holy Bible and wrongly apply them to their followers. And this is the case with the Jehovah's Witnesses in their doctrine that forbids any human blood transfusions for the saving of human life. Sadly, as a result, more than one member of the Jehovah's Witnesses religion has probably died before their time just because they didn't believe in blood transfusions.

Where in the Bible do Jehovah's Witnesses get the backing for their twisted doctrine which forbids blood transfusions?

In the Old Testament laws of Moses for the nation of Israel, we see more than one passage which forbid the Jews to eat any meat which had not been properly drained of blood (Leviticus 7:23–27, 17:10; Deuteronomy 15:23; 1 Samuel 14:34). And it is easily admitted that according to Acts 15:20–21, the apostles of the New Testament also taught that even New Testament Christians should not eat any animals which had not been properly bled either. In fact, even before the nation of Israel existed through Abraham, we find that God commanded the righteous to not eat any meat which had not been properly bled (Genesis 9:4).

As far as our discussion here is concerned, it is really rather irrelevant as to just *why* God commanded this and we won't take the time to get into all that. However, the real question is, how do these commands of God to eat animals properly drained of their blood have anything at all to do with forbidding humans to get blood transfusions? One really has to get out the scripture twister to even remotely get these commands of God to mean that the Church cannot receive any human blood transfusions. First of all, the plain context of these commands of God only involve humans eating animal blood, not humans just receiving human blood to save their lives.

About the only thing both scenarios have in common is that they both involve blood. Other than that, they are completely unrelated, not to mention that when God gave those commands, man did not even have the medical capabilities to save lives through blood transfusions. So why would God prohibit blood transfusions when he already knew those he commanded wouldn't even have that medical capability? Any way one looks at it, it really makes very little sense to base such a hard life and death doctrine off of these commands which only had to do with how man eats animal meat.

However, since we know from scripture that Satan has come to kill, steal, and destroy (John 10:10) and that all false doctrines are ultimately hatched from the demonic realm for this purpose (1 Timothy 4:1–2), then this misinterpreted legalistic evil of "no blood transfusions" begins to make some real sense. And to the contrary, since we know Jesus came to give mankind life and life more abundantly (John 10:10), we also know that such a doctrine prohibiting life-saving blood transfusions simply cannot be of God. The Pharisees accused Jesus of breaking the Sabbath laws of God when he healed people on the Sabbath. But Jesus asked them, *"Is it lawful on the Sabbath days to do good, or to do evil? To save life, or to destroy it?"*

In other words, Jesus taught that all the laws of God were for the purpose of doing good and saving life, not to destroy it! And because of their misinterpreted legalism, the Jehovah's Witnesses with their no blood transfusions doctrine have really left a wake of *bad fruit* behind them which is just the opposite of being a good Samaritan to their fellow man who is dying! God's Word plainly teaches us, *"Withhold not good from them to whom it is do, when it is in the power of thine hand to do it"* (Proverbs 3:27).

"As we have therefore opportunity, let us do good to all men, especially unto them who are of the household of faith" (Galatians 6:10).

Why, even the civil court truth is that when we do not save the life of our fellow man when it is clearly in our power to do it that it's the very same as murder!

Objection 51
I'm a Jehovah's Witness

The Jehovah's Witnesses with their no blood transfusions doctrine have really left a wake of bad fruit behind them which is just the opposite of being a good Samaritan to their fellow man who is dying!

Testing Jehovah's Witnesses against its divine power demonstrated

Many of the Jehovah's Witnesses teachings are in stark contrast to the main doctrines taught within the New Testament. This is very likely why after the late hour their religion was founded, they saw the need to create their own New World Translation Bible, which according to the Bible itself is not the Word of God at all because it has been changed (Galatians 1:6–9; 2 Timothy 3:16; 2 Peter 2:1–2; Revelation 22:18–19). But one must certainly ask the reasonable question: Since the Jehovah's Witnesses didn't always have their New World Translation, what did they do for an accurate version of the Bible before they came out with their New World translation? Here, again, we see a religion which has evolving truth as not only its doctrines but even its source of truth changed as time went on. This, too, should be a major red flag which shows that the Jehovah's Witnesses could not have been set up by our perfect eternal creator who could never contradict himself. The following are just some of the basic doctrinal differences between the Jehovah's Witnesses and biblical Christianity:

Salvation by works

Like most all cults, the Jehovah's Witnesses may well believe that faith (even faith in Christ) is essential for salvation, but since they also insist that *good works* are also necessary to obtain God's eternal salvation, this of course, nullifies the true Gospel of *faith in Christ alone* which Christ and his apostles preached (Galatians 1:6–9; Ephesians 2:8–9). Quite a number of different references within their teachings easily expose the fact that they believe eternal salvation must be partially earned through a variety of religious good works (see *Studies in the Scriptures, Vol. 1*, p. 150, 152). This alone should easily disqualify the Jehovah's Witnesses as the one true faith.

Jesus Christ

Strangely enough, Jehovah's Witnesses believe that Jesus Christ was actually Michael the Archangel before he became a man. But that is not their only violation of Christ's clear identity given to us in the scriptures, for neither do they even believe him to be God who created all as the Bible clearly teaches (Colossians 1:16–17). They merely believe him to be a god and not our one and only true creator as part of the trinity. This alone is damning heresy and easily disqualifies the Jehovah's Witnesses as the one true faith as well.

The Trinity

The Jehovah's Witnesses only believe in God the Father as our supreme God and basically reject Jesus Christ and the Holy Spirit as members of the biblical *Godhead*. They not only believe Jesus to just be a god who was the first created being but also believe that the Holy Spirit is just some kind of an impersonal force who is not even God at all! However, there is much scripture within the Bible (which severely predates their New World Translation) that teaches us the sure reality of the three-person divine Godhead. Thus, their clear rejection of Christ's and the Holy Spirit's deity is damning heresy of the worst kind. Just some obvious biblical references to the trinity or *Godhead* within the Bible are Genesis 1:26 (*us*), Genesis 3:22 (*us*), Genesis 11:7 (*us*), Matthew 28:19, John 10:30–33, John 14:6–9, and Romans 1:20. Once again, this heretical rejection of the trinity easily disqualifies the Jehovah's Witnesses as the one true faith as well as it goes directly against the scriptures of God's infallible Word.

A literal and eternal punishment hell

Like the Seventh-Day Adventists and other cults, the Jehovah's Witnesses totally reject the Bible's clear teaching on a literal and eternal punishment hell, which is the sure destination of all those who finally reject Christ. Often, if you notice, cults will only reject and subtract *the unpleasant realities* of God's Word which pertain to those who reject the biblical Christ. How convenient for them, right? Many times, if it is not eternal punishment in hell which they subtract from God's Word (through the doctrine of annihilation), it will be the seven-

Objection 51
I'm a Jehovah's Witness

year tribulation judgment of Revelation they subtract (through false doctrines like Historicism and Preterism).

According to the Bible itself, this teaching of *no eternal punishment hell* is not only a major heresy because it is essentially subtracting from God's Word, but it is also what we'd call a Catch-22 deception. For, ironically, according to Revelation 22:19, all those who flatly reject Christ and the apostle's clear teaching on a literal eternal punishment hell will actually go to the very hell they don't believe in if they don't mend their beliefs! And, of course, this is precisely the devil's ploy to destroy as it concerns the false doctrine of annihilation which attempts to subtract eternal punishment from biblical hell.

> Ironically, according to Revelation 22:19, all those who flatly reject Christ and the apostle's clear teaching on a literal eternal punishment hell will actually go to the very hell they don't believe in if they don't mend their beliefs.

And since no Jehovah's Witness has ever demonstrated the miraculous power of God our creator as Christ and his disciples clearly did many times in front of many public witnesses, who should we reasonably trust as it concerns all those basic Jehovah's Witness doctrines that obviously conflict with the Bible? Especially considering the original Greek of the New Testament predates all their extrabiblical literature and their New World translation by thousands of years going all the way back to Christ himself?

While the answer should be obvious to those being only reasonable, the very unreasonable nature of the entire Jehovah's Witness religion is quite apparent in that its leaders would have us blindly just take their word for it over the word of the divine Christ and his apostles. When Christ and his apostles all walked the earth, they not only fully demonstrated the power of God through major supernatural miracles hundreds of times over in front of many public eyewitnesses, but additionally, the Bible itself is laced with over 2,000 future predicting prophecies which have already been accurately fulfilled, all proving Jesus is far more than Michael the Archangel who was just a created being! And this awesome divine power displayed is something unique to biblical Christianity *alone*. As the saying goes:

Jesus did not at all expect the world to follow him blindly... He publicly healed the blind to prove his deity!

Conclusion

The Jehovah's Witnesses as a religion has many other unsolvable problems as well which neither time nor written page permits us to expose. But quite sufficient should be the evidence which we've discussed. All in all, in the spiritual sense, we can only conclude that like all other self-defeating man-made religions, the Jehovah's Witnesses is truly a spiritual mess and likely remains an *extreme minority* in the world's population because of it. Statistics are always changing, and depending upon the source for one's statistic, presently, there are roughly 8.3 million people worldwide who have been deceived into the Jehovah's Witnesses cult.

If the Jehovah's Witness religion is the truth, that would be only about an eighth of 1 percent of the world's overall population who is even able to recognize the truth! Is that hard for you to believe? If not, it should be! If Jehovah's Witnesses is the one true faith, then reasonably, all others (99.85 percent of the world's population, and, of course, all those who lived prior to 1870) will not obtain God's eternal life. And considering Jehovah's Witnesses narrow the gap even further by claiming *only 144,00* make it into God's kingdom, that really makes God look hard, narrow, unloving, and not to mention quite unable to reach his own lost world!

If you happen to presently belong to the Jehovah's Witness religion, I strongly encourage you to even look up online for yourself and see just why many know the Jehovah's Witness religion to be a dangerous cult which ultimately endangers the salvation of those who belong to it. But just as Jesus proved his divinity to the honest soul many times over when he walked the earth, so too is his Word completely trustworthy when it plainly teaches us that *all* who simply believe in what Christ did for them on the cross will be saved without any religious good works attached!

The Jehovah's Witness religion constantly heaps heavy burdens on the backs of its members teaching that one must go door to door,

Objection 51
I'm a Jehovah's Witness

evangelizing their false religion and do and not do many other things in order to obtain their version of eternal salvation. And even then, only 144,000 are promised to inherit God's kingdom! On the other hand, Jesus plainly taught that his salvation is equally obtainable for all who simply believe that he took the punishment for their sins on the cross. Jesus said in Matthew 11:28–30:

> *"Come unto me all you that labor and are heavy laden, and I will give you rest. Take my yoke upon you, and learn of me; for I am meek and lowly of heart: and you shall find rest for your souls. For my yoke is easy and his burden is light."*

You see, God doesn't need slaves who try to continuously work their way into his everlasting kingdom. Nor is he impressed with any of man's attempts to earn his eternal life with their good religious works. Why would he be when he himself is perfect and all powerful? On the contrary, he only created all mankind to just have a loving and trusting relationship with himself! You see, our creator is perfect love and is easy to please. All we have to *do* for God's eternal salvation is have faith in the finished work he accomplished for us on the cross. And this gives God glory and not man.

God teaches us plainly within his Word that *"he will give his glory to no other"* (Isaiah 42:8). And three days later, after Christ died on the cross, he rose again to prove he was just who he claimed to be. Did Charles T. Russell ever prove through the power of God in any way that he was more than a mere man who was just creating his own religion with the influence of the demonic realm? No. Where are the miracles he did as Christ did? Where are all his fulfilled prophecies? Where is there any real evidence (beyond the normal weak abilities of man) that God was even working through him? Since there really isn't any sound evidence, it is quite plain to see that Charles T. Russell just expected man to follow him quite blindly. Jesus, on the other hand, proved his divinity, and his apostles all proved through the supernatural power of God that God was working through them.

As we have sufficiently shown, the Jehovah's Witnesses religion can be nothing other than a man-made cult which quickly fails all reasonable tests when they are applied to it. On the other hand, the Holy Bible which has always stood up to all the same reasonable tests plainly teaches us that if anyone believes that even *one small good work* of their own (added to the Gospel) will save them, according to the scriptures of the Holy Bible, they will simply *not be saved* (Galatians 1:6–9)!

If you are one who is unwilling to let the false doctrines in the Jehovah's Witness religion destroy your chance for eternal life in God's kingdom, then I would encourage you to embrace the true biblical gospel of salvation. If you are one who can easily see through the deception of the Jehovah's Witness religion because it miserably fails the reasonable tests we've applied to it and would like to be right with God and be assured of your place in God's awesome eternal kingdom to come, I invite you to just take that first small step of faith by sincerely praying the prayer of salvation located at the end of this book. Even if you've been a Jehovah's Witness for many years, you can still break away from that obvious cult today which threatens your true salvation through Christ.

And don't be concerned with what your family members may think of you because, simply put, they will not be your judge on judgment day! This decision is between you and God (your creator) alone. No matter what your past is like, God loves you and sincerely wants you to be a part of his awesome eternal kingdom! However, the Bible teaches us plainly that *only through Christ* can we obtain God's eternal life. Jesus said, *"I am the way and the truth and the life. No one comes to the Father except through me"* (John 14:6).

Someone once asked Jesus how many will be saved. And Jesus replied, *"Make every effort to enter through the narrow door, because many, I tell you, will try to enter and will not be able"* (Luke 13:24).

> *Jesus said, "I am the resurrection and the life. He who believes in me, will live even though he dies; and whoever lives and believes in me will never die."* (John 11:25–26)

Note: Another helpful resource on this subject would also be *Answers to My Jehovah's Witness Friends* by Thomas F. Heinze.

OBJECTION 52
I'm a Seventh-Day Adventist

A loving reminder: Before each false belief system we discuss, just so my loving intentions cannot be misunderstood, I will *once again* remind the reader that it's certainly *not the adherents* of any false belief system which the true Church is against but rather just the *false teachings* within them which deceive men away from the one and only true God and his eternal salvation (Ephesians 6:12). You see, God loves everyone, and everyone *has the right to know* if a religion or belief system is truly steering people away from him and his eternal salvation. In fact, if the true Church did not expose false belief systems which do not pass the reasonable tests which we can apply to them, then it most certainly would be a reflection of its love!

Therefore, my dear reader, please know that our discussion of these various different religions or belief systems is very much a *love* issue! However, with that said, even though one confirms that a given religion is false by way of combing through the honest evidence, that is certainly not to say that there could not be some true believers in Christ within that false religion. This is especially true with those false religions which are *closest* to the biblical truth. In such cases, the Bible teaches us that "the Lord knows them that are his" (2 Timothy 2:19). However, if, in fact, there are true believers in Christ within any false religion, it is certainly *despite* their official doctrines, not *because* of them! And to be sure, God would have such a true believer in Christ leave that false religion before they lose their own stability in Christ (Romans 16:17; 1 Corinthians 5:11–13; 2 Corinthians 6:14; Galatians 5:19–21; 1 Timothy 6:3–11; 2 Timothy 3:2–5; Titus 3:9–11).

The origin of the Seventh-Day Adventist religion

Like most all false religions, the first and most obvious problem with the Seventh-Day Adventist religion is also its late starting date in the history of the human race. Unlike biblical Christianity which goes all the way back to the first man Adam (Genesis 1:26–27; Matthew 19:4; 1 Corinthians 15:45), the Seventh-Day Adventist (SDA) religion (again, I can't call it a church) was basically founded in the 1800s by a man named William Miller.

Originally, the SDA religion was known as the Millerite movement. It wasn't until later when the Millerite movement fell apart into splinter groups:that one of them became known as the Seventh-Day Adventists. Again, the embarrassing question for the SDA Religion is: If the SDA religion with all its peculiar doctrines is the real truth, how did the entire human race obtain that truth (and God's eternal salvation according to Adventists) prior to its late starting date within the human race, seeing there was no such organization prior to its start? Would a perfect God really be so neglectful of his own creation?

And, again, the SDA religion can't at all claim that Christ and his apostles actually spear headed their particular religion with all its unique doctrines because neither Christ nor his apostles never once even mention their religion by name or taught any of their unique SDA doctrines in the entire New Testament. Nor can the SDA Religion claim that Christ's Church went into complete apostasy and needed to be restored or that the New Testament lost its accurate content through mistranslations because there is simply no *professional* historical evidence for such claims.

In 1818, after having studied the Bible *only two years*, Miller announced to the world that Christ would return in 1843 or 1844 based on Bible texts like Daniel 8:14 and one Hebrew calendar. By the time 1843 rolled around, amazingly enough, Miller had a following of 50,000 people who actually believed in his false prophecy of Christ's return! When, much to their disappointment, Christ did not return by March 1844, Miller recalculated the new and more specific date

Objection 52
I'm a Seventh-Day Adventist

of Christ's return to be October 22, 1844. Then, when Christ did not return right on October 22, 1844, what they called The Great Disappointment resulted, and essentially, Miller's whole movement collapsed.

To cover up his false prophecy, Miller once again scrambled to gain control of his followers by insisting that Christ did in a sense return on October 22, 1844, but Miller had just not understood that Christ first had to stop at the heavenly sanctuary to clean it up before actually returning to earth! Unfortunately, many were ignorant and unwise enough to keep believing Miller's lies and the pathetic religion survived just on that ignorance alone. For Daniel 8:14 only talks about the cleansing of the earthly tribulation temple prior to Christ's return and mentions nothing about God's heavenly temple being cleansed. After all, why would anything in the third heaven (where God resides) even need to be cleansed at all?

> In 1818, after having studied the Bible only two years, Miller announced to the world that Christ would return in 1843 or 1844.

And the obvious problem with all this is that anyone who could read the Bible for themselves could also easily see that the Bible itself doesn't breath a word about such a double stage return for Christ (other than the rapture of the Church, which has nothing to do with the cleaning of God's heavenly sanctuary and obviously didn't happen in 1844).

1. First of all, the Bible teaches us plainly that Christ was seated at the right hand of the Father (in the third heavens) ever since his ascension after his death and resurrection with no indication that he'd be anywhere else until his return to earth during the entire church age. For plain verification of this fact, please read the following verses: Acts 2:34–35, 7:55–56, Romans 8:34, Hebrews 1:3, 13, 1 Peter 3:22, 1 John 2:1.

2. Secondly, there are no scriptures teaching us that the sanctuary of God in the third heavens needs any cleaning whatsoever as God himself is absolutely perfect and cannot even live in the presence of any sin or spiritual uncleanness (Psalm 5:4).

3. Thirdly, there are no scriptures in the Bible teaching us that Christ has to go to any other part of the third heavens before he returns to earth. Any way one looks at it, the whole prophecy of Christ's return on a specific date was obviously false, and Miller then just desperately concocted another false story just to cover up his first obvious blunder.

In 1845, the deceived Millerite followers (who bought into Miller's lie that Christ was just cleaning up heaven first before he returned to earth) then met to discuss the future of their disappointed movement. Because of the the Great Disappointment, instead of folding completely like it should have to save further embarrassment, the Millerite movement just broke up into smaller cult groups such as the Seventh-Day Adventists, The Christadelphians, The Followers of Herbert Armstrong, The Bible Students, and the Church of God (Seventh Day), Salem Conference, etc. However, it would seem that none of them actually learned what they should have from the Great disappointment, which was that Miller was a false prophet because he did originally prophesy that Christ would physically return to earth in 1843 or 1844 *with no mention of Christ first cleaning heaven.*

Even if Miller's unbiblical lie that Christ was actually cleaning heaven's sanctuary was true, there's nothing in the Word of God that teaches us that any prophet of God can just change their original prophecy and be off the hook because they simply misunderstood it! If that was the case, then I would say most all of us could qualify as a prophet of God any time we wanted to! Unfortunately, many Seventh-Day Adventists today remain completely *ignorant* of the fact that their entire religion actually got its start through a liar and his very false prophecy of Christ's return on a specific date which he set.

> There's nothing in the Word of God that teaches us that any prophet of God can just change their original prophecy and be off the hook because they simply misunderstood it.

Then after the death of Miller, in 1849, a new false prophet took control of the movement, but this time, a woman by the name of Ellen G. White who Miller had also groomed to believe in his false prophecy that Christ had somehow returned in 1844 by just cleaning up heaven

Objection 52
I'm a Seventh-Day Adventist

first before his actual return to earth. And to this day, Adventists consider the teachings of Ellen G. White to be equal with scripture. The SDA religion declared it in their *Ministry Magazine* of October 1981 and has never retracted it:

> "We believe the revelation and inspiration of both the Bible and Ellen G. White's writings to be of equal quality. The superintendence of the Holy Spirit was just as careful and thorough in one case as in the other."

However, if we notice, 2 Timothy 3:16–17 does not say "*All scripture* plus the writings of Elen G. White *is given by inspiration of God and is profitable for doctrine, for reproof, for correction, for instruction in righteousness*. It just says *All scripture (of the Bible)*! According to Revelation 22:18, anyone adding like that to the authority of God's Word cannot be right with God and will be left behind in the tribulation period to experience all of its awful *plagues* (or judgments).

> Adventists consider the teachings of Ellen G. White to be equal with scripture. The SDA religion declared it in their Ministry Magazine of October 1981 and has never retracted it.

Testing the Seventh-Day Adventist religion against man's true moral condition

Like many man-made cults, the SDA religion basically rejects the Bible's clear teaching that all men have a sin nature which is inherited from the first man and woman, Adam and Eve. They may believe all men can presently choose good or evil, but they basically reject the reality of an *inherited sin nature* from birth. While it is certainly true that all men can choose good or evil, the Bible has always clearly taught that all men are also born into inherited sin from Adam as well (Job 5:7; Romans 5:12; 1 Corinthians 15:22). Therefore, any religion which teaches against *inherited sin* is going directly against the basic teachings of God's Word, proving itself to be false right there on the spot.

Additionally, the SDA religion also believes in a doctrine of theirs called *sinless perfection* which essentially teaches that man can actually become sinless while he or she is still living in their natural state. And presumably, this doctrine would apply only to Seventh-Day Adventists, just because they believe one has to belong to the SDA religion in order to even be saved.

This is similar to the Roman Catholic belief that its leaders can actually reach a state of being which is perfect or infallible. My friend, anyone who believes such obvious nonsense clearly contradicts all past human history wherein mankind has always been plagued with a sin nature, not to mention the common sense of even a ten-year-old! Also, their teaching on *sinless perfection* directly contradicts the Bible which they also *claim* to believe in.

As we already stated, the Bible not only teaches that all men are born into sin (Job 5:7) but that all men continue to sin throughout the entire course of their natural lives. In fact, when the Apostle John (who was probably one of the most spiritual men who ever lived) was even nearing the end of his days, he clearly taught that if any man (which would have included himself) should say that they were without sin that the truth was not in them and they were not even saved (see 1 John 1:7–10)!

> The SDA religion also believes in a doctrine of theirs called sinless perfection which teaches that man can actually become sinless while he is living on earth in his physical body.

Testing the Seventh-Day Adventist religion against self-contradictions

Like so many other cults or false religions, even the *basic* doctrines held by the SDA evolved over time. For example, the doctrine that Saturday was the true Sabbath was not even preached by William Miller but came much later. Nor did Miller even preach about or believe in vegetarianism which also came later through Ellen G. White when her husband got sick in 1864. However, even despite their vegetarian diet which Ellen supposedly got in a *vision* from the Lord, James, her husband, nevertheless died in 1881. Obviously, there's nothing wrong with trying to better one's health through a better diet. But when a religion attaches salvation to that venture as the SDA religion has, then that's where they part company with God's inspired Word as well as common sense.

The SDA religion today also teaches that keeping the Sabbath (not doing any work on the Sabbath) is essential for one's salvation. So if the SDA religion teaches that today, then we must conclude that all SDA

Objection 52
I'm a Seventh-Day Adventist

followers prior to that doctrine being established in their religion must have been damned because they clearly didn't believe (or live) that! Not to mention the whole human race prior to the late starting date of their religion!

So we can easily see that all such religions which have evolving doctrines over time essentially end up contradicting themselves just because the former adherents of their religion could not have believed or lived like the latter adherents. Especially if those doctrines concern the eternal salvation of men can we see the gross self-contradiction within that evolving religion. Not only does their doctrine of keeping the Sabbath (not doing any work on the Sabbath) for salvation contradict the beliefs and lifestyles of earlier Adventists, but it directly contradicts the Bible which they also *claim* to believe in.

Let's get this right. It was the *unsaved Pharisees* who came against Jesus and his disciples for going through the cornfield and eating corn on the Sabbath. It wasn't Jesus and his disciples who came against the unsaved Pharisees for such a thing (Matthew 12:1–2)! So it looks like the SDA religion is following in the footsteps of the unsaved Pharisees, not Christ, as many New Testament scriptures (like Matthew 12:1–2) make it abundantly clear that the New Testament Church no longer adhered to such Mosaic laws (Acts 1:12).

Actually, if the truth be told, the Old Testament law for Israel also states in Exodus 16:29 that no Israelite was to even leave their home on the Sabbath! And we know the SDA religion does not keep that law, for then they couldn't even go to their so-called church on the Sabbath. And, again, many other passages like Ephesians 2:8–9 equally make it quite clear that no man can obtain God's salvation through good works of any kind.

We can easily see that all such religions which have evolving doctrines over time essentially end up contradicting themselves just because the former adherents of their religion did not believe or live like the latter adherents.

The SDA religion itself doesn't even keep their own Sabbath law for salvation

If the truth be told, the Hebrew Sabbath laws of Moses from which the SDA Sabbath doctrine is taken was only intended for the nation of Israel during Old Testament times (Exodus 31:12–17). In the New Testament, the Apostle Paul makes it crystal clear that the true Church can meet for worship *any day*, and the Lord will receive it. Please consider Romans 14:4-6:

> *"Who are you to judge someone else's servant? To his own master, he stands or falls. And he will stand, for the Lord is able to make him stand. One man considers one day more sacred than another; another man considers every day alike. Each one should be fully convinced in his own mind. He who regards one day as special, does so to the Lord. He who eats meat, eats to the Lord, for he gives thanks to God; and he who abstains, does so to the Lord and gives thanks to God. For none of us live to himself alone and none of us dies to himself alone. If we live, we live to the Lord; and if we die, we die to the Lord. So whether we live or die, we belong to the Lord."*

Additionally, the Apostle Paul said to the Church in Colossians 2:16–17, *"Let no man judge you in meat, or drink, or in respect of a holy day, or of the new moon, or of the Sabbath days: Which are now a shadow of the things to come; but the body is of Christ."*

However, Christian cults (like the Seventh-Day Adventists) quite often try to make the New Testament Church keep the Old Testament Mosaic laws which God only intended for the nation of Israel before Christ. But when they do, failure to keep those laws (and guilt) is always the result, just like the nation of Israel itself proved for thousands of years (Acts 15:7–11)! And God gave the nation of Israel his impossible laws to keep quite on purpose so that they would finally realize they couldn't keep them and be driven to Christ their Messiah for salvation when he did finally come (Galatians 3:23–24).

The Sabbath laws of Moses state that the Israelites were not to work on the Sabbath, which actually included not making anyone else work on the Sabbath either (Exodus 20:8–10)! So if Adventists today even use any utilities such as water, electricity, or natural gas (or go to the hospital) on the Sabbath to the breaking of their own doctrines, they are always making someone else work on the Sabbath! It may be convenient for them to do so but, of course, quite hypocritical if they insist that they can't do any work on the Sabbath.

Thus, technically, according to their own doctrine of salvation connected to keeping the Sabbath, they are always causing others within utility plants and hospitals to lose their own salvation! Even those Adventists who are farmers milking their cows on the Sabbath are also breaking the Sabbath laws of Moses because that, too, is work *which could technically be done just during the other days of the week.* It's not like it would kill the cow to *not* milk them on Saturdays! And, technically, the Sabbath laws of Moses additionally state that the Israelites were not to even make any fires on the Sabbath either.

But as soon as a member of the SDA religion jumps into their car to drive to their meeting place on the Sabbath, they actually combust plenty of fire within the engine of their car and technically break the Sabbath laws of Moses on the no fires basis as well. Therefore, even the Sabbath laws of the SDA have never really been kept by even its own members, even though they insist on it for salvation! This, too, is a major self-contradiction within their religion.

Christian cults quite often try to make the New Testament Church keep the Old Testament laws which God only intended for the Nation of Israel. But when they do, failure to keep those laws is always the result.

No mediator?

The SDA religion believes that all men will have to stand in the presence of the living God for judgment without a mediator. However, this directly contradicts the Bible (that they also *claim* to believe in) which clearly teaches that there is one mediator between man and God who is Christ Jesus (1 Timothy 2:5). This, too, is a self-contradiction within their religion. Let's all be honest: either they believe in the Bible or they don't!

Seventh-Day Adventists make a grave error with their soul sleep doctrine

The SDA religion also believes that the souls of believers in Christ are not in heaven (as the Bible they *claim* to believe in clearly teaches) but are actually just sleeping in their earthly graves. However, there is not only more than one verse in the Bible which plainly teaches us that the spirit/soul of all believers in Christ go right to heaven when they die, but there are also many verses which teach us that the spirit/souls of believers could not just stay in some earthly grave as well. Among Luke 23:43, 2 Corinthians 5:6–8, and Revelation 7:9–17, please consider the following additional verses of God's word:

1. Luke 16:22: *"And it came to pass, that the beggar died, and was carried by the angels into Abraham's bosom."*

Obviously, *Abraham's bosom* here and the earthly grave are not one and the same thing. According to Jesus here, the spirits/souls of *Old Testament righteous* men did not stay in some earthly grave until the resurrection but went into *Abraham's bosom* (obviously a large place where both Abraham and the *rich man* were located), which certainly rules out Lazarus's earthly grave.

2. Luke 16:22–23: *"[T]he rich man also died, and was buried; and in hell he lift up his eyes, being in torments."*

According to Jesus, the spirits/souls of *Old Testament unrighteous* men are definitely not confined to some earthly grave (dormant) until the resurrection. Even though the rich man was *buried* in an earthly grave (v. 22), his spirit/soul was immediately brought to *hell* in the center of the earth upon his physical death. According to the Bible, all the Old Testament *unrighteous* dead are still in hell (in the center of the earth) and will continue to be *tormented* there until they are finally *cast into the lake of fire* after the 1,000-year reign of Christ is over (Revelation 20:11–15). Let us read another verse:

3. Matthew 17:3: *"And behold, there appeared unto them Moses and Elias talking with him."*

Here, again, if earthly grave soul sleep were true, how is it that the disciples testify here in Matthew 17:3 that they were eyewitnesses of both Moses and Elijah, talking with Jesus on the mountain of transfiguration? Unlike Elijah, we can be sure that Moses did die a physical death just like everyone else (see Deuteronomy 34:5–6).

4. Psalm 90:10: *"The days of our years are three score years and ten…for it is soon cut off and we fly away."*

Other verses, such as Psalm 90:10 and Ezekiel 13:20, also teach that the spirits/souls of men certainly do not lie dormant in the grave. And if the spirits/souls of righteous men are carried away by angels as soon as they die (like Christ's account in Luke 16:22 teaches), then these scriptures teaching that *we fly away* also fully cooperate with that reality as well.

> 5. Hebrews 12:1: *"Wherefore seeing we also are also compassed about with so great a cloud of witnesses, let us lay aside every weight, and the sin which doth so easily beset us, let us run with patience the race that is set before us."*

Here, again, it should be obvious that the spirits/souls of all the righteous men and women which Paul talked about in Hebrews chapter 11 (Abel, Enoch, Noah, Abraham, Sarah, Isaac, Jacob, Joseph, Moses, Rahab, Gedeon, Barack, Samson, Jephthae, David, Samuel, and countless others) do not lie dormant in an earthly grave in unconscious soul sleep before their resurrection. Scripture teaches that Christ even brought all Old Testament saints with him to the third heavens after his resurrection from the dead. In fact, they (and all New Testament saints who have died) are depicted as those intensely interested in watching the lives of all saints who are still in their natural state. In the book of Revelation, scripture also plainly teaches that the spirits/souls of the tribulation saints go right to heaven after physical death as well (Revelation 6:9–11).

However, another problem with the unbiblical SDA doctrine of earthly grave soul sleep is, where do the souls of men go if they are not at all buried in the ground with a normal burial? For example, many today are cremated and their ashes are sprinkled all over. Many men have undoubtedly lost their lives at sea, only to become fish food. Many have probably also died in the wilderness without burial, only to be eaten by scavengers. And many have probably died in fires, only to have their ashes scattered. So just where does their soul then sleep according to SDA doctrine? Wow, that's awkward. Since their beliefs about soul sleep in the graves clearly contradict many plain scriptures of God's Word which they also *claim* to believe in, why should we believe such lies which are quite apparent through their own self contradictions?

However, with that problem exposed, it should be mentioned that the whole problem with SDA soul sleep doctrine is quite easily solved when one realizes that it is largely based on a misunderstanding of the Hebrew word for Sheol in the King James version of the Old Testament. Just because the King James often reads *the grave* for Sheol in the Old

Testament, Adventists just ignorantly assumed that the grave it refers to is just six feet down and not in the center of the earth as many other Old Testament verses confirm. But even though the King James often reads *the grave* for Sheol, it is still difficult to understand why the Seventh-Day Adventists have mistakenly thought that biblical soul sleep actually takes place in the earthly graves of men here *on earth* instead of *in Sheol* located in the center of the earth.

Ephesians 4:8–10, Psalms 68:18, 1 Samuel 28:14, and Luke 16:19–31 should all easily clarify to the honest reader that all those in Old Testament times went to the great divided pit of Sheol in the center of the earth. And Hebrews 12:1, Matthew 17:3, and Luke 16:22 should all easily clarify to the honest reader that all Christians in New Testament times go directly to the third heavens when we die.

Again, one must always remember that correct doctrine will always satisfy *all scripture* which pertains to it (2 Timothy 3:16)!

The SDA religion believes that the spirits/souls of all deceased believers in Christ actually just sleep in their earthly graves. However, the Bible plainly teaches us that the spirit/soul of all believers in Christ go right to heaven after death.

Again the SDA religion contradicts the Bible they profess to believe in

The Seventh-Day Adventists also typically hold to a doctrine called "Historicism." This non-biblical doctrine maintains that the future tribulation period as described in the book of Revelation has already taken place to a large degree throughout the entire church age so far. However, to accomplish such a doctrine, they must *over symbolize* much of God's plain word, even when symbolism isn't at all indicated by the scriptures they are symbolizing.

Their over symbolized version of Revelation's tribulation period starts all the way back in AD 70 when Titus, the Roman emperor, took control of Jerusalem. Since they way oversymbolize the book of Revelation, they can awkwardly force the historical events of centuries past to *somewhat resemble* the actual events of Revelation's tribulation period. However, for those who know God's Word (which they also *claim* to believe in), it's a false theology which is easily exposed. For just

Objection 52
I'm a Seventh-Day Adventist

one example of many, let's see for ourselves that it simply cannot be reconciled with verses like Revelation 22:18 which states:

"For I testify unto every man that heareth the words of the prophecy of this book, if any man shall add unto these things, God shall add unto him the plagues (or judgments) that are written in this book."

Obviously, according to this passage, if any man during the entire church age (even today) adds to the book of Revelation, God will add to him the plagues (which just means judgments in the Greek) that are written in the book of Revelation (which obviously includes all the judgments of Revelation's tribulation period). But the Seventh-Day Adventist doctrine of historicism makes no sense with this inspired verse of God's Holy Word because how could someone today who adds to the book of Revelation possibly have all the judgments of Revelation's tribulation *added to them* if *most of them* have already taken place back in the history of the church age?

The only eschatology position which makes any sense at all with this plain verse of God's Word is the futurist position which says the entire tribulation period of Revelation is yet future. And Revelation 22:18 not only insists that the tribulation period of Revelation is yet future but also only makes sense with a Pre-Tribulation rapture which teaches that the entire true Church walking with Christ *will not* go through any part of the Tribulation period of Revelation (Luke 21:34–36; Revelation 3:10, 22:18).

Obviously, according to Revelation 22:18–19, those adding to or subtracting from the book of Revelation are not right with God and not part of the true Church when doing so. Thus, because the judgments of the tribulation period are only prescribed for those adding to the book of Revelation and are *not added* to those who are *not adding* to the book of Revelation (meaning the true Church), we can be sure that those adding to it are *left behind* when the true Church is raptured away and cannot experience any of the tribulation judgments. Any way one would look at it, only the futurist position and a pre-Tribulation rapture makes any sense at all with Revelation 22:18!

Since the Bible specifically teaches that all correct doctrine must check out with *all of God's Word* (2 Timothy 3:16), we know that not only the preterist and historicist positions but also all *internal tribulation rapture positions* instantly crumble when tested against Revelation

22:18. So, once again, we see that the SDA religion contradicts itself simply because it consistently claims to believe in the Holy Bible which simply cannot be reconciled with many of its strange doctrines.

> Since the SDA religion way over symbolizes the book of Revelation, they can awkwardly force the historical events of centuries past to somewhat resemble the actual events of Revelation's tribulation period.

Testing the Seventh-Day Adventist religion against the character of its founders

We've already discussed the fact that William Miller, the founder of SDA, clearly gave a false prophecy and then made it worse by lying about it. And Ellen G. White proved to be no better with her false prophecies. In fact, she even lied for William Miller as well by teaching his same lie about the return of Christ requiring the cleaning of heaven's sanctuary. Additionally, it can also be shown that Ellen committed much plagiarism when writing her many books (which supposedly came from the Lord). This, too, has been a common practice among cult leaders.

The SDA religion today tries to justify her plagiarism with the fact that there were no copyright laws back then. But such laws have always been made for moral reasons, and it still does not excuse her taking the words of others and selling them as though they were her own from God Almighty if she has a Christian conscience! Just how does a spirit-filled woman do that and not only sell them but claim her teachings within them came from the Lord? Hmm…since that's obviously not possible, then what is the only other obvious reality left to us?

> William Miller, the founder of SDA, clearly gave a false prophecy and then made it worse by lying about it. And Ellen G. White proved to be no better with her false prophecies.

Objection 52
I'm a Seventh-Day Adventist

Testing the Seventh-Day Adventist religion against its prophetic predictions of the future

As we've already cited in the origin of Seventh-Day Adventists, William Miller, who was founder of the Millerite movement from which the Seventh-Day Adventist religion came, falsely predicted Christ's return in the years 1843 or 1844. During her years as the seer for the SDA church, Ellen G. White also prophesied more than one prediction which proved false because it did not at all come true. Just one of the most obvious false prophecies which she made was when she predicted before the American Civil War that the union would not be preserved but that the United States would be divided and slavery would not be abolished. She, like Joseph Smith, also prophesied that England would actually intervene and declare war on the United States. So, actually, this false prophecy of hers has at least four smaller false prophecies which did not at all come true. But, like so many other cults, the Adventists have just swept their false prophecies under the rug and kept rolling.

As a result, many Adventists today do not even know about them and continue to blindly believe that Ellen G. White's teachings (and prophecies) are equal with scripture. It is interesting indeed that the Seventh-Day Adventists have always had a strong emphasis put on prophecy when, ironically, their whole religion actually started through a major false prophecy of a specific date for Christ's return.

As we already mentioned in the previous objection, when any false religion in the world which gives prophecies, not many of them *can be correct* because the only source that they can be influenced from for their prophecies is really the demonic realm as God himself would have no part of any such thing. That's why in Isaiah 41:22–23, God himself also teaches us that it is rather impossible for false religions to be accurate in their prophecies of the future as it states:

"Let them bring forth, and show us what shall happen: let them show the former things, what they be, that we may consider them, and know the latter end of them; or declare us things to come. Show us the things that are to come hereafter, that we may know that you are gods: Yea, do good, or do evil, that we may be dismayed, and behold it together."

Before the American Civil War, Ellen G. White prophesied that the union would not be preserved, slavery would not be abolished, and that England would actually intervene and declare war on the United States.

Testing the Seventh-Day Adventist religion against the fruit it has produced

Any time a false religion produces false prophets, the fruit produced by those false prophets over time is usually destructive to man both spiritually and physically. And all this just makes sense if Satan is the one who is actually inspiring those false prophets and not the Holy Spirit as they usually claim. For example, most all false religions which adamantly teach that God's eternal salvation is achieved in part (or wholly) through human performance can only subject its adherents to constant guilt, simply because no one in their religion (not even their leadership) can keep all their ordinances. Thus, it only makes sense that many Adventists would struggle with constant guilt.

In truth, there are all kinds of destruction left in the wake of false religions. For yet another example, David Koresh in the 1990s was a self-proclaimed Seventh-Day Adventist prophet. And, of course, the fruits of his spirituality ended up hurting and destroying his followers. At the time, I don't think it was even publicized in the news during his last stand against our government forces that he was even a Seventh-Day Adventist. But he was, and those in the world watching the news who may not have even known that he belonged to an obvious cult may very well have thought less of true Bible-believing Christians as a result!

This is how Satan has always tried to work because he's always trying to discredit the true Church in the eyes of those who are actually ignorant of what the Bible really teaches. However, since David Koresh himself strongly opposed the doctrinal beliefs of the true Christian Church outside his brand of the Seventh-Day Adventist religion, it would make little sense indeed to fault the true Church for his nonbiblical beliefs and non-Christlike violent behaviors.

Objection 52
I'm a Seventh-Day Adventist

David Koresh, in the 1990s, was a self-proclaimed Seventh-Day Adventist prophet. And, of course, the fruits of his spirituality ended up hurting and destroying his followers.

Testing the Seventh-Day Adventist religion against its divine power demonstrated

Not only have we discussed the fact that many false prophecies have been given within the SDA religion so far (which, of course, shows the lack of divine power), but, of course, like all cults, there has been the complete lack of any genuine miracles performed by its adherents which, of course, does not do much for their testimony that God himself has worked through their leaders. Shall we all just blindly take their word for it? It's easy for *small* false cults to insist that only their particular name brand religion is the one true faith from the one true God, offering the only way of salvation; but, really, where's the supernatural power behind that claim which even remotely compares with the miracles that Christ and his apostles performed? Just an honest question for an honest soul.

And, again, false cults such as the SDA religion can't at all claim that Christ and his apostles actually spearheaded their particular religion with all its unique doctrines because they never once even mention their religion by name or taught any of their unique doctrines (like keeping the Sabbath for salvation) in the entire New Testament. Yes, Adventists claim that there were miracles which accompanied Ellen G. White and her prophecies. But if her prophecies were at all wrong, as we've already exposed, then where does that leave the supposed miracles of God which are ultimately connected to the same source as her prophecies?

We must remember that even the demonic world has some miraculous powers to deceive the ignorant with. In the one true faith, everything (prophecies, miracles, character of leaders) must be all without flaw; otherwise, we do have the perfect right to conclude it could not have come from our perfect creator.

Conclusion

As we can honestly see, the SDA religion also fails many reasonable tests when sincerely explored. And, actually, we've just uncovered the tip of the iceberg as it concerns the many plain deceptions of the Seventh-Day Adventist's religion (and even the other false religions we've discussed). Thus, in order for one to remain deceived in the Seventh-Day Adventist religion (like all the false religions which we've discussed), one is rather forced to throw their good conscience under the bus to a very large degree. Statistics are always changing, and depending upon the source of one's statistic, presently, there are roughly 20 million people worldwide who claim to be members of the Seventh-Day Adventist religion. This is *far less than* half of 1 percent of the world's overall population. This would mean that 99.5 percent of the world's population today (not to mention all those who lived prior to 1820) is deceived and unable to find SDA eternal salvation!

Such a reality should be hard for anyone to accept. If you happen to be one who is just ignorant of the major evidence which points to the fact that the Seventh-Day Adventist religion is a true cult which endangers one's salvation, I would strongly encourage you to do some real searching in the Bible on your own so you can see once and for all that the eternal salvation of God cannot at all be obtained by any religious good works on our part (Ephesians 2:8–9). On judgment day, all of us will only be judged by God's Word alone, not any man-made doctrine which contradicts it (John 12:48)! I can also assure you that on that day, neither Ellen G. White nor any other SDA leader will be of any aid to you whatsoever. What you do with the true Gospel message of God's eternal Word will ultimately be up to you, and I sincerely hope you will only put your full trust in Christ alone and what he did for you on the cross for your own eternal salvation.

There are, of course, many other Christian cults which have been ultimately hatched from the demonic host for the sole purpose of deceiving men away from the one true God and his eternal salvation (1 Timothy 4:1–2). The list goes into the hundreds, all of which will only use *parts* of the Bible, which makes them most deceptive simply because they are probably closest to true Christianity among all the false religions of the world. Some of the main cults among them include:

Objection 52
I'm a Seventh-Day Adventist

Worldwide Church of God, Unity Church, Unification Church, The Way International Church, Christian Science Church, and many others which may not be so prominent as the ones we've discussed more thoroughly in our objections. However, no matter which Christian cult they may happen to be, they all have these very real problems which certainly should be a major red flag to the honest soul:

1. They all completely disagree with each other as well as the true New Testament Christian faith.
2. They all insist that man has to earn God's eternal salvation through different good works.
3. They all most certainly fail the reasonable tests which we've employed.
4. They all have a very *tiny* following compared to the world's overall population (too small to be the truth, their numbers being far less than one-fourth of 1 percent of the world's population).
5. They all have very late starting dates within the church age we live in.
6. They are all quite lacking of the real power of God, whether demonstrated through real miracles or prophecies which come true with 100 percent accuracy.

Did William Miller ever prove through the power of God in any way that he was more than a mere man who was just creating his own religion with the influence of the demonic realm? No. Where are the miracles he did as Christ did? Where are all his fulfilled prophecies? Where is there any real evidence (beyond the normal abilities of man) that God was really working through him? Or Ellen G. White, for that matter? All of us can eat vegetables!

Since there really isn't any sound evidence, it is quite plain to see that both he and Ellen G. White just expected man to follow them blindly. Jesus, on the other hand, proved his divinity, and his apostles all proved through the supernatural power of God that God was working through them. And to top it off, if anyone believes that even *one small good work* of their own (added to the Gospel) will save them, according to Scripture, they will simply *not be saved* (Galatians 1:6–9)!

If you are one who is unwilling to let the legalistic doctrines of the Seventh-Day Adventist religion destroy your chance for eternal life in

God's kingdom, I would encourage you to embrace the true gospel message of salvation in the Bible (which doesn't have the works of men added to it). If you are one who can easily see through the deception of the Seventh-Day Adventist religion and would like to be right with God and be assured of your place in God's eternal kingdom to come, I invite you to just take that first small step of faith by sincerely praying the prayer of salvation located at the end of this book. Even if you've been a Seventh-Day Adventist for many years, you can still break away from that obvious cult today which threatens your true salvation through Christ.

And don't be concerned with what your family members may think of you because, simply put, they will not be your judge on judgment day! This decision is between you and God (your creator) alone. No matter what your past is like, God loves you and sincerely wants you to be a part of his awesome eternal kingdom! However, the Bible teaches us plainly that *only through Christ* can we obtain God's eternal life. Jesus said: *"I am the way and the truth and the life. No one comes to the Father except through me"* (John 14:6), Someone once asked Jesus how many will be saved. And Jesus replied, *"Make every effort to enter through the narrow door, because many, I tell you, will try to enter and will not be able"* (Luke 13:24).

> *Jesus said, "I am the resurrection and the life. He who believes in me, will live even though he dies; and whoever lives and believes in me will never die."* (John 11:25–26)

OBJECTION 53
I Believe in Satanism

A loving reminder: Before each false belief system we discuss, just so my loving intentions cannot be misunderstood, I will *once again* remind the reader that it's certainly *not the adherents* of any false belief system which the true Church is against but rather just the *false teachings* within them which deceive men away from the one and only true God and his eternal salvation (Ephesians 6:12). Therefore, my dear reader, please know that our discussion of these various different religions or belief systems is very much a *love* issue!

Defining Satanism

The world is, of course, full of all different conflicting ideas about Satan. However, since we have already established in Objection #28 that the Holy Bible has certainly proved to be the inspired Word of God through its many miraculously fulfilled prophecies, our study of Satanism in this objection will be from a *biblical perspective*. No other so-called holy book in the world can compete with the 100 percent prophetic accuracy of the Holy Bible which, of course, would include any satanic bibles as well!

Additionally, since the Holy Bible itself is really the oldest historical record, which we have of Satan, mentioning him in the very beginning of creation, it is only reasonable to acknowledge it's authoritative and unique qualifications to actually define Satan. Some Satanists may try to convince you that Satanism is the oldest religion because men worshipping Satan *may* predate Judaism, which technically started with the patriarch Abraham around 2000 BC (Genesis chapters 1–25). However, according to the Bible, long before Abraham, God had covenant relationships with mankind all the way back to the very first man Adam who worshipped God his creator only. Thus, biblical Christianity (which realizes that even God of the Old Testament was the Pre-incarnate Christ) is truly the oldest religion, simply because it was the very first religion.

Thus, Christianity which would also be founded upon the preincarnate Christ in the Garden of Eden before the fall of man certainly predates any variety of Satanism which has ever existed. Other modern Satanists today even deny that Satanism is a religion at all simply because they claim to be atheists and technically any "religion" requires a belief in God or gods. Nevertheless, whether or not one considers Satanism a religion or not, even as a belief system, it is certainly not the oldest. As once again, according to the Holy Bible (which proves its divine authorship over and over again), the preincarnate Christ, our creator, having unhindered relationship with Adam and Eve certainly predates their fall into sin as a result of Satan's influence upon them. Not to mention Christ himself predates Satan by eternity past!

> Since no satanic Bible has proved to be more powerful than the Holy Bible is through its many miraculously fulfilled prophecies, our study of Satanism in this objection will be from a biblical perspective.

Additionally, Christ himself validated the Bible as the inspired written word of the living God and that it can be fully trusted as such (Matthew 4:4). And unless some Satanist in history displayed more divine power than Christ did through the hundreds of miracles he did (and the fulfillment of over 300 Messianic prophecies), then why should anyone believe a Satanist over Christ? Not to mention, God also performed many powerful miracles through Christ's apostles as well who all plainly taught that the Holy Bible was, in fact, the inspired

Objection 53
I Believe in Satanism

written Word of the living God, and it can be fully trusted as such (2 Timothy 3:16). And unless some Satanist displayed more divine miracles in the open public than did Christ and his apostles, then honestly, why should anyone believe a Satanist over all their combined public miracles and testimonies? What are we saying? As it concerns our search for the one true faith among all the conflicting religions of the world, the greatest power revealed certainly equals the greatest trustworthy authority.

> Unless some Satanist displayed more divine miracles in the open public than did Christ and his apostles, then honestly, why should anyone believe a Satanist over all their combined public miracles and testimonies?

According to quite a number of biblical references which all agree with each other, Satan himself is nothing more than the created fallen angel Lucifer (Isaiah 14:12–16). The Hebrew word for Satan is *saw-tawn* and essentially means "adversary" or "archenemy" (Job 1:6). Some biblical titles given to Satan *before* his rebellion against God may include "anointed cherub" and "son of the morning." Other titles given to him *after* his rebellion against God include: the serpent, the great dragon, the devil, and Satan (Ezekiel 28:2, 12–19; Genesis 3:1–5; based on Revelation 12:9 and 20:2).

In all, there are over sixty references to the devil within the Word of God, and there are over fifty references to Satan, all of which refer to the very same cursed fallen angel who's pathetically resigned himself to aiding the physical and spiritual destruction of all mankind; thus, he is truly our greatest adversary, just as the word Satan means.

According to the Bible, however, while Satan can just *facilitate* man's spiritual destruction, he himself cannot actually prevent any man from having a right relationship with God and actually *cause* them to go to eternal hell (James 4:7; 1 Peter 5:8–9). And we can praise God for that! Ultimately, that is only a *free will choice* for each individual person which Satan cannot take away. Thus, any man must really be a willing participant and fully cooperate with Satan if, in fact, they would be led astray by him! And as is evident within the Satanist religion, one of Satan's biggest deceptions is that he himself is actually a good guy. But they must, of course, overlook the fact that our English word, *devil*, is just the word evil with a "D" in front of it, and the "D" undoubtedly represents the dragon of Rev. 12:9!

> While Satan can just facilitate man's spiritual destruction, he himself cannot actually prevent any man from having a right relationship with God and actually cause them to go to eternal hell.

Historically, the actual worship and following of Satan can be traced all the way back into the Old Testament times when heathen nations (and even Israel at times) worshiped Baal, Baal-zebub, or Beel-zebub, which are all just other names for Satan who is just the chief of evil spirits (Judges 2:13; 2 Kings 1:2; Matthew 12:24). But, technically, when it comes to mankind encountering and following Satan, as we have already mentioned, we can easily see that it even goes all the way back into the Garden of Eden when Eve was first deceived by him (Genesis 3:1–6).

However, to suggest that both Adam and Eve were Satanists, just because they were influenced by him in their fall is, of course, absurd. There is absolutely no indication in God's Word that Adam and Eve worshipped Satan or adopted anything like Satanism for their belief system as it indicates they believed in God even after their fall into sin (Genesis 4:1, 25).

Satanism as a whole belief system probably took root much later in man's history. And when it did take root, it must be also said that men adhering to some form of Satanism did not just seek to encounter Satan but also the whole demonic realm as well. This involved a variety of witchcraft, such as *necromancy* (an attempt to communicate with those dead through demonic beings), *divination* (seeking insight into the future through demonic beings), *enchantments* or *incantations* (the casting of spells on others carried out by demonic beings), etc. However, all such demonically aided practices have always been forbidden by God throughout the Bible, and in Old Testament times, those within the nation of Israel who practiced them at all were, in fact, put to death (Exodus 22:18; Leviticus 20:6, 27; Deuteronomy 18:9–14)! And this was simply because God knew it just deceived men away from a right relationship with himself and his eternal life (Revelation 21:8).

Objection 53
I Believe in Satanism

In Old Testament times, God commanded those within the nation of Israel who practiced Satanism to be put to death.

Modern Satanism

Some say that modern-day Satanism was basically founded in 1966, so we'll be addressing that notion to some degree as well. However, no matter *when* in history some form of Satanism can be found, it should be pointed out that religious practicing Satanists (especially ever since Christ) have always been an *extreme minority* in the world's overall population! In fact, like most all small false belief systems, professing Satanists make up *far less* than 1 percent of the world's population today. And today, they are not only an extreme minority among all the different religions in the world, but they are also quite divided among themselves as to what a real Satanist even is.

For example, today, there is reactive Satanism, LaVeyan Satanism, Theistic Satanism, Luciferianism, Temple of Set, the Satanic Temple, and I'm sure even more satanic cult groups which even choose to remain anonymous to the general public. And despite the Holy Bible's clear and long record of just who *Satan* is, many modern Satanists today (such as the Church of Satan or LaVeyan Satanism) just choose to completely reject any belief that Satan is even an angelic being created by God at all. Instead, they define themselves as atheists who neither believe in God nor the devil and contend that Satanism itself is rather just some kind of a philosophical self-serving belief system (not a religion), which they admittedly take great pride in.

However, since just our first five objections in Part 1 of our series give us *overwhelming honest evidence* that there is indeed an intelligent creator behind all the superior intelligence to our own, which we repeatedly find in nature, the adamant belief in atheism which many Satanists have adopted loses its credibility right there rather quickly. And so, if, in fact, we have a creator which is confirmed over and over again through much honest evidence, could those *atheist* Satanists who also reject the belief that Satan is a real fallen angel be equally as wrong about him?

Professing Satanists make up far less than 1 percent of the world's population.

The selfish attractions of Satanism

Some of the selfish attractions of Satanism may include unlimited sexual pleasures with unlimited consenting adults. Other attractions may include money and a variety of drugs taken during their rituals. Ultimately, to many modern Satanists, it's all about serving self. Hmm...that is about as polar opposite of biblical Christianity as it can get as biblical Christianity teaches Christians to deny self in order to genuinely love God and others. Not to mention, it should be easy to see that the motives of self-serving Satanists, then, is pretty far from *a sincere search for the truth.*

Along with pursuing sex, money, and drugs, many modern Satanists (like those Satanists of old) certainly seek to tap into the powers of the demonic realm as well. And this is so they can request those things they want from the demonic realm, even though they may very well claim to the general public not to even believe in the devil or demons! The truth is that many people attracted to Satanism are attracted to the supernatural for the power they *think* it will give them. Even LaVeyan Satanists (those who follow the deceased Anton LaVey) consider themselves black magicians and request many personal desires from the forces of darkness in their rituals. In those rituals, they summon, communicate, and make pacts with demonic beings just to achieve their desires. And, again, with some Satanists, drugs may be preferred to just aid the ritual mindset.

Some Satanists may try to convince others that most all Satanists believe demonic beings to be just some trick of the mind and do not believe them to be literal beings. But, LaVeyan Satanists certainly do believe in demonic beings as Anton LaVey himself taught his followers to treat all demonic beings with respect and friendship; one just has to read it for themselves in LaVey's satanic bible.

While some Satanists believe they are their own god, other Satanists even believe Satan to be our one and only true creator! Nevertheless, it would certainly seem that most Satanists do believe in the demonic realm as there is a real reason they continue to refer to themselves as Satanists and not just regular atheists! In fact, let's be honest, normal

Objection 53
I Believe in Satanism

modern atheists typically reject the spirit world altogether. But this is certainly not the case with even LaVeyan Satanists who do, in fact, make pacts with demonic beings in their rituals. If demonic beings were just some philosophical idea or a trick of the mind as some Satanists may claim, then just how does one make a pact (or agreement) with a philosophical idea or a trick of the mind anyway?

Nevertheless, one cannot only easily see that the differences between basic Satanist cults are rather major (which in itself is discrediting) but that their members are quite secretive and do not always reveal their *true* beliefs to the general public. And, generally speaking, when someone is purposely hiding something, it usually means they have something to really hide which is hardly ever good!

Along with pursuing sex, money, and drugs, many modern Satanists certainly seek to tap into the powers of the demonic realm.

When it comes right down to it, LaVeyan Satanists can really believe in whatever demonic beings they want to, for LaVey himself built that freedom into his *so-called church*. Reasonably, if it's all about self, he'd have to have taken that doctrinal stance. In fact, the golden rule within his satanic bible is, "Do what thou wilt shall be the whole of the law." Thus, it would be rather impossible for any LaVeyan Satanist to insist that all followers of LaVey do not believe in literal demonic beings if, in fact, they are free to believe what they want on that issue. However, it is certainly typical for false religious cults to misrepresent their actual beliefs just to get the unsuspecting public involved. Then once they are involved, by the time they find out the truth, they just won't care because of what's in it for them and the social ties they have already made.

However, with all that said, ultimately, it would seem Satanists simply fail to understand at least two basic biblical realities:

1. Satan and most of his demonic hosts are very intelligent masters of deception and quite able to deceive even Satanists into hell through their own selfish desires.
2. Satan and his demonic hosts ultimately hate *all men* and sincerely want them to be in the lake of fire for all eternity. And this, of course, includes Satanists. And even if demonic

beings have to *pretend* to be the *friend* of a Satanist in order to accomplish their destructive end, they are very willing participants!

For an example of #1 above, when Satanists practice necromancy and call up the dead to talk with them, they are really being deceived into believing they can actually talk to dead relatives, etc. However, the biblical truth is that no man living can possibly converse or even see anyone who has departed because *all those departed* are either in the center of the earth, hell, awaiting the Great White Throne Judgment and the lake of fire or they are in the third heaven until the rapture of the Church occurs. Either way, according to the very plain teachings of the Bible, all deceased men *are absolutely inaccessible to living men on earth!*

So, in all reality, those calling up the dead are really only speaking with a deceiving demonic spirit who was, in fact, very *familiar* with the dead person they are trying to communicate with. And such demonic spirits are so clever and deceptive that they can imitate most anything about those deceased they were familiar with. That's why the Bible refers to such demonic beings as "familiar spirits." They can even imitate a dead relative's voice, appearance, mannerisms, personality, and smell!

In 2 Corinthians 11:13, the Apostle Paul reminds us of the deceptive powers of the demonic realm by teaching us that Satan can even transform himself into an *angel of light* in order to deceive ignorant men for his evil purposes! Ultimately, Satanists, in general, are quite deceived as their view of Satan (if they even believe in him) is *far, far better* than who he actually is!

> In all reality, those calling up the dead are really only speaking with a deceiving demonic spirit who was, in fact, very familiar with the dead person they are trying to communicate with.

For example, as we pointed out in #2 above, Satan actually hates all men and just wants to kill them before they even get a chance to be right with God, and again, this, of course, includes Satanists. But, obviously, Satanists do not at all believe that; thus, they are far more deceived and unsuspecting because if it. The very nature of deception (when one is truly deceived) is not knowing one is actually deceived!

Objection 53
I Believe in Satanism

Thus, they play a very dangerous cat and mouse game with demonic spirits, just so they can get the power they want or the things they want (like sex, drugs, and money). And even though serious Satanists keep delving into the demonic realm for intrigue and imagined power, ironically, it is really only God and the good angels (whom they don't believe in) who are protecting them the whole time from the deadly harm always intended by the demonic realm! According to the Bible, demonic beings can only cause harm to man by specific permission of God who alone knows the hearts of all men (Job chapters 1–2).

Many Satanists may really think they are in control and can become friends with demonic beings, but from a biblical perspective, demonic beings would just deceptively portray such false friendships if they could deceive that person away from God in the process. Demonic beings are, in fact, far more clever and deceptive than Satanists realize! In fact, anyone who rejects the truth of God's Word opens themselves up to be deceived and double-crossed by the demonic world. Because once one is on Satan's playground with God's protection even more limited, there is simply no way to win.

Satanists don't realize it, but Satan and his demonic host don't at all care *just how* they deceive mankind into hell, just as long as they accomplish that same end result! If you want to be a humanist, that will serve their evil purpose just fine because your eternal fiery fate *as a humanist* is sealed, and Satan knows that. If you want to be a Hindu, Buddhist, or a New Ager, that's just fine with the devil too because he still accomplishes his same evil objective, which is always to deceive you away from the one true God and his eternal salvation.

If you want to be a Muslim, the demonic realm will welcome you into the Muslim religion with open arms! In fact, Satan doesn't mind if you want to give yourself to *any false religion or belief system in the world* which he has created for those rebelling against God because his same evil objective is achieved any which way! Just don't be a Bible-believing Christian because then you'll be worshipping your true creator and he does not get his evil way with your eternal destiny! And Satanism is probably his favorite simply because those belonging to that are not only deceived away from their perfect loving creator and the awesome eternal life he has for them, but also the closest to worshipping Satan openly, which has always been Satan's ultimate goal with humanity in his very insane diluted competition with God.

> Satanists don't realize it, but Satan and his demonic host don't at all care just how they deceive mankind into hell, just as long as they accomplish that end result.

Straight talk

According to the Bible, if Satan and the demonic realm had their way, they would just kill all mankind (including Satanists) off instantly before we even got a chance to be right with God through Christ and we'd all go straight to hell. And as we've already mentioned, our loving creator and the good angels are really the only reason any of us are still alive! Yes, according to the Bible, God our loving creator and two-thirds of the angels (which did not rebel and are not cursed by God) actually protect us from demonic beings 24/7! And scripture indicates that God's good angels are much stronger than Satan and his demonic host, simply because they were not cursed by God in any rebellion against him (Revelation 12:7–9, 20:1–2).

My friend, no one loves us more than our very own creator, which just makes good sense if you think about it at all. And the little bit of money, sex, drugs and pleasure Satanists might be given in their short lives in their natural state doesn't even begin to compare with all that God our creator would give them throughout their eternity with him (1 Corinthians 2:9)! Only God loves his own creation because he is, in fact, the only source of real love, period. In fact, if you call yourself a Satanist, God loved you enough to actually come down out of heaven to earth and die a brutal death on the cross just to take the punishment for all your sins upon himself! Not to mention, he's the one who created you in the first place so you even could have his eternal life!

And that's exactly what Christ did for all Satanists and all of us whom he created. But, my friend, according to the Bible, Satan doesn't even know how to love at all! And he would certainly never die for you or anyone because it's always been all about himself, even though he deceptively tries to get Satanists to believe it's all about themselves! But true love has always been just the opposite of serving self as we can clearly see there is no selfishness in what Christ did for all of us on the cross. However, from the very start of when Satan fell into sin, he's insanely just tried to take God's place, even though he is just a created being and only a cursed one at that!

Objection 53
I Believe in Satanism

So what better way for Satan to deceive Satanists than to tell them it's all about them when it is really *all about him* and they are just pawns in his ultimate war with God? And what better way for Satan to deceive Satanists than to tell them that they can become a god when really that has only been his personal misguided agenda from the start of his rebellion against God? Fortunately, no one has to believe Satan's lies. It's all about the personal power of freewill choice which our loving creator gave us. None of us have to believe lies and all of us can believe the loving truth of God supported by plenty of honest evidence if we want to! And not even Satan can take that power of freewill choice away from you.

> God and the good angels are really the only reason any of us are still alive, simply because if Satan had his way, he'd really just kill all mankind instantly, including Satanists!

So not only are Satanists robbed of experiencing their very own creator's real love for them simply because the demonic realm is completely incapable of God's love, but they are also robbed of the real supernatural power of God which is always constructive and life giving. The Bible teaches us plainly that *every good gift* (which is always accompanied by good intentions) comes from God, not the demonic realm (James. 1:17). Yes, the demonic realm may indeed give Satanists access to wealth, sex, materialism, etc. in continued exchange for their eternal soul, but that isn't exactly a *good gift* or *real love* if the end-result is eternal punishment in hell, is it? And, believe me, my Satanist friend, Satan knows all this quite well which is very strong evidence for his pure hatred of the human race. If you are a Satanist, you not only need to know that Satan is real but that he really does hate you! Jesus said in Matthew 16:26, *"For what is a man profited, if he shall gain the whole world, and loose his own soul? Or what shall a man give in exchange for his soul?"*

Even much of the supposed supernatural power demons entice men with is simply smoke and mirror deceptions, which is actually no power at all. And that's exactly why demonic power given to Satanists almost never manifests for all to see in the form of substantial life-giving miracles in the real world. And when demonic spirits do actually give men a certain amount of real supernatural power, it is only for the sole evil purpose of bringing them into further deception and leaving them further away from God. And, sometimes, God actually allows the demonic realm to have a certain amount of power to deceive men away from himself if he already knows quite well that those men do not want the truth or a right relationship with himself.

Thus, in an overall sense, demonic beings will only give men what they want if they know they can hurt them spiritually in the process. This is the case simply because, my friend, that *is their only continuing and ultimate goal!* Whether Satanists realize it or not, Satan and his demonic host hates all mankind and it has always been just as 1 Peter 5:8 states, *"Be sober, vigilant; because your adversary the devil, as a roaring lion, walks about seeking whom he may devour."*

Demonic beings not only want to deceptively portray themselves as good but also want men to believe all kinds of lies about God as well, mainly that God isn't a God of love or, better yet, that he doesn't exist at all! And this is because they do not want men to be reconciled with God in a right and loving relationship. For if that happens, they will actually be with God for all eternity and truly live happily ever after with indestructible bodies and *countless* other blessings which far exceed anything the demonic host could offer the lost during this life. And Satan doesn't want *any man* to have God's eternal life, simply because he knows he can't have that himself!

Since Satan already blew his chance for eternal life and is headed for the fires of hell, he just wants to wreck the opportunity all men have for God's eternal life as well. What a great guy, huh? So please don't let yourself be deceived by him and his lies about Christ whether you are a Satanist or not! For as we've already exposed, Satan and his demonic host are behind all false religions or belief systems, including just plain old humanism and self-reliance. Now that we've discussed just some of the basics of Satan and Satanism, let's briefly see how Satanism fairs as a belief system when tested.

> In an overall sense, demonic beings will only give men what they want if they know they can hurt them spiritually in the process.

Objection 53
I Believe in Satanism

Testing Satanism against the true moral condition of man

While many modern-day Satanists may have already believed one of Satan's greatest lies—that he doesn't even exist—they essentially do believe in self-worship and the delving into the demonic realm for their own purposes. And because self or me-ism is largely at the very center of modern-day Satanism cults, their actual moral view of mankind is far better than the biblical view that man himself is born with an obvious fallen sin nature. However, the ironic thing about promoting self while at the same time rejecting the basic sin nature of man is that according to the Bible, the promotion of self is the very definition of sin because loving others is simply not a priority! Therefore, the more Satanists promote self and feed their selfish nature with sex, money, drugs, and pseudo-demonic powers, the more they make it obvious that they, too, have an inborn sin nature which Christ their creator had to die on the cross for.

> The ironic thing about promoting self while at the same time rejecting the basic sin nature of man is that according to the Bible, the promotion of self is the very definition of sin!

Remember when I mentioned that most all false religions attract their members with money, immoral sex, drugs, or pseudo-power from the demonic realm? Well, Satanism as a belief system fits this whole profile quite perfectly. And this, of course, makes no sense with Satanism's underlying insistence that man himself is basically good. While it may be easy to see just why some may be attracted to Satanism for the selfish things it offers, rarely does one become a Satanist because of any honest evidence which confirms Satanism as the one true faith. As is very evident within Satanism, we learn that people can most certainly join false religions for purely emotional and selfish reasons.

While Satanism may be good at offering a variety of immoral attractions to its adherents, the one thing it completely fails to do is to clearly demonstrate any real love or any real power, which can only come from our creator if you reasonably think about it. Since when has any Satanist (or even demonic being) ever openly demonstrated his power or love to all mankind as Christ did? And as their doctrinal stance remains that man is basically good and is not plagued with a sin nature from birth, then this, of course, goes directly against the very reality of wide spread moral failure in the world, which we all experience every day to some degree in our lives. Therefore, that form of modern-day Satanism which would promote self and simply deny the sinful condition of man would certainly fail this very reasonable test of man's true moral condition.

Testing Satanism against self-contradictions

As we've already mentioned, modern-day Satanism, which would promote self and simply deny the sinful condition of man, is an obvious contradiction because the more man becomes steeped in selfishness, the more any conscientious society would pronounce moral failure upon him! Those Satanism religions which centrally promote self also often teach that pride is a good thing and not a sin as the Bible teaches. However, once again, the more man becomes puffed up in his own pride, the more any conscientious society would also pronounce moral failure upon him. Thus, in this basic respect, the majority of modern Satanism groups which sincerely believe these contradicting doctrines about mankind easily fail this very reasonable test as well. And as we've already mentioned, while some Satanist groups actually deny the existence of Satan and his demonic host, they at the same time delve into the demonic realm just to get what they want.

So do they believe in the demonic realm or not? And if some Satanist groups really don't believe Satan exists (like they claim), then why would they even call themselves Satanists (and not just regular atheists)? This, too, is a contradiction within some Satanist groups.

In LaVeyan Satanism, members of the Satanic church are free to really believe whatever makes them happy because this is what LaVey himself taught. But at the same time, they have rules, like no sex with children, etc. So they can believe whatever they want as long as they keep all the basic membership rules of their church? Obviously, they cannot just believe whatever makes them happy; they must keep all the rules. Otherwise, they will be kicked out for good!

This, too, is a contradiction within their so-called *church*. Additionally, if all members can believe anything they want, then obviously, they would, of course, constantly contradict each other within their church on many issues. And, finally, as we've already mentioned, all the different Satanist cult groups even disagree with each other *on the very basics* of what a Satanist even is. So, all in all, we find that Satanism as a belief system is one of the most self-contradicting belief systems, even compared to other false religions which also prove to be quite self-contradicting, like the New Age movement which could be looked at as just another brand of Satanism if, in fact, they too delve into the demonic realm through channeling, etc.

Testing Satanism against its prophetic predictions of the future

Again, since Satan and his demonic host are just cursed created beings and not like God who is all-knowing, their ability to see into the future is most certainly limited and skewed. Does that mean that they are never correct? No, but it means that they are wrong a lot, and one simply can never be sure when the demonic realm would transfer accurate information about the future. All down through human history, false prophets controlled by demonic beings have mostly proved to be wrong with only *some* scattered exceptions. They must be correct to *some degree* in order to deceive and convince, just like all false religions must have some real truth in them in order to deceive. If they didn't, no one would get deceived and believe in them! However, when your eternal destiny is on the line, my friend, *some truth* certainly shouldn't be good enough! And the truth is that no Satanist (or even group of Satanists) in history has even come close to giving as many detailed prophecies as did the prophets within the Holy Bible and proven to be 100 percent flawless in their predictions of the future. Thus, Satanism, as a whole, fails this very reasonable test as well.

No Satanist (or even group of Satanists) in history has even come close to giving as many detailed prophecies as did the prophets within the Bible and proven to be 100 percent flawless in their predictions of the future.

Testing Satanism against divine power demonstrated

Anyone could verbally claim to be God who is the creator of all. But Jesus came down to earth and proved it through hundreds of miracles done publicly in front of many unbiased witnesses. For those Satanists who believe Satan is actually our one and only true creator, when in human history did Satan come and live among men in visible sight and prove his loving deity through hundreds of undeniable life, giving miracles in front of many witnesses? For those Satanists who believe they are their own God, since when has any Satanist even come close to all the different miracles Christ and his apostles did out in public where everyone can see? Both Christ and his apostles did all their miracles *instantly* and *out in the open for everyone to see,* but whenever you hear of modern Satanists supposedly raising the dead to life, they *claim* to have done it in their very private secret rituals which take hours.

So, with Satanists who never perform any consistent large public miracles of any kind, we're just supposed to take their word for all of reality? I don't think so! And since when has Satan or any Satanist risen from the dead like Christ did and was seen by more than 500 witnesses (1 Corinthians 15:6)? Obviously, every Satanist (including the deceased Anton LaVey) was quite mortal (even if they claimed to be their own god) because, unlike Christ, they never appeared to many men in their resurrected state. All in all, Satanism completely lacks any real power which would go beyond the normal powers of weak misguided human men who are just being deceived by the demonic realm.

> When in human history did Satan come and live among men in visible sight and prove his loving deity through hundreds of undeniable miracles in front of many witnesses?

What is your final authority on all truth?

Because it has thoroughly proven itself to be divinely authored, the inspired Word of God is really our only trustworthy source when it comes to understanding Satan or Satanism. Satanists can choose to believe their doctrines and/or false bibles over the Holy Bible, but until any of their sources can legitimately demonstrate the divine power which the Bible has revealed through its thousands of fulfilled prophecies and miracles, why should we believe them over the Word of God? Since Satan is not all-knowing, he cannot even compete with God on telling the future with any consistent accuracy. And since he cannot create one single thing, all he can do is try to destroy what God has created and/or try to imitate what God has created through counterfeit means.

Objection 53
I Believe in Satanism

While the long historical belief system of Satanism has proven to be both false and spiritually destructive to mankind when tested, the one thing it does do is validate the Bible in respect to its teaching that the demonic realm is both real and evil! And what we mainly can know about the demonic realm is revealed to us by God in the Bible, simply because God doesn't want any man to be deceived by it! Thus, our loving creator is playing very fair.

So, then, in light of all this, how does it make any sense for any Satanist to even follow Satan or tap into the demonic realm if God himself is the only one who can give them the real love, power, eternal life, and hope they really need? Statistics are always changing, and depending upon the source of one's statistic, presently, there are roughly only about 200,000 people worldwide who claim to believe in some form of Satanism. Satanists will, of course, claim that their numbers are much greater, but do some real searching on your own because if we consider just what the Bible has always taught about Satan, if nothing else, he is a master at deception and the father of lies (John 8:44).

My friend, even if one would double this number (200,000) six times, it would still represent *far less* than 1 percent of the world's population!

And one of the biggest lies he may try to get Satanists to believe is that he doesn't really even exist as a fallen angel just as the Bible teaches he does (Isaiah 14:12–16). And even if men believe he actually does exist, another lie he tries to deceive them with is that he's the keeper of souls in hell and actually has access to hell in the center of the earth. But the biblical truth is that Satan himself has never yet set foot in the center of the earth hell and will only be bound there for 1,000 years (during the millennial reign of Christ) before he is finally cast into the lake of fire for all eternity. The real truth that Satan does not want people to know is that he's actively seeking out men right on earth, constantly trying to deceive them away from the one true God and his eternal life with false religions, cults, money, immoral sex, and any other thing he can dangle in front of our fallen human nature!

Conclusion

My friend, if you presently call yourself a Satanist, I strongly urge you to try to see the big picture of your eternal life which only Jesus your creator can give you. All the fleeting pleasures of this short life will soon fade as you get older and cannot even partake of them. Or who knows? Anyone of us could die tomorrow. And if one does not know Christ as their Lord and Savior, then their spirit will go immediately to center of the earth, hell, until they will stand before their creator to give an account of their life at the Great White Throne Judgment which takes place right after the 1,000-year reign of Christ on earth.

While Satan doesn't want the unbelieving to know all this, God does, so they can avoid it and be in right relationship with him. All through the gospels, Jesus commanded the demonic world and put demons in their place, simply because he himself is the ultimate source of all power as their creator. When Christ and his apostles all walked the earth, they fully demonstrated the power of God through major supernatural miracles hundreds of times over in front of many public eyewitnesses. Additionally, the Bible itself is laced with over 2,000 future predicting prophecies which have already been fulfilled, all proving Jesus is just who he claimed to be! And this awesome divine power displayed is something unique to biblical Christianity alone.

By the way, where is any satanic bible with such fulfilled prophecies? There is none. As the saying goes:

"Jesus did not at all expect the world to follow him blindly… He publicly healed the blind to prove his deity!"

And as we've already mentioned, in the end of this present age we live in, the entire demonic world will be tossed into the lake of fire at Christ's command where they will be tormented day and night forever (Revelation 20:10). The truth is that only God loves you (and those who follow him, loving you with his love) because he's the only one who created you! And just as Jesus proved his divinity to the honest soul many times over when he walked the earth, so too is his Word completely trustworthy which foretells the awesome eternity which God has for all those who love him. As Revelation 21:3–4 clearly teaches:

Objection 53
I Believe in Satanism

"[B]ehold, the dwelling place of God is with men, and he will live with them, and they shall be his people, and God himself shall be with them, and be their God. And God shall wipe away all tears from their eyes; and there shall be no more death, neither sorrow, nor crying, neither shall there be any more pain: for the former things are passed away."

"No eye has seen, no ear has heard, and no mind has imagined, what God has prepared for those who love him." (1 Corinthians 2:9)

But the Bible teaches us plainly that *only through Christ* can we obtain God's eternal life. Someone once asked Jesus how many will be saved. Jesus said, *"I am the way and the truth and the life. No one comes to the Father except through me"* (John 14:6).

And Jesus also said, *"Make every effort to enter through the narrow door, because many, I tell you, will try to enter and will not be able"* (Luke 13:24).

If you are one who can easily see through the deception of Satanism and would like to be right with God and be assured of your place in his awesome eternal kingdom, I invite you to just take that first small step of faith by sincerely praying the prayer of salvation located at the end of this book. Even if you've been in Satanism for years, you can still break away from that obvious false cult today which threatens your true salvation through Christ.

And don't be concerned with what your fellow Satanists may think of you because, simply put, they will not be you're judge on judgment day! This decision is between you and God (your creator) alone. No matter what your past is like, God loves you and sincerely wants you to be a part of his awesome eternal kingdom!

Jesus said, "I am the resurrection and the life. He who believes in me, will live even though he dies; and whoever lives and believes in me will never die." (John 11:25–26)

OBJECTION 54
I Believe in Scientology

A loving reminder: Before each false belief system we discuss, just so my loving intentions cannot be misunderstood, I will *once again* remind the reader that it's certainly *not the adherents* of any false belief system which the true Church is against but rather just the *false teachings* within them which deceive men away from the one and only true God and his eternal salvation (Ephesians 6:12). You see, God loves everyone, and everyone *has the right to know* if a religion or belief system is truly steering people away from him and his eternal salvation. In fact, if the true Church did not expose false belief systems which do not pass the reasonable tests which we can apply to them, then it most certainly would be a reflection of its love! Therefore, my dear reader, please know that our discussion of these various different religions or belief systems is very much a *love* issue.

The origin of Scientology

Scientology started as a religion in 1950 with the publishing of the book *The Modern Science of Public Health* by Lafayette Ron Hubbard. According to Hubbard's dianetic theory in his book, the human mind is just made up of mental image pictures of all events within a person's life. Hubbard refers to all past events marked with pain as engrams. Supposedly, according to Hubbard, all painful events of a person's life

Objection 54
I Believe in Scientology

(engrams) can be completely erased, restoring man to perfect physical and mental health which enables deeper analytical thought. And the person whose engrams have all been erased is referred to as a clear. Thus, it is the very purpose of Scientology to clear our entire planet through dianetic processing. Since, according to Hubbard, in 1954, all men were also reincarnated (having hundreds of past lives), all our past lives must also be cleared as well. Hubbard was also convinced that all members of Scientology would eventually remember those past lives, minus all the engrams, of course.

Also according to Hubbard, the real person is also invisible (similar to the human spirit and soul according to the Bible), which he decided to label the thetan. And as a person's *thetan* becomes relieved of their *engrams*, they will actually regain all the godlike powers which were inherently theirs. According to Hubbard, some of these godlike powers would include telepathy (nonverbal mind-reading and communication), exteriorization (an ability to separate from one's body with full perception), and telekinesis (an ability to move objects with just thought), etc. Thus, Hubbard believed man is actually quite ancient in his age and was once godlike and just deteriorated over time.

But he also believed that through Scientology counseling, which he called auditing, a person can regain their godlike status and abilities. And Hubbard called a thetan who has been restored to their godlike status an OT or an operating thetan. People today within the *very small* religion of Scientology actually pay exorbitant fees of $1,000 an hour just to have their engrams erased through auditing so they can reach their OT (or operating thetan) status and acquire their godlike abilities! But, of course, the problem is that no one has ever met any Scientologist with godlike abilities, which would obviously surpass that of a normal weak human being! At least, I'm not aware of anyone who has; are you? So as we can see, Satan not only wants men to be deceived, but he actually gets them to pay for their own deception and gives them no real results in return!

> People today within the very small religion of Scientology actually pay exorbitant fees of $1,000 an hour just to have their engrams erased and acquire their godlike abilities!

According to Hubbard, when a person dies, their thetan (or spirit) has been preprogrammed to return to what he calls an implant station located somewhere in outer space. According to Hubbard, there in the implant station, their thetan will have all the memories of their recent life erased before their thetan will be sent back to earth to pick up a new body and start a new life. But Hubbard also promises Scientology members that with precise (and very expensive) auditing, a person can actually erase their return command so that they will never have to return to an implant station again and thus be a free agent. This, of course, means that they will be able to drop off an old body and pick up a new one all on their own without the aid of an implant station and is done with full consciousness and self-determination. Hmm…that sure is a lot of self-determination or something else! Therefore, members of Scientology following Hubbard believe that they themselves are, in fact, very ancient alien beings which have memories from literally millions of years ago and that they are essentially immortal once the objects of immortality (engrams) have been erased.

Thus, Scientology members believe themselves to be a god who's just in the process of regaining their lost powers. And the main reason the entire human race (within all of recorded human history) has not reached its godlike potential is simply because we were not smart enough to realize all that Hubbard himself did in 1950! But then one most certainly has to ask the reasonable question: Why didn't at least Ronald Hubbard ever reach his godlike status in any way obvious to the whole world if he was the actual founder of Scientology? And if he didn't ever reach his godlike status as the actual founder of Scientology, what hope is there for his followers and the rest of humanity?

Once again, if unlike biblical Christianity which goes all the way back to the first man, Adam (Genesis 1:26–27; Matthew 19:4; 1 Corinthians 15:45), the Scientology religion was basically founded by Ron Hubbard around 1950, then one must certainly ask the very reasonable question: How indeed did all mankind have access to the vital truth which pertains to their godlike status prior to the late birth of Scientology? Obviously, the whole Scientology religion cannot be found anywhere in our history books prior to L Ron Hubbard. And if we all have the same godlike potential, why has Ron Hubbard been the only one in all of recorded human history to realize his whole specific Scientology claim?

Objection 54
I Believe in Scientology

Members of Scientology claim that they themselves are, in fact, millions of years old and that they are essentially immortal once the objects of immortality (engrams) have been erased.

Testing Scientology against the true moral condition of man

Scientology doesn't believe in man's sin because it doesn't even teach that we are humans created by a moral God. According to Scientology, we are all actually ancient alien beings (even though for some reason, we've always called ourselves humans!) who are millions of years old evolving through reincarnation. And the only thing holding us back from our true alien potential are our engrams or painful memories! As we've already discussed in our Objection #18, evil or sin could be accurately defined as *"the lack of spiritual good in the free will choices of man when he goes against his God given conscience."*

However, Scientology fails to even recognize man's moral failure to do good all throughout human history because of freewill choice and instead blames everything evil on just engrams or painful memories. Additionally, our Objection #19 thoroughly exposes the fact that mankind (including those tangled in the Scientology religion) has always had a problem with moral failure. Because a painful memory could hardly be considered a moral failure of any kind, Scientology completely fails this very reasonable test against the true moral condition of man, which has proven to be quite morally fallen throughout all recorded human history.

Testing Scientology against the well-known facts of science

It is a well-documented fact that the foundation under the Scientology religion of Hubbard was basically just old-fashioned Satanism, which just used scientific sounding terms and had a front door decorated with scientific absurdities. Just like the cereal Grape-Nuts has never had neither grapes or nuts in it, Scientology really has nothing to do with real observable science or even true spirituality, for that matter. Implant stations in outer space for all the spirits of men (who are actually ancient aliens) are no more scientifically verifiable than the cosmic sea turtle of Hinduism! It's quite easy for Hubbard to teach that we are all actually ancient alien beings who are millions of years old, evolving through reincarnation, but, my friend, such a belief has nothing to do with real observable science and simply cannot be confirmed through any honest evidence whatsoever! And to stake one's eternal salvation with such ridiculous beliefs would be literally insane. But Scientologists might ask: Are the teachings of the Bible any less fantastic to believe in? Yes, for at least two simple reasons:

1. First of all, Scientology ultimately relies on the theory of evolution for even its alien origins. And the Theory of evolution itself must ultimately rely upon the insane belief that everything in nature having intelligent design literally came from *nothing* or was always just there. My friend, as we've already discussed within our first five objections of part one of our series, such beliefs could not be more unreasonable or unscientific. However, in stark contrast, biblical Christianity teaches us that everything in nature having intelligent design came from an intelligent perfect eternal divine being who has fairly and honestly revealed himself to all mankind, not only through nature which easily reveals his intelligence but also through thousands of fulfilled Bible prophecies as well as the divine Christ and his apostles who openly demonstrated Christ's divinity right in front of humanity through hundreds of miracles.

So, ultimately, Scientology teaches that intelligence came from nothing while biblical Christianity teaches that intelligence came from an intelligent source who has revealed himself openly for the whole human race to see. Scientology, based on evolution, must also teach that all the order we see in nature came from disorder, a special imaginary reality which science has never been privileged to observe! But biblical Christianity has always believed all the order we see in nature came from an orderly intelligent divine being. My friend, which one *honestly* sounds more scientific and reasonable to you?

> Scientology ultimately teaches that intelligence came from nothing while biblical Christianity teaches that intelligence came from intelligence—which one honestly sounds more scientific and reasonable to you?

Objection 54
I Believe in Scientology

2. As we already covered well enough in Objection #5 of Part 1 in our series which discusses evolution, the Holy Bible is in complete compliance with the natural sciences, and many of our greatest scientists have, in fact, been Bible-believing Christians because of it. Sir Isaac Newton and literally hundreds of other prominent scientists like him could be listed as we already partially did in our Objection #5. However, since Hubbard started Scientology in 1950, no scientists prior to 1950 could have even believed in his Scientology. In fact, I can assure you, even very few evolution-believing scientists after 1950 have believed in Hubbard's Scientology with its fantastic ideas of reincarnation and outer space implant stations!

While many scriptures of the Bible have proven to be in compliance with the natural sciences, there is very little within the writings of Hubbard which can even be confirmed by the natural sciences. For example, he teaches that our minds *are just* made up of mental pictures. Hmm...sounds a bit simplistic and unverifiable to me. How does he actually know, especially when all scientists before him never made such a claim? And if he can't give us any honest evidence for such a claim or back up his claim with the supernatural power of his own godlike status, then why should we ever begin to believe him?

Again, it's a classic case of a cult leader just wanting us to take his word for all his strange beliefs while completely escaping his responsibility to provide any honest evidence for them. Additionally, he claims that all our bad memories can be completely erased, plunging us into godhood? Have you honestly ever met anyone who managed to completely forget all their bad memories? Have you honestly ever met anyone who became a god, just because they managed to forget their painful past? Real science or fantasy? You decide. I've already decided, and the choice was not that difficult to make!

> While many scriptures of the Bible have proven to be in compliance with the natural sciences, there is very little within the writings of Hubbard which can even be confirmed by the natural sciences.

Testing Scientology against the character of its founder

While our previous discussion of what those in Scientology actually believe may sound too ridiculous to even consider valid, Hubbard's followers not only believed him but also actually had him on a lofty pedestal because of it. And, certainly, his fake biographies which he presented to his followers just added to the larger-than-life image which he portrayed for himself. The only problem was that many of his many amazing claims within them were a total fabrication produced by his overactive imagination!

As we will easily show, L. Ron Hubbard was, in fact, *a chronic liar.* He not only claimed to have learned to read *and write* by the age of three (which itself would be quite amazing indeed) but claimed to have read and understood *many* of the world's greatest classics by the age of twelve. Also, he portrayed himself in his youth as an expert horseman, claiming he grew up on a ranch in Montana which covered one quarter of the state!

Additionally, he portrayed himself as some kind of a heroic world explorer who hunted coyote, became blood brothers with the Blackfoot Indians, explored the coast of China several times, lived with bandits in the mountains of Tibet, made friends with an old magician whose ancestors served in the court of Kublai Khan, and made friends with the ruling warlords of western Manchuria (by demonstrating his superior horsemanship) and discovered an ancient burial ground steeped in the tradition of heroic warriors and kings deep in the jungles of Polynesia— all by the age of 18! However, none of it was, of course, true as the true L. Ron Hubbard was a high school dropout who struggled academically and only went on some steaboat rides with his mother and just went camping at some nearby campgrounds! Now do you see what I mean by a chronic liar? And if we know Hubbard lied all about himself to gain followers, then why wouldn't he also lie about the supposed spiritual realities he taught?

After being discharged from the Navy in December of 1945, Hubbard did not return home to his wife and two small children in Bremerton, Washington, like all other normal married men after the war. Instead, he essentially ignored his wife and children and went directly to Pasadena, California, where he met up with a satanic organization called the Ordo Templi Orientis, which was just the US name for Aleister Crowley's organization back in England. There, he and Jack Parsons (who was the leader of the cult) actually organized sexual rituals with women in an attempt to create the moonchild they believed in. What a faithful husband, huh? But, keep in mind, all such sexual freedoms are typical of any satanic group because that's exactly what Satan often uses to attract them to it!

Remember when I mentioned that most all false religions attract their members with money, immoral sex, drugs, or pseudo-power from the demonic realm? Like Satanism itself, Scientology as a belief system fits this profile quite perfectly as well. While it may be easy to see just why some may be attracted to Scientology for these self-serving emotional reasons, none of these things, of course, have anything at all to do with any honest evidence which confirms Scientology as the one true faith. So we cannot only see that many must be attracted to Scientology for the wrong reasons but also that the very founder of Scientology certainly lacks the trustworthy character which we would expect of the founder of the one true faith which explains eternal reality for everyone else!

> We can not only see that many must be attracted to Scientology for the wrong reasons but also that the very founder of Scientology certainly lacks the necessary character which we would expect of the founder of the one true faith which explains reality for everyone else!

Testing Scientology against its divine power demonstrated

As we already mentioned, it is a well-documented fact that the underlying religion of Hubbard was just old-fashioned Satanism. The simple truth is that Scientology as a belief system completely rejects a creator God and just taps into the demonic realm. In fact, Hubbard's mentor as a young man was the infamous English black magician, Aleister Crowley. Crowley's most famous work was called *The Book of the Law*, where he expressed his main philosophy of life: "Do what thou wilt shall be the whole of the law." While this was indeed a belief Hubbard would live by for the rest of his life, we can also see it influenced many other men caught up in Satanism as well such as Anton LaVey who essentially adopted the same philosophy in his satanic bible.

In fact, it is obvious that Hubbard incorporated many of Crowley's beliefs into his own Scientology religion later on, especially in the secret upper levels of Scientology, which are referred to as the OT Levels. And following Crowley's footsteps, Hubbard of course adopted many of his black magician practices which included the use of many illegal drugs and what they called affirmations given to them from the demonic realm. According to Hubbard's own son, his father regularly used amphetamines, barbiturates, and hallucinogens such as cocaine, peyote, and mescaline. Some of the written affirmations of truth which Hubbard received were, "All men shall be my slaves! All women shall succumb to my charms! All mankind shall grovel at my feet and not know why!" Sounds like Satan himself, does it not? Wow, what a guy!

> According to Hubbard's own son, his father regularly used amphetamines, barbiturates, and hallucinogens such as cocaine, peyote, and mescaline.

While Scientology may be good at offering a variety of immoral attractions to its members, the one thing it completely fails to do (just like Satanism) is to clearly demonstrate any real selfless love or divine power. Since when has any alien being even openly demonstrated his power or love to all mankind as Christ did in human history? However, Christ came down to earth and literally lived among us, fully proving that he was, in fact, our loving divine creator in front of many historical witnesses. And God even worked many powerful public miracles through his apostles as well in order to demonstrate his love. And whenever Christ or his apostles did a miracle, it was always to help or heal mankind, never to do man harm.

Additionally, the Bible itself is laced with over 2,000 future-predicting prophecies which have already been fulfilled, all proving Jesus is just who he claimed to be! However, in comparison, none of Hubbard's writings contain any such powerful prophecies which prove any kind of divine aid within them. The truth is this awesome divine power displayed by Christ and his apostles is something unique to biblical Christianity alone. As we've already mentioned in our earlier objections:

> Jesus did not at all expect the world to follow him blindly... He publicly healed the blind to prove his deity!

But with L. Ron Hubbard, who never walked in any consistent large public miracles of any kind, we're just supposed to take his word for all of his supposed take on reality? I don't think so. In fact, off stage, it is very doubtful that the magician, Aleister Crowley, even displayed anything like a real miracle. All in all, Scientology completely lacks any power which would go beyond the normal powers of the demonic realm bent on spiritually destroying mankind. As in the case with all false religions, trust is broken quite rapidly if one should actually take the time to study them out at all and test them against the very reasonable tests which we have discussed.

And as we can easily see, Scientology as a belief system is no exception as it, too, fails even the four basic tests we've just employed. Like all the false religions we'll discuss, Scientology has many other unsolvable problems as well, which neither time nor written page permits us to expose. However, just what we have exposed should be sufficient to convince the *honest soul* that Scientology as a religion has no more to do with the spiritual truth than it has to do with real *observable* science.

Conclusion

Scientology leaders today will try to convince the world that there are over 10 million people worldwide who now believe in Scientology. Even if such a boast was close to true, that would still be *far* less than one-fourth of 1 percent of the world's entire population. Such statistics are always changing, but if one looks into a variety of nonbiased sources, they will quickly discover it is much closer to a mere 40,000 than 10 million. Of course, one way false religions try to attract their members is to overinflate the true number of their serious adherents. But just like there is a huge difference between 10 million and 40,000, there is also a big difference between the real truth and what Scientology teaches.

If you happen to really believe in Scientology right now and are actually deceived by what it teaches, please realize that, really, none of its claims can really be verified through real science or history as in the case with biblical Christianity, which can be historically traced all the way back to the beginning of creation. However, in stark contrast, Scientology as a religion really only goes back to the very recent mind and imagination of the very imperfect self-deceived man, Ron L. Hubbard.

> One way false religions try to attract its members is to overinflate the true number of their adherents.

The truth is our creator is far more loving and creative than Ron Hubbard, and the future he has planned for those who believe in Christ is far greater than any alien evolutionary future outlined by Scientology. The Bible reveals that all believers in Christ will not only have resurrected perfected bodies (which will never feel any pain again) but will also be able to walk through solid objects, travel at the speed of thought, and probably have the angelic ability to be invisible at will. And even far beyond all what the Bible reveals to us, God sincerely promises us that, *"Eye hath not seen, nor ear heard, neither has it entered into the heart of man, the things which God has prepared for them that love him"* (1 Corinthians 2:9).

However, in stark contrast, Scientology, which is ultimately based on Darwin's Theory of Evolution, is confined to the constant pain, bloodshed, and death which evolution always requires. Don't be deceived. Evolution is no more true than is reincarnation which has no real scientific backing either. But if you give Christ a chance, he will not only prove to you that he is just who he claimed to be but will also give you the eternal life he promised all men who believed in the awesome love he showed them on the cross. And just as Jesus proved his divinity to the honest soul many times over when he walked the earth, so too is his Word completely trustworthy, which foretells the awesome eternity which God has for all those who love him. As Revelation 21:3–4 clearly teaches:

> *"[B]ehold, the dwelling place of God is with men, and he will live with them, and they shall be his people, and God himself shall be with them, and be their God. And God shall wipe away all tears from their eyes; and there shall be no more death, neither sorrow, nor crying, neither shall there be any more pain: for the former things are passed away."*

Objection 54
I Believe in Scientology

But the Bible teaches us plainly that *only through Christ* can we obtain God's eternal life. Jesus said, *"I am the way and the truth and the life. No one comes to the Father except through me"* (John 14:6).

Someone once asked Jesus how many will be saved. And Jesus replied, *"Make every effort to enter through the narrow door, because many, I tell you, will try to enter and will not be able"* (Luke 13:24).

If you are one who can easily see through the deception of Scientology and would like to be right with God and be assured of your place in his awesome eternal kingdom to come, I invite you to just take that first small step of faith by sincerely praying the prayer of salvation located at the end of this book. Even if you've been in Scientology for years, you can still break away from that obvious false cult today which threatens your true salvation through Christ. And don't be concerned with what fellow Scientologists may think of you because, simply put, they will not be you're judge on judgment day! This decision is between you and God (your creator) alone. No matter what your past is like, God loves you and sincerely wants you to be a part of his awesome eternal kingdom!

> *Jesus said, "I am the resurrection and the life. He who believes in me, will live even though he dies; and whoever lives and believes in me will never die."* (John 11:25–26)

OBJECTION 55
I Believe in Freemasonry

A loving reminder: Before each false belief system we discuss, just so my loving intentions cannot be misunderstood, I will *once again* remind the reader that it's certainly *not the adherents* of any false belief system which the true Church is against but rather just the *false teachings* within them which deceive men away from the one and only true God and his eternal salvation (Ephesians 6:12). You see, God loves everyone, and everyone *has the right to know* if a religion or belief system is truly steering people away from him and his eternal salvation. In fact, if the true Church did not expose false belief systems which do not pass the reasonable tests which we can apply to them, then it most certainly would be a reflection of its love! Therefore, my dear reader, please know that our discussion of even this religion is very much a *love* issue!

The origin of Freemasonry

While the complicated and often debated history of Freemasonry as a religion is certainly beyond the scope of our short objection, we can say its roots do go all the way back *at least* into the Middle Ages, around AD 1390. And from there, we could say that the secretive fraternal organization evolved into what it is today. But, once again, one must certainly ask the very reasonable question: If the Freemasonry religion (with all its peculiar beliefs) is, in fact, the one true faith for all mankind, how indeed did all mankind have access to the vital truth which pertains to their eternal salvation prior to the late birth of Freemasonry? Would a perfect God really be so neglectful of his own creation?

Ironically, the term *Freemason* actually does refer to those young men in medieval times who were trained to work with limestones or sandstones suitable for ornamental masonry. And the adjective *free* attached to it back in medieval times just indicated that the mason was not enslaved but worked for payment.

And, strangely enough, the medieval stone construction organization actually mutated into today's Freemason religion which still portrays itself to be good through its good works, even though it no longer has anything at all to do with stone construction. So, just like Scientology really has nothing to do with real observable science, the modern Freemasonry religion really has very little to do with stone or brick construction.

It is also interesting to note that many false religions which reject the main correct teachings and doctrines of the Bible often hypocritically use what scriptures they can from the Holy Bible, just so they can deceive and appear more credible. You'll find this is also quite true with Freemasonry. But reasonably, if their false religion is really the one true faith, why on earth do they even need to borrow any scriptures or doctrines from the Holy Bible in the first place? I can assure you that biblical Christianity certainly does not borrow any of the unique teachings of Freemasonry, just to appear more credible. Not just because biblical Christianity easily predates Freemasonry, but also because its spiritual truths are complete all by themselves, just as we would expect of the one true faith (2 Peter 1:3).

> Strangely enough, the medieval stone construction organization actually mutated into today's Freemason religion, even though it no longer has anything at all to do with stone construction.

Testing Freemasonry against the true moral condition of man

Freemasonry maintains that man *is basically good* and can obtain salvation through his own good works without faith in Jesus Christ.

This belief, of course, is not only in direct contrast to the true fallen moral condition we can plainly observe in the heart of man throughout all of human history but also goes directly against the clear teachings of the Bible that man is born into sin and can only get redemption and salvation by believing in what Christ did for us on the cross (Ephesians 2:8–9; Acts 4:12; John 14:6). Thus, it should be quite obvious Freemasonry fails when tested against man's true moral condition.

Let's all be honest: if mankind was basically good and did not have an inborn sinful nature to wrestle with, the prisons would not be full, there would be little need for governments, we wouldn't have to teach children to be good, there would be no wars, and the news and newspapers would all be mostly good news!

Testing Freemasonry against self-contradictions

Probably one of the biggest contradictions within Freemasonry (and all false religions) is that it portrays itself to be so good on the outside of the cup being actively involved with helping their fellow man in a large variety of ways. Mormonism and Jehovah's Witnesses both also excel at a good outer appearance. However, the sad thing, of course, is that these very deceiving organizations just lead many away from their true need for Christ and into eternal hell which, by the way, Masons don't believe in either. Other self-contradictions within Freemasonry, of course, would include their hidden violent practices against their members when they break their secret oaths and the fact that they tap into the demonic realm during their rituals as well.

Let's be honest: neither of these realities gel too well with the good Samaritan portrayal of their organization to the world! There are, of course, many other self-contradictions as well, which neither time nor written page permit us to explore. Thus, all in all, Freemasonry as a religion easily fails this basic test as well.

> Other self-contradictions within Freemasonry, of course, would include their hidden violent practices and their pursuing of the demonic realm, even though they portray themselves to be good to the outside world.

Objection 55
I Believe in Freemasonry

Testing Freemasonry against the fruit it has produced

And like its title even indicates, the Freemasonry religion as a whole is simply not what it portrays itself to be! The very fact that its truths are bound under the secret oaths of its members is just further proof that their true beliefs and upper-level practices are largely hidden from the outside public world which, again, is true of most satanic cults which delve into the demonic realm. In fact, the upper members of Freemasonry must swear secret oaths that even involve mutilation and murder if broken (Duncan, *Duncan's Masonic Ritual*, p. 35, 65, 96)! While it is common knowledge within the true Church that the Bible forbids all men to make any oaths at all, simply because it just leads to evil (Matthew 5:33–37), the related doctrines within Freemasonry throw all such caution to the wind. Even though Freemasonry started in Europe and England, it was later brought to America in the colonial days. However, no matter where the religion took root, it was characterized with secrecy, hidden violence, and connections with Satanism in its upper levels.

> The upper members of Freemasonry must swear secret oaths that even involve mutilation and murder if broken.

In 1826, one man, William Morgan, disappeared from Batavia, New York, after threatening to expose Freemasonry's secrets. This caused much suspicion in the US that he had, in fact, been murdered by his fellow Masons. To this day, the public never did find out what happened to William Morgan. Quite reasonably, after that, Freemasonry declined as a religion the next forty years in America until it was popularized again after the Civil War in the supposed Golden Age of Fraternalism.

As an organization, the Masonic Lodge not only rejects almost all critical basic teachings of biblical Christianity but also clearly taps into the demonic realm as well, having its rituals, etc. However, while its swearing of oaths goes back to the earliest records of organized Masonry, the first recorded rituals were not until later in about 1696. Since the Bible has always taught that all false religions are ultimately hatched from the demonic realm (1 Timothy 4:1–2), it should not then surprise us if many of them should eventually teach their members to tap into the demonic realm.

Since the Bible has always taught that all false religions are ultimately hatched from the demonic realm, it should not then surprise us if they should eventually teach their members to tap into the demonic realm.

Testing Freemasonry against its divine power demonstrated

Again, any supernatural power which Freemasonry has displayed would not have exceeded that of the demonic realm simply because, like Scientology and even Satanism itself, that is its only source of power the members can be tapped into as the divine Christ is clearly rejected. Thus, just like Satanism and Scientology, Freemasonry also fails to even compare to the divine power Christ and his apostles openly displayed to the world. While Freemasonry (like many other false religions) may do *some* good in the world and/or teach *some* truth, we can see that it still falls horribly short of what we would expect of the one true faith backed by the one true God who himself must be morally perfect in order to be eternal. And the fact that false religions like Masonry have *some* truth and do *some* outwardly good things is exactly what make them so deceptive and dangerous. If they didn't actually do *some* good and teach *some* truth, they probably would not deceive very many people at all.

But even Satan knows that a good glass of water with only one small drop of poison in it is just as deadly as a full bottle of pure poison which has the label on it! And, again, Satan's ultimate goal is to destroy us in the process of giving us just what our fallen human nature wants. Picture it this way: Satan and his demonic realm will always try to reach out and offer you something quite tempting. But right while you are giving in to their temptation, they are also making sure that you are cutting off your own creator and your only source of eternal life! The demonic realm has to have some good enticements to draw you into their trap, just so they can make you share their own miserable fate in the lake of fire.

Objection 55
I Believe in Freemasonry

Conclusion

Statistics are always changing, and depending upon the source for one's statistic, presently, there are roughly only about 5 million people worldwide who may claim to belong to the religion of the Freemasons. Again, that is *far less than* one-fourth of 1 percent of the world's entire population. But it should be quite difficult for anyone to believe that, for according to this fact, 99.75 percent of the world's population (plus all those who lived before the 1300s) is deceived and does not have the truth!

My friend, if you happen to belong to the Freemasons, please see through its thin outward veneer of good humanitarian works which it deceptively portrays to outsiders and know that it is indeed a demonic-based cult which threatens the very salvation of its adherents. If the Bible has always taught that the salvation of men cannot in any way be obtained by doing good religious works of any kind (Ephesians 2:8–9) and that a works-based salvation will damn a soul (Galatians 1:6–9), then all Masons certainly have a choice to make before they stand in front of their true creator who actually proved his divinity with mankind many times over.

If you can see through the obvious deception of the Freemasonry cult and choose to trust in Christ alone and what he did for you on the cross for your salvation, I can *honestly* assure you that you will never be disappointed with your choice (Romans 10:11)! Not to mention the big burden which will be lifted off you because you no longer have to try and earn your eternal salvation through good works! And this is not to say that good works will not be the honest *result* of your saving faith in Christ; they will just not be the *cause* of your salvation anymore. And, of course, there is a big difference between the two!

Just as Jesus proved his divinity to the honest soul many times over when he walked the earth, so too is his Word completely trustworthy which foretells the awesome eternity which God has for all those who love him. As Revelation 21:3–4 clearly teaches:

> *"[B]ehold, the dwelling place of God is with men, and he will live with them, and they shall be his people, and God himself shall be with them, and be their God. And God shall wipe away all tears from their eyes; and there shall be no more death, neither sorrow, nor*

crying, neither shall there be any more pain: for the former things are passed away."

But the Bible teaches us plainly that *only through Christ* can we obtain God's eternal life. Jesus said, *"I am the way and the truth and the life. No one comes to the Father except through me"* (John 14:6).

Someone once asked Jesus how many will be saved. And Jesus replied, *"Make every effort to enter through the narrow door, because many, I tell you, will try to enter and will not be able"* (Luke 13:24).

If you are one who can easily see through the deception of the Masonic Lodge religion and would like to be right with God and be assured of your place in his eternal kingdom, I invite you to just take that first small step of faith by sincerely praying the prayer of salvation located at the end of this book. Even if you've been a Freemason for years, you can still break away from that obvious false religion today which threatens your true salvation through Christ. And don't be concerned with what your fellow Masons may think of you because, simply put, they will not be your judge on judgment day! This decision is between you and God (your creator) alone. No matter what your past is like, God loves you and sincerely wants you to be a part of his awesome eternal kingdom!

Jesus said, "I am the resurrection and the life. He who believes in me, will live even though he dies; and whoever lives and believes in me will never die." (John 11:25–26)

OBJECTION 56
I Believe in Nothing

Believe in Nothing

It is easy to see why some may get so discouraged with all the contradicting religions in the world and simply conclude that there is really nothing to believe in after all. In fact, this may be the very way they've found to escape the spiritual confusion in the world around them. After all, believing in nothing *may actually seem* much easier than trying to sort out the one true faith in the midst of a bunch of deceptive false religions. And those who are this discouraged may not even realize it, but that is the very reason the demonic realm has even created all the false contradicting religions in the first place: to discourage men to the point of throwing out even the one true faith (1 Timothy 4:1–2)!

However, if one does actually bother to ever test all the main contradicting religions in the world with just the simple tests which we've discussed in our previous objections, they will be surprised at just how quickly the one true faith will stand out among all of Satan's counterfeit religions which miserably fail when tested! But perhaps you've not been only discouraged but actually been hurt by a particular false religion and simply have concluded that there is really nothing to believe in after all, just because of your hurtful experiences.

If you happen to be one who has resolved to believe in nothing, just because of your hurts, you must realize that the devil is truly the enemy of our soul, and that's why he's tried so hard to stain the true reputation of the biblical Christ in this world and cause people to rebel against him. And, sadly, in such cases, when people do rebel against Christ, many times, their rebellion is really just against a lie or a false portrayal of Christ which the demonic world has also created in order to deceive men away from God!

Thus, strangely enough, they aren't even rejecting the true biblical Christ, even though they may think they are. Perhaps because you were raised in a hurtful cult or false religion of some kind, you've been in rebellion against God for years because of it. But whatever your particular situation is, what if it is not the real biblical perfect Christ which hurt you? And what if it is not the real biblical Christ which you have been rebelling against all these years but rather just *a false portrayal of Christ* which you mistook for your eternal creator who really must be *perfect* love by definition in order to even be eternal? In fact, that's exactly what the devil wants, for when you reasonably think about it, how else could he deceive men away from the one true God and his eternal salvation other than hatching unbiblical lies about him? But just like we've already mentioned in Objection #40, there are really only two basic realities to be aware of in such cases:

> When people do rebel against Christ, many times, their rebellion is really just against a lie or a false portrayal of Christ which the demonic world has created in order to deceive men away from God!

1. First of all, *there are actually false Christians in the world* who may claim to live for Christ but, in reality, do not because they live in some lifestyle of sin (1 Corinthians 6:9–10). Judas Iscariot became one such counterfeit among Christ's true disciples, and this is the way it has been ever since Christ's Church started. And to be sure, this sin can even include those who cling to false unbiblical doctrines, even while claiming to be a Bible-believing Christian. Or it could be a professing Christian who's really living for money and not God, and you can see that. Or it could be a professing Christian who's living in sexual sin. But whatever the case, my friend, why let another person's hypocrisy deceive you away from the true biblical Jesus and rob you of eternal life? As the saying goes:

Objection 56
I Believe in Nothing

Never let very imperfect man rob you of your perfect God

Trust me because God is all-knowing and perfect, they won't get away with anything (Matthew 10:26)! Every person makes their own decisions and those counterfeit Christians not really living for Christ will surely reap the results (Galatians 6:7–8). The Bible clearly teaches us that the hearts of all men are *open and laid bare to the eyes of Him with whom we have to do* (Hebrews 4:13). Or perhaps your family is trapped in some kind of a cult and you really want to help them out of their deception but don't know where to start. So then you must ask yourself, will it really help them more to believe in nothing? Or would it help them much more to at least genuinely believe in the true Christ yourself and belong to the true faith which alone has the power to give men eternal life? In other words, even you must decide if you are going to be a part of the solution or part of the problem, to love men in the right direction or the wrong one. It's good that you may have rejected all false religions, but you need to also take responsibility as well by believing in the truth of Christ. Let's be honest: if we are not part of the solution, we really are still part of the world's problems! There really is no neutral middle ground to hide in.

    2. Secondly, perhaps you've just been hurt by *true Christians who have not always lived like Christ*. Yes, admittedly, even the true Church is full of imperfections. Even the Apostle Paul, one of the most spiritual men who walked the earth, said that it was the perfect Christ which he was preaching, not himself, because he himself was still very imperfect and need Christ's forgiveness every day (2 Corinthians 4:5). In fact, the Apostle John also said that if anyone who is a professing Christian claims he is without any sin that the truth is not even in him (1 John 1:8)! And if you were to honestly search your own soul, you'd probably have to admit that you, too, are also very imperfect and have probably hurt others as well at times. So, if you were to reject the perfect biblical Christ, just because of the many imperfections you've seen in other true Christians or even because you've been hurt by imperfect true Christians,

then wouldn't you yourself be just falling into hypocrisy because you, too, are imperfect?

The sad truth is that at times, we all hurt others! We may not have hurt others in just the same way others may have hurt us, but to God who is morally perfect, it is all the same, simply because sin is sin. And that's exactly why we ourselves also need Christ's forgiveness as he is the only one who is perfect and it is his moral standards which we've all violated. The bottom line is only God, who is perfect, can live all his own perfect moral standards! And that's why no man has to be *perfect* in order to be right with God and have his eternal life. They only have to be *forgiven* through the cross of Christ. And because our perfect creator is willing to forgive us for our many sins from the cross, then should we not also be willing to forgive others who may have hurt us?

Truly the only way you are going to get to know the true biblical perfect Christ (and not some false portrayal of him) who would never hurt you in any way is to take some responsibility yourself by reading the New Testament and meeting him. If you have never sincerely sought to know the true Christ by reading the whole New Testament, I would strongly encourage you to do so as it is probably one of the most important things a person can do in this life before they meet their creator! Then, if you still reject Christ, at least you will be rejecting the perfect biblical true Christ and not just some false portrayal of him created by the demonic world and/or false Christians.

You see, the devil knows that Jesus Christ is your only source of real truth and eternal life, simply because he is, in fact, also your only creator. And if you just give the real biblical Jesus a chance, he will certainly prove that to you!

Sometimes a horse will actually be afraid of his own shadow, even though we all know a shadow could never hurt anyone. And sometimes man can be afraid of his own creator, even though by definition, his creator could never hurt him because he must actually be perfect in love in order to even be an eternal being. The fact that our very own creator can actually love and bless us far better than we could ever love and bless ourselves rarely occurs to those in rebellion against him. But when you just think about it at all, it's the reasonable truth. If you have presently resigned yourself to believe in nothing because of your past hurts, I sincerely appeal to you right now because someday, you and I

Objection 56
I Believe in Nothing

will stand before our own loving creator and give account to him for either our reasonable surrender to him or our unreasonable rejection of him.

We won't be judged for the bad spiritual choices others may have made. We'll be only judged for what we ourselves decided to do with Christ. If we reject our very own creator who is himself the very source of perfect love and our eternal life, then how can he possibly ever give us the very thing we are rejecting?

> The fact that our very own creator can actually love and bless us far more and better than we could ever love and bless ourselves rarely occurs to those in rebellion against him.

It's actually impossible to believe in nothing

Additionally, when one thinks about it at all, it's really not quite that easy to believe in just nothing after all. In fact, in all actuality, it may be much harder than believing in the real truth! For example, even a person *claiming* to believe in nothing doesn't like being lied to, stolen from, disrespected, or beat up, etc. In this basic respect, they would at least believe in the Ten Commandments of the Bible and Christ's golden rule (Exodus 20; Luke 6:31). And if one believes in the Ten Commandments and Christ's golden rule, they technically also believe in most all other teachings and/or moral standards of God's Word because they are just detailed explanations which actually just expound upon God's Ten Commandments and the golden rule (Matthew 22:37–40). In this real sense, then, it is literally impossible for anyone to actually believe in nothing, even though some may claim that they have no spiritual beliefs at all.

Perhaps you are one who just has a difficult time with attending a formal church. I understand completely. Well, this may surprise you, but there is nothing in the Bible which teaches that you have to attend a formal church in order to be a Christian who is right with God and heaven-bound. The biblical truth is that the New Testament Church largely started in just regular homes! Today, we call them home churches, and many may actually prefer them to bigger organized churches.

The main thing according to the Bible is that the truth of God's Word is taught without compromise, and God is worshiped in spirit and truth. So, if you can find a home church to attend, it's perfectly okay with Christ who said, *"Where two or three are gathered together in my name, there I am in the midst of them"* (Matthew 18:20). Or you could actually just attend a Bible study in someone's home if that is where you'd like to start.

> It is literally impossible for anyone to actually believe in nothing, even though some may claim that they have no spiritual beliefs.

Conclusion

As we've already mentioned in previous objections, *many people* choose their particular spiritual beliefs just for emotional reasons, and it has nothing at all to do with a genuine search for reality based on honest evidence. The following are just some of the reasons some may *claim* to just believe in nothing:

1. As we've already mentioned, some may claim to just believe in nothing to escape the spiritual confusion in the world around them. However, as we've already pointed out, the confusion is quickly lifted when one sincerely searches out the one true faith by testing all major religions with just the very simple tests we've just discussed in our previous objections. Additionally, it is literally impossible to believe in nothing, and to claim such a belief would be just adding to the spiritual confusion in the world and not even escaping from it.

2. And still others may claim to believe in nothing because they've either *been hurt* or they simply do not want to know the truth because they may be afraid the truth will somehow *take away from their personal happiness*. But as we've already discussed in other objections, when we reflect on this a little deeper, it is not really the truth which ever truly hurts us; it is only lies and deceptions which actually hurt us. Since the real truth connects us with

Objection 56
I Believe in Nothing

reality, we can then make personal choices which actually respect reality, give us life, and allow us to avoid the real harm of deception. It's no different than if someone turns on the light when you are trying to walk through a dark room. The light (representing the truth) enables you to not run into anything and get hurt.

Ever really stub your little toe in a dark room? Well, a lot worse can happen to us spiritually if we stumble around in the spiritual darkness of this fallen world without the truth. Therefore, in light of that, would not the truth actually be man's greatest friend? Jesus said, *"I am the way, the truth, and the life"* (John 14:6); thus, *the truth* is really the person of Christ himself. And since Jesus proved his deity many times over through the hundreds of miracles, he and his disciples did in front of many witnesses, we can trust him when he said, *"You shall know the truth and the truth shall set you free"* (John 8:32).

But since when has *nothing* ever set anyone free? And just as Jesus proved his divinity to the honest soul many times over when he walked the earth, so too is his Word completely trustworthy which foretells the awesome eternity which God has for all those who love him. As Revelation 21:3–4 clearly teaches:

> *"[B]ehold, the dwelling place of God is with men, and he will live with them, and they shall be his people, and God himself shall be with them, and be their God. And God shall wipe away all tears from their eyes; and there shall be no more death, neither sorrow, nor crying, neither shall there be any more pain: for the former things are passed away."*

But the Bible teaches us plainly that *only through Christ* can we obtain God's eternal life. Jesus said, *"I am the way and the truth and the life. No one comes to the Father except through me"* (John 14:6).

Someone once asked Jesus how many will be saved. And Jesus replied, *"Make every effort to enter through the narrow door, because many, I tell you, will try to enter and will not be able"* (Luke 13:24).

If you are one who presently believes in *nothing* for the afterlife of mankind but also know in your heart that there must be a loving God who's sustained all delicate life on earth millennia after millennia, I would encourage you to give Christ a chance to reveal himself to you.

After forty years of being a Christian, I can personally testify that it was God's love which ultimately changed my life for the better. But if I had never given Christ a *real chance* to even reveal himself to me, then I know I would have never gotten the real love and healing I needed.

If you are one who is tired of running from God and you want to personally experience his awesome unconditional healing love for you, I invite you to just take that first small step of faith by sincerely praying the prayer of salvation located at the end of this book. No matter what your past is like, God loves you and sincerely wants you to be a part of his awesome eternal kingdom!

> *Jesus said, "I am the resurrection and the life. He who believes in me, will live even though he dies; and whoever lives and believes in me will never die."* (John 11:25–26)

OBJECTION 57

As Long as You Are Sincere, What Does It Really Matter What You Believe?

Sincerity

Sincerity itself is a very commendable quality. Many people in today's world have lost it. If you are sincere with good intentions in your beliefs, your sincerity itself is something which I don't believe God would want you to change. People in today's world are often hardened by life's trials and just lose their desire to remain sincere. And some people you meet in life will literally treat most everything as a joke, especially when it comes to finding the spiritual truth. So sincerity certainly has value because it actually enables people to find the spiritual truth if they are headed in the right direction.

However, while sincerity itself is something to greatly esteem, it does not necessarily guarantee that we have found the truth or that we will find the truth. It's kind of like a clipper ship out at sea. While sincerity could be compared to a strong wind in its sails, it still has to have its rudder pointed in the right direction in order to arrive at the correct destination. It doesn't matter how full the sails are; if its rudder is not pointed in the right direction, it will never reach its correct destination. And in order to have its rudder in the right direction, one has to first determine the right direction by way of a trustworthy compass and map which will not deceive and lead one astray. And when it comes to our spiritual beliefs, the Bible, which has proven itself to be the infallible Word of God many times over through fulfilled prophecy, is truly the only trustworthy spiritual compass and map.

Are there any other so-called holy books in the world which prove their divine authorship through such fulfilled prophecies (as the Holy Bible contains) which confirm our perfect creator has communicated clearly to us? If you find one, I give you permission to destroy my ignorance.

> While sincerity itself is something to greatly esteem, it does not necessarily guarantee that we have found the truth or that we will find the truth.

There are probably many things which we all *sincerely* believed growing up, but now know they are simply *not true*. More than one young boy has *sincerely* believed they were going to be astronauts or pro-football players when they grew up. But as they got older, the reality of who they really are proved to be quite different. And this process of discovering true reality in every facet of life just continues as we get older and collect more information.

At one time, as a young man, I sincerely believed I was to become a truck driver. I even went to school for it which cost me $7,500. I took my truck driver's test and even passed it (by one point—ha!). But the whole time, I was so uncomfortable that I finally had to be *honest* enough with myself that it really wasn't me, even though I had invested all that time and money. The truth is that even though we may be *sincere*, we can all be *sincerely wrong* if, in fact, we are not decently connected to reality. Thus the saying, "Even strong faith disconnected from reality is faith misplaced!"

Either we are gifted to be a natural truck driver or we are not. I was not, and the real truth was that is not who I was created to be, even though I probably could have painfully forced myself to do it for a season of time. Maybe you could even recall some things in your own life that you believed with all your heart, but later, you were rather forced to conclude it simply was not true based upon further evidence or even painful experience.

For an extreme example, I suppose even Adolf Hitler himself was very *sincere* in his brand of socialism which he really wanted the world to adopt. However, a short time not only proved to the world that

Objection 57
As Long As You Are Sincere, Does It Matter What You Believe?

his beliefs were in great error, but also, the world would have been far better off if he had *sincerely* acknowledged that he was wrong long before he raked as much death and destruction as he did! The truth is sincerity is like a good sturdy rope. You definitely need it to climb a mountain, but that's not all you need. You also need Tee-tons with rope clips anchored into the steep mountain all the way up if you are going to make it to the top!

Similarly, when it comes to our spiritual beliefs, we all do need to have sincerity, but we also need to be anchored into the truth of reality with our sincerity as well. Otherwise, we will not only get hurt, but we'll probably just hurt others as well. After all, one can find very *sincere believers within all the conflicting religions of the world,* which we know cannot all be correct because of their *conflicting basic doctrines.* And since, logically, only one or none can be correct (as we discussed in our Objection #41), any way one would look at it, there are an awful lot of people in this world who are *sincerely wrong* and in for a very rude awakening when they step into eternity! But the good news is, my dear reader, you don't have to be among them!

> Because of all the conflicting religions, any way one would look at it, there are an awful lot of people in this world who are in for a rude awakening throughout all eternity!

Some may sincerely believe that one religion is just as good as another and the world is just one big happy family, simply because it doesn't at all matter what we choose to believe spiritually. But *simple logic* and *a little bit of honesty* should tell us that the truth of reality can never contradict itself, and all the different conflicting religions in the world simply cannot be connected to reality. And the moment the truth contradicts itself, it is no longer the truth which can be relied upon to give man life. And if it is not the truth, then it is really only deception (that only *claims* to be the truth of reality) which causes mankind harm.

As history has plainly shown, if we are not decently connected to reality in our beliefs, great pain is almost always the result! And we must all certainly admit that being deceived into physical and spiritual harm has nothing to do with real love either! Therefore, it certainly does very much matter what we believe spiritually in as much as it does very much matter if we are connected to reality and not deceived into physical or spiritual harm!

Again, true love is very much the issue with our desire to be connected to reality, simply because I cannot claim to love you if I do not tell you the truth! Thus, the simple saying:

> One cannot claim to love others while compromising the truth.

For another example of *sincerity gone wrong*, one may sincerely believe they are to get married to someone, only to find out several children later in divorce court that the person was definitely not a healthy choice! Since the long list of all the examples of *sincerity gone wrong and the pain it has caused man* could, of course, go on and on, we must conclude that this world we live in can be very deceptive if we do not have the proper discernment we need. And it would seem that the more a thing could affect our personal well-being, the more we should want to *sincerely* search it out with all our hearts if we don't want to experience the potential great pain attached to a possible wrong choice with that critical thing. And when it comes to our spiritual beliefs, this is exactly why *sincerity itself is never enough*, and it really does matter greatly just what we *choose* to believe because either we are connected to actual reality with our spiritual beliefs or we are not.

My friend, truly, it is the difference between having solid ground under our feet and stepping off the edge of a cliff! What we chose to believe spiritually then will not only greatly affect our whole natural life but also, according to every religion, it will make or break our eternity as well.

> What we chose to believe spiritually then will not only greatly affect our whole natural life but also, according to every religion, it will make or break our eternity as well.

OBJECTION 57
AS LONG AS YOU ARE SINCERE, DOES IT MATTER WHAT YOU BELIEVE?

Conclusion

Many who are now believers in Christ may have at one time sincerely believed things about Christ and the Bible which were simply not true until they found out that they were *sincerely wrong*. Perhaps you've even been given a *skewed view* of the biblical Christ in some way or another. Given the demonic realm is always bent on deceiving men away from the one true faith, it wouldn't at all surprise me. But the only way to really know is to just read the New Testament for yourself and meet the real Jesus somewhere where it is just you and God alone. The book of John in the New Testament is a good one to start with. If, in fact, the Holy Bible is really God's Word to all mankind as it claims over 3,000 times, and one is not decently connected to that reality by truly believing in Christ, then the very consequences described for all unbelievers within the Bible could become our reality if we were *sincerely wrong*. For if you are like me, you've also noticed one thing about reality—it doesn't seem to move much for anyone, even if we are *sincere!*

But just like we've already discussed in our Objections #41–56, there are many conflicting misrepresentations of reality within all the conflicting religions of the world. Therefore, the main thing necessary for one to actually find the spiritual truth isn't so much just having sincerity but also *making sure we are connected to reality with our sincerity* by simply just testing our present spiritual beliefs with the basic tests we've just discussed in this Part 3 of our series. However, after 40 years of being a Bible believing Christian, I can also personally testify that it wasn't just the truth supported by honest evidence which confirmed I was connected to reality but also God's unconditional love shown to me! But if I had never given Christ a decent chance to even reveal himself to me, then I know I would have never gotten the love, healing, and life-giving truth I needed.

The Prayer of Salvation

Because the Bible also teaches us that it is sin which separates us all from God (Isaiah 59:2), our sins must first be dealt with before our relationship with him can be restored. And the Bible teaches us plainly that *only through Christ* can our relationship with God be restored so he can grant us his eternal life. Jesus said, *"I am the way and the truth and the life. No one comes to the Father except through me"* (John 14:6).

Someone once asked Jesus how many will be saved. And Jesus replied, *"Make every effort to enter through the narrow door, because many, I tell you, will try to enter and will not be able"* (Luke 13:24).

Jesus said, *"I am the door: by me if any man enter in, he shall be saved."* (John 10:9).

"For God so loved the world, that he gave his one and only Son, that whoever believes in him shall not perish, but have eternal life." (John 3:16).

If you already know in your heart that just any old false religion will never give you the life, love, and fulfillment you need, and you'd like to know for certain that you, too, are right with God and have his eternal life, I invite you to take that first small step of faith by praying the following prayer of salvation sincerely from your heart. No matter what your past is like, God loves you and sincerely wants you to be a part of his awesome eternal kingdom!

Dear Lord Jesus,

"I easily admit that I cannot come close to keeping all the perfect moral standards of your Word through my own efforts, and this is what your Word, the Bible, calls sin. And because my sin is what separates me from you, I believe that in your great love for me, you humbly came to earth and died a brutal death on the cross, taking my punishment for me, even though you yourself are perfect and didn't even deserve it. Just because I believe in what you did for me on the cross that I could not do for myself, I believe according to your own Word that the justice of the Father is now satisfied and my relationship with you is now restored. I ask your forgiveness for all my sins, and I humbly give you the rest of my life from

Objection 57
As Long As You Are Sincere, Does It Matter What You Believe?

here on, no longer living for myself but only for you to the best of my ability. Thank you for what you did for me on the cross and your free gift of eternal life!"

Amen.

Jesus said, "I am the resurrection and the life. He who believes in me, will live even though he dies; and whoever lives and believes in me will never die." (John 11:25–26)

1 John 1:9 says, "If we confess our sins, he is faithful and just to forgive our sins, and cleanse us from *all unrighteousness.*"

And now that you have come into a right relationship with God through Christ, for your personal spiritual growth, it is important to:

1. *Talk to God* (pray) as much as you can every day with thanksgiving and praise (Romans 12:12; Philippians 4:4–7; Psalm 145:3).
2. *Read God's Word* (the Bible) as much as you can every day to get to know the Lord better. Ask the Holy Spirit to help you understand, and don't be discouraged if there are some things you don't understand for a while. The book of John and the other gospels are good books to start with (John 8:31–32, 15:7; 2 Peter 3:14–18; (2 Timothy 3:14–17).
3. *Attend a Bible-believing church* and stay in fellowship with them and other Christians as much as you can. If the church you attend has small groups or home groups, this will greatly aid your spiritual growth as well (Hebrews 10:25; Acts 2:42; Ephesians 2:19). If you are one who'd prefer not attending a traditional church in some church building, a home church with just friends is a very good option which many do not even know about. In fact, such a church model is just as biblical as the first Christians also met in homes (Matthew 8:14–17; Acts 28:30–31). Jesus plainly stated that when two or more are gathered in his name, there he is in the midst of them (Matthew 18:19–20).

Let's face it: the entire worldwide Church will not fit into one building! When it comes to a quality church experience, bigger is not necessarily better. The main thing is that there is at least one elder who's teaching the Bible accurately with the literal method of interpretation and Christ is worshiped in Spirit and in truth. There's absolutely nothing in God's Word which insists that teachers or even pastors, for that matter, must graduate from some Bible seminary school in order to be qualified to teach in church. In fact, many Bible seminary schools today are even teaching false doctrines because they've drifted from the truth of God's Word through the allegorical method of interpretation. We must remember it's all a heart issue with God, not an issue of high education.

4. If one truly believes in what Christ did for them on the cross in their heart, they will actually show it by *following after Christ* and not sin. This, of course, does not mean as a Christian, you will be perfect (if you were, you would not need Christ), but the rudder on your ship should be basically pointed in the direction of Christ and not sin (2 Corinthians 5:15; 1 John 2:6). If you just remember that God always loves you and that nothing can separate you from his love (Romans 8:35–39), then you will just be inspired from the inside to live for him with all your heart.

5. *Share your faith with others* so they, too, can know Christ and have his eternal life. The Christian faith was never something which God intended the Christian to keep to himself. If we truly love God, we'll love others. And if we love others, we'll want them to have God's eternal life too! Truly, there is a grand variety of ways we can share our faith. Choose the one which uses the gifts which God gave you and have a good time doing it.

May God truly bless you in your new relationship with him, and always remember God's love for you is far greater than any of your problems, and Christ's future for you is far better than anything this world can offer! As Revelation 21:3–4 clearly teaches:

"Behold, the dwelling place of God is with men, and he will live with them, and they shall be his people, and God himself shall be

with them, and be their God. And God shall wipe away all tears from their eyes; and there shall be no more death, neither sorrow, nor crying, neither shall there be any more pain: for the former things are passed away."

"No eye has seen, no ear has heard, and no mind has imagined what God has prepared for those who love him."

(1 Corinthians 2:9)

ABOUT THE AUTHOR

Not having been raised with any particular religion at all, it wasn't long before author, Ted Even, did discover real hope when at age eighteen, he decided to give Christ a chance and become a Bible-believing Christian. If the Christian faith did not really make good sense, Ted Even is probably one of the first to say that he most certainly would have abandoned his faith long ago. But while he diligently studied the Holy Bible (as well as other sources) during the last forty years which followed his conversion, he only found that God's Word gave reasonable solid answers to even the harder questions which many skeptics have probably wrestled with ever since Christ.

In his *Answers for the Honest Skeptic* four-part series, Ted Even reveals just what he has discovered as he responds to eighty-five different objections which skeptics often have had to biblical Christianity.

[1] Doctrine and Covenants 84:3-4.
[2] Bent Corydon, L. Ron Hubbard: Messiah or Madman (Secaucus, New Jersey: Lyle Stuart, 1987), pp. p. 219–220.
[3] Russel Miller, Bare-faced Messiah: The True Story of L. Ron Hubbard (Penguin Books, Ltd.), p. 26.
[4] Bent Corydon, L. Ron Hubbard: Messiah or Madman (Secaucus, New Jersey: Lyle Stuart, 1987).